Ten Times Calmer

'With Dr Kirren's warm, practical and expert advice for managing anxiety, you'll learn how to stop surviving and start thriving.'

Vex King, *Sunday Times* bestselling author of
Closer to Love* and *Good Vibes, Good Life

'I've had an awful lot of help with my mental health over the years from a number of therapists and psychologists. If only I had come across Dr Schnack's work sooner. Now we can all enjoy her wisdom and experience thanks to *Ten Times Calmer*. Follow her practical advice and straightforward strategies and you might not have to take the scenic route like me.'

Rachel Kelly, bestselling writer and mental
health advocate, ambassador for SANE
and Rethink Mental Illness

'An educational, nurturing and practical guide that really will change your life. Dr Kirren's words are warm, packed with knowledge and gently guiding. In a time where there is a lot of stress and uncertainty, this book will be a gift to all that read it.'

Clare Bourne, pelvic health physiotherapist
and author of *Strong Foundations*

Ten Times Calmer

Beat Anxiety
and Change
Your Life

Dr Kirren Schnack

FLATIRON
BOOKS
NEW YORK

www.flatironbooks.com

The Library of Congress Cataloging-in-Publication Data is available upon request.

ISBN 978-1-250-34126-6 (hardcover)
ISBN 978-1-250-34127-3 (ebook)

Our books may be purchased in bulk for promotional, educational, or business use. Please contact your local bookseller or the Macmillan Corporate and Premium Sales Department at 1-800-221-7945, extension 5442, or by email at MacmillanSpecialMarkets@macmillan.com.

Originally published in the United Kingdom in 2023 by Bluebird, an imprint of Pan Macmillan

First U.S. Edition: 2024

10 9 8 7 6 5 4 3 2 1

*To every person who's ever felt troubled by anxiety.
I'm truly inspired by your courage. Never give up.*

Disclaimer: This book aims to provide general educational information and is not tailored to any specific individual. It should not be relied upon as a substitute for professional advice. The information presented in this book is based on research evidence and my clinical experience at the time of writing.

Each individual's experience of anxiety is unique and their ability to use the information in this book may also differ. Therefore, the outcomes and changes achieved will vary accordingly. Since I cannot know the personal circumstances of each reader, neither I, nor the Publisher, can accept liability for the consequences of the information provided. To address your specific circumstances, it is recommended you consult with your doctor to find an approach specifically tailored to you.

If you experience physical symptoms, it is crucial not to self-diagnose and instead seek confirmation and guidance from your doctor, including assessing if anxiety plays a role.

Additionally, follow your doctor's guidance on when to schedule further consultations for any symptoms you experience. Please note that using alcohol or drugs as coping mechanisms for anxiety can lead to addiction and other issues so, if you have concerns about this, please consult your doctor.

Throughout this book, various patient examples are used to enhance readability and relatability. Although these may be inspired by my clinical experiences, they do not depict specific individuals. They are composite narratives that illustrate key concepts and ideas.

Contents

Introduction

One of the most wonderful things I've had the privilege to witness in my professional life is the capability people have to beat anxiety and change their lives. They just need to know how to do it and this is exactly what you and I are going to do in *Ten Times Calmer*. You may have been struggling with anxiety for most of your life or just more recently. Perhaps you've tried a range of quick fixes or therapeutic approaches, yet none have provided a real solution for your struggles. The help you need is within the pages of this book and I'll guide you on the path to overcoming your anxiety. I want you to imagine yourself sitting with me in my clinic room, as I share with you simple, clear and detailed strategies for beating anxiety and transforming your life.

Though the experience of anxiety is different for everyone, clinically it's recognized that certain anxiety problems share common features. Because they share these characteristics, the ways in which they are managed and treated can also overlap. The *Ten Times Calmer* programme will guide you through a series of ten essential components to help you beat your anxiety. Whether this is general anxiety, health anxiety, panic or social anxiety. The strategies in this book will help you learn how to deal with your anxiety in the best way possible, so that you can heal yourself. These strategies are the best ones, because they're drawn from clinical guidance, supported by scientific evidence, and have been clinically validated through my extensive experience with patients. By consistently using the strategies and following the ten stage programme I've designed, you'll be able to conquer your anxiety and achieve lasting change.

You may be curious about my expertise and authority on this topic, and might be wondering why you should listen to me. So let me give you a little background and explain what qualifies me to give you this advice. I am a Clinical Psychologist, trained at the University of Oxford. I've lived and worked in Oxford ever since I qualified, though I'm a northerner at heart. I continue to work in clinical practice with both adults and children. Over my twenty-year career as a psychologist I've treated thousands of patients with anxiety disorders, as well as those with many other mental health problems.

In addition to my clinical work, I share practical advice with a large following on my social media platforms. My social media journey started during the pandemic, and the response from people struggling with anxiety was incredible. My followers related to my content and expressed that they felt understood, often remarking that they'd never encountered someone discussing anxiety in such a relatable manner. What I saw through my social media work corroborated what I'd observed: that so many people just don't have access to the mental health care they need.

Anxiety can be influenced by various life stages, although each person's experience is distinct, and not everyone will encounter anxiety during these periods. It's important to recognize that feeling anxious during certain life transitions is normal, but if the anxiety becomes overwhelming or significantly impacts daily functioning it may have become a bigger problem. Here are some typical life stages and events that are often associated with anxiety:

- Adolescence: Hormonal and physical changes during puberty, along with the challenges of transitioning into adulthood.

- College or university: Academic pressures, social adjustments, and increased responsibilities.

- Starting a career: Job interviews, performance expectations, career uncertainties and workplace conflicts.

- Relationship changes: Starting or ending romantic relationships, conflicts, divorce or separation.

- Parenthood: Becoming a first-time parent or adjusting to the demands and uncertainties of raising children.

- Empty Nest Syndrome: When children leave home, parents may experience a sense of loss or purposelessness.

- Menopause: Hormonal changes during this stage can impact mood and increase the risk of anxiety for some women.

- Ageing and retirement: The process of ageing, health concerns, and transitioning into retirement can introduce anxieties related to identity, health and financial stability.

- Significant life changes: Moving, changing careers, experiencing bereavement, financial difficulties, or trauma can also trigger anxiety problems.

At the time of writing this book, anxiety is affecting approximately 284 million people worldwide – and that's just the number of cases we know about. Unfortunately, this number is expected to increase. Regardless of where you look in the world, it's troubling to note that there's a significant gap between the demand for treatment and its availability. Shockingly, 85 per cent of people suffering from anxiety never receive the help they need. People don't have access to good-quality help, because public services are overburdened, and the waiting times are often extremely long. Even when people get to the front of the queue, they often don't get the help they really need. I'm truly grateful for where I am today. As someone who has faced adversity, I know how challenging it can be to overcome life's toughest obstacles. I also recognize that private help is not an option for most individuals.

All these experiences have shown me time and again that there's a pressing need to broaden clinic-based treatments, and tailor them for self-help purposes. To show people the way to help themselves. Self-directed skills have a remarkable ability to alleviate stress and foster resilience, making them an ideal approach for beating anxiety. For decades, reading to support mental health or 'bibliotherapy' has been an influential therapeutic tool in managing many mental health problems. It brings me great joy to be able to contribute to this, and to every single one of you reading this book right now.

Just as with my patients in the clinic, our shared aim is to break free from problematic anxiety. You have come here with the desire to move from point A to point B, and it is my privilege to guide you through this process with my expertise. I will equip you with the strategies you need, and support you in working through things at a pace that is comfortable for you. As you get better you might experience a setback; if you do, then please remember, it's natural to feel hopeless at times and setbacks are a normal part of progress. Don't let a setback be the reason for giving up. Many people who suffer from persistent anxiety have been able to make a full recovery.

It's important to keep going with kindness, compassion and an open mind towards yourself. Even if you feel scared, weak or lost, acknowledge the courage within you. Your bravery is apparent in the ways you've faced your challenges, persistently trying your best even when anxiety has left you feeling mentally and physically exhausted. By reading this book, you're showing your resourcefulness, your courage, your willingness to help yourself and your belief in your ability to recover. This is truly admirable.

Maybe you resonate with the feeling that you've been struggling for so long, and question whether things can ever get better. I've met and worked with people from all walks of life with different levels of suffering. By the time they come to meet me, people have suffered for weeks, others for months, even years and decades. Let me share a story with you to give you hope and inspire courage. One September, a patient who was eighty-two years old, and had been struggling with travel anxiety for decades, asked me if there was any chance of improvement. I assured them that there was, and by Christmas that same year, they'd conquered their anxiety and taken their first flight in thirty-five years! This patient's success is just one of many examples that show how remarkable changes can be achieved by ordinary people through manageable steps. I want you to know that you can experience these transformations too. Although recovery can happen quickly, it's important not to put unnecessary pressure on yourself by setting strict time frames for progress. Every single one of us is different: we all have our own ways of thinking, feeling and processing. We all get there via our own path. While it's important not to set rigid deadlines, it's also important to understand that the work you need to put in to overcome anxiety is not endless.

What you'll learn

Ten Times Calmer is designed to follow a specific format. In laying the book out, I've mirrored the work I do in the clinic with my own patients. I've incorporated the same strategies I use with my patients and modified these so you can use them for self-help. As you progress through the book, integrate these self-help strategies into your personal toolkit. This toolkit serves as a valuable resource, equipping you with a wide array of skills to draw upon to effectively confront and manage your anxiety. The chapters here follow the same sequence as I do in my clinical approach. To get the most out of this book, approach it with a sense of openness and flexibility. I'd like to encourage you to work through each chapter before moving on to the next. From this you'll gain a strong understanding of the foundational concepts I discuss early on, as these serve as building blocks for some of the later sections. Everyone's needs and circumstances are different, and certain chapters or exercises may not feel as relevant to you as others. It's perfectly fine to skip over them if they do not apply to you at all. On the other hand, if you find some chapters resonate strongly with you, I recommend revisiting them as needed, and especially if you notice that you're slipping back into anxiety. By doing this, you'll be able to reinforce the concepts and strategies that have helped you the most. Remember, the goal of this book is to provide you with the tools and strategies you need to improve your anxiety. As you work through the chapters you'll find what works best for you, and you can customize this to fit your individual needs.

In the ten stage programme, we'll start by exploring the root causes of your anxiety in Chapter 1. Moving on to Chapter 2, we'll delve into the skill of acceptance, which will empower you with the freedom and flexibility needed to make progress.

When anxiety becomes problematic, your nervous system is under stress. This stress can be brief, or it can be chronic (persisting for a long time or recurring). When this stress is chronic it can result in physical symptoms that persist even when you're not feeling anxious or panicky. Chronic anxiety can feel like a leaky tap that slowly drains your energy and leaves you feeling exhausted. It can be challenging to shake off the constant worry and anticipation of anxiety, even when you're not actively experiencing it. Just like a leaky tap that keeps dripping water when you're not using it, anxiety can keep your mind racing even when you're not in an anxious situation. This constant drain on your mental and emotional resources can lead to feeling depleted and overwhelmed. But, just as you can fix a leaky tap to prevent water waste, you can also learn to manage your anxiety and conserve your energy. To tackle this problem, it's crucial to understand how to trigger the relaxation response in your body. In Chapter 3, we'll explore various strategies you can utilize to achieve this goal.

Anxious thoughts can range from fears about serious illness, death (either your own or that of a loved one), losing control, panic attacks, heart attacks, passing out or not being able to breathe, to finding yourself in embarrassing situations like peeing or losing control of your bowels. It's as if your mind is consumed with endless possibilities of negative outcomes. In Chapter 4, which is the largest chapter, I'll provide you with my most effective strategies for managing anxious thoughts.

Anxiety can narrow and intensify your focus on the things that trigger your fear. To overcome this fear, it's vital to learn how to redirect your attention and broaden its scope. In Chapter 5 I'll provide you with specific strategies to help accomplish this. By expanding the scope of your attention, you can decrease the power of anxiety-provoking thoughts and sensations.

The way you handle your emotions can perpetuate your anxiety problems too. Because anxiety gives rise to terrifying thoughts, this naturally generates intense emotional distress, which can be difficult to endure. This intense emotional distress can make you feel different in your body. You might then interpret this distress as a sign of something being wrong, leading you to react in ways that reinforce your anxiety. Learning effective skills for regulating these intense and distressing emotions can help break this cycle, as we'll see in Chapter 6.

Chapter 7 is all about uncertainty, which is closely linked with anxiety, and if you struggle with tolerating uncertainty, you're more likely to experience high levels of anxiety. It's impossible to completely eliminate uncertainty from life and attempting to do so is not only a temporary fix but it also makes anxiety worse as your intolerance reduces further. It's important to learn how to live with and tolerate uncertainty, as this can really help reduce the impact of anxiety.

Avoidance is a common coping mechanism for those with anxiety, as it provides a sense of safety from feared situations. But this avoidance can actually worsen anxiety. In Chapter 8 I'll guide you through a step-by-step process to overcoming avoidance so you can return to activities that are important to you.

Experiencing traumatic events can often, but not always, lead to the development of anxiety-related problems. It's essential to explore the relationship between trauma and anxiety and explore effective strategies to manage it. People who have experienced trauma often struggle to accurately assess safety and danger, and their anxiety levels can remain high even when they're objectively safe. So it makes sense that people become hyper-vigilant and hyper-sensitive to potential threats. We will cover a number of tools in Chapter 9 to help you manage anxiety related to trauma and soothe your nervous system from its effects.

Anxiety can take up a lot of mental space, but once it dissipates, there's room for new and more positive experiences. After beating anxiety, you may discover a renewed sense of self, or newfound space for activities you previously couldn't do. We'll explore how you can maintain your progress and introduce things you love into your life. Lastly, in Chapter 10, I'll share strategies to protect yourself from future stressors and setbacks.

Throughout my years of clinical experience, I have encountered thousands of patients displaying among them a vast array of anxiety symptoms. Anxiety can manifest differently in each person's body and mind. Despite these variations, there are many shared experiences and symptoms that you'll recognize as you work through this book. By recognizing these symptoms, you'll gain a better insight into your own anxiety and this will help you learn how to cope more effectively. I will present all the information in a way that is easy to understand and, throughout the book, will use numerous real-life patient examples from my clinical experience to illustrate the concepts.

The strategies in this book are all based on well-researched, evidence-based, scientifically proven methods, including the following:

- Cognitive behavioural therapy (CBT). This helps people develop alternative ways of dealing with their difficulties, by managing thoughts and behaviours in other ways.
- Acceptance and commitment therapy (ACT). This has a strong focus on behaviour change, moving you away

from being trapped by the negative, and towards the life you want.

- Exposure and response prevention (ERP). This is a skill through which you learn to face your fears while refraining from doing things that reinforce them.

- Breathing exercises. These are effective in reducing the respiratory abnormalities seen in people with anxiety-based disorders.

- Mindfulness-based interventions. We will also use these to help engage the body's relaxation response.

When people discuss their anxiety problems with me, they often ask, 'What can I do to fix this?' My commitment to you is to equip you with all the necessary strategies to overcome your struggles with anxiety. I've laid these out for you in this book, and in return, I ask that you make a commitment to yourself to use the skills I've provided as best you can. Throughout the book there are lots of tasks. I encourage you to complete these exercises to the best of your ability, so you can pave the way towards achieving the success you truly want. Completing them is fundamental to your success. To begin with, you may find it helpful to work through the tasks in the order they follow, which will help you build your confidence gradually. As you become more familiar with the material you can then work on different tasks at the same time, particularly those that you find most helpful. I suggest you get a notebook for the tasks or use a digital notes app on your phone or computer. I love pen and paper, but more recently I've come to prefer digital notes, which are easier to find, store and look back at. In addition to the more detailed tasks aimed at anxiety recovery, you'll discover some quick hacks, a first aid kit of sorts, which provide you with skills to manage anxiety when you need a quick solution. These hacks, ten in total, are spread throughout the book at the end of chapters. So keep an eye out for them! I understand that adding more tasks to your daily routine can seem overwhelming and inconvenient, especially with everything else you're already dealing with. But consider this: your anxiety has probably taken up huge amounts of your time and energy. The tasks I'm asking you to do are minimal in comparison, and the benefits you'll gain from completing them are well worth the effort. Not only will you find these tasks enjoyable and some even relaxing, they'll also provide you with permanent alternatives to managing your anxiety. As you practise these new skills, you'll start to feel lighter and calmer. You'll also be better equipped to handle future anxiety and prevent it from becoming a bigger problem. So keep practising, and remember that the more you do, the easier it will become and the more progress you'll make.

Think of your anxiety as a story, where you are both the actor and the audience. As the actor, you might engage in behaviours that your anxiety tells you to do, like avoiding certain situations, or checking yourself excessively. But as the audience, you can observe how these actions impact the storyline and the consequences they bring. When you follow anxiety's script, the outcome is often negative and unfulfilling. You have the power to change the plot by becoming aware of your role as the actor, and taking small steps to shift your behaviour. That is exactly what the tasks in this book are about. By practising these tasks with persistence, you can gradually build your confidence and create a more positive outcome for yourself. By viewing your anxiety as a story, you can take control and become the author of your own narrative. With time, you'll watch your story unfold with a happier ending, and feel more empowered in managing your anxiety.

Getting the Basics Right

Before delving into those specialist tools, I want to emphasize the importance of the basic aspects of good mental health. These include sleep, diet, physical activity and how you spend your time, all of which have a significant impact on your emotional well-being. We won't devote a lot of time to this topic, but it's important to recognize that paying attention to these things will help you succeed in beating anxiety. Perfection is not the goal here, but rather doing the best you can. As you read, keep in mind that during difficult times, taking care of yourself by getting enough sleep, eating healthily and taking time out for yourself are the essential basics. The details I provide are simply suggestions to help you, so please just do what you can. Remember, as with all things, it's natural to fall off track occasionally, and when that happens, don't be too hard on yourself. Just pick up where you left off and keep going.

Sleep

Let's begin with the importance of sleep. Getting enough quality rest at night has a huge benefit for your mental health and can reduce your anxiety too. It's crucial to establish a consistent sleep routine that works for you. Try to create a soothing sleep environment. Aim to go to bed and wake up at roughly the same times each day. As you doubtless already know, avoid smoking or consuming caffeine, sugary drinks or alcohol before bedtime. All these things can stimulate your body and disrupt your natural sleep pattern. Avoid using screens approaching bedtime too, as these can also affect your ability to fall asleep. If you struggle with the urge to use your phone, consider leaving it in another room and using a physical alarm clock instead of relying on your phone. If you have any worries that play on your mind before bedtime, writing them down to deal with the next day can also help – keep your notebook or journal handy. If all this seems overwhelming, start with small changes, and gradually add more to your routine as you become more accustomed to the changes. For example, begin by turning off all screens by 10 p.m., and after a few weeks, incorporate more wind-down activities into your routine.

A good routine might involve an hour, or half an hour, of winding down, depending on how long you need. During this time, dim the lights, put on some calming music or maybe a podcast, brush your teeth, take a calming shower or bath, and complete any night-time grooming. After this you can do something relaxing, like reading a book, meditating, drawing, doing a puzzle, listening to an audiobook or doing some gentle yoga and stretching. Then get in bed and go to sleep! If you find it difficult to calm your mind, there are simple techniques you can try to help yourself to settle, such as counting backwards from a random number in the thousands. Another strategy is to visualize your favourite place in as much detail as possible. If you can't sleep and find yourself tossing and turning for more than thirty minutes, it can help to get out of bed and go back to a calming activity like reading until you feel sleepy again, then return to bed. Lastly, try to avoid looking at the time during the night, because this is known to increase anxiety, making you alert and then interrupting sleep further.

Diet

Food is fuel not only for your physical health, but also for your mental health. What you eat makes a difference to how many helpful nutrients your body gets. A good diet not only improves your mood, it also provides you with increased energy and, importantly, it enables your mind to think with increased clarity. The better you eat, the better your body works, and the better your brain works. The goal isn't about having an Instagram-worthy, picture-perfect diet; I'm quite sure my simple Marmite and toast snack wouldn't meet that standard, and that's okay. We're not striving for perfection, but simply doing our best with the resources we have available to us.

During anxiety crises, some of my patients may not be able to maintain a healthy diet for a day or two. I'm not going to pull them up about it, but I will support them and encourage them, because we have to accept that life is tough sometimes, and things like this will happen. Through my clinical work I know that appetite can often be suppressed by fear and anxiety. If this is the case for you, try to eat something small, something that is palatable. If you go through harder times and struggle with eating, just eat healthily when you can, and keep going. Where possible, try not to skip meals, and eat regularly throughout the day, so your body has enough fuel to keep working well. A quick and easy dietary hack is to have a piece of fruit (or vegetable) at each meal if you can. This not only helps you get your 'five a day', but research shows that eating raw fruit and vegetables is one of the pillars of good mental health. Aim to have a healthy, balanced diet, one that includes lots of fruits and vegetables, wholegrains, protein, healthy fats such as omega-3 and -6 fatty acids (to feed your brain). These foods contain many of the vitamins and minerals and much of the fibre you need. As well as your food intake, make sure that you're well hydrated by drinking plenty of fluids throughout the day. Keep in mind that anxiety can impact your digestive system, causing it to slow down or even speed up; it's important to support your body when anxiety is high, by consuming foods that are easy to digest. If you need specific advice on a healthy balanced diet see the NHS's Eat Well site or speak to your doctor.

Physical Activity

Physical activity is widely recognized as having significant positive impacts on both mental and physical health. Research studies overwhelmingly demonstrate that engaging in physical activity can help protect against anxiety and enhance overall mental well-being. Research also shows that physical activity can reduce the symptoms of anxiety and stress-related disorders, including post-traumatic stress disorder (PTSD) and panic disorder. If that isn't convincing enough, physical activity also reduces physical tension, enhances sleep quality, redirects attention, creates a sense of accomplishment, elevates your mood, decreases blood pressure, accelerates learning and enhances memory. So, try to engage in some form of regular physical movement, even if this is something small. You don't need to join a fancy gym or splash out on expensive equipment. There are so many free and easy ways to get moving both outdoors and indoors. Free exercise videos are widely available online, making it easier to engage in physical activity from the comfort of your own home. You can also take a brisk walk, cycle, swim, do some gardening, dance, and so much more. Getting outdoors will also give you additional benefits: exposure to green spaces has been shown to positively impact mental well-being. It's important that you find something you actually like doing, so it's fun as well as helping with your anxiety and mental health. Is there anything you used to enjoy in the past that you could start doing again? Can you look into local groups or sports teams?

Fun Activities

Participating in activities that you find enjoyable can have significant mental and physical health benefits. Anxiety should not consume your entire life or identity – when this happens you can lose sight of yourself and find that days, nights, weeks and months revolve solely around anxiety. Engaging in activities that provide alternative experiences for you can be hugely beneficial. Having enjoyable activities in your life can help you cope better with your more mundane daily tasks, reducing feelings of being overwhelmed by stressors. Anxiety is mentally and physically draining. By engaging in some fun activities, you will boost your energy levels, reduce tiredness and feel more confident. Doing fun things also reduces cortisol, a stress hormone that is elevated in people who suffer with anxiety problems. Taking time out for fun activities increases serotonin, another hormone. Serotonin helps with your mood, sleep, digestion, memory and the health of your body. The decrease in cortisol and increase in serotonin can increase mental energy, improving your clarity of thought and memory. These benefits are so desirable to us and will help us with the work we're going to do in beating anxiety.

Like many people, you may have stopped doing things you used to enjoy since anxiety took over. Take a moment to consider activities that you used to do but have stopped since anxiety took hold. Can you make a list of these activities and look at ways to reintroduce at least one back into your life?

Carve out time in your week to really commit to doing something you love. As time goes on, and you work through this programme, you can add more of these activities into your life. If you need some inspiration, take a look at the '100 Fun Activities' section starting on page 378.

Connection

The people and connections in your life can also have a positive impact on your mental health and overall well-being. They might be family members, friends, neighbours, colleagues or others. Through our connections we experience joyful moments, find support during difficult times, and we learn from one another too, whether from spending time talking, doing something fun or interesting together, exploring our emotions, getting a different perspective, getting someone's opinion on a problem, and so much more. Remember that it's okay to ask for help. But it's impossible for people who love and care about you to help you if they don't know what you need, so avoid isolating yourself and suffering in silence; reach out instead.

Both research and my own clinical experience with patients show that those suffering from anxiety tend to isolate themselves from others, which can worsen their problems. As you become more and more preoccupied with your anxiety, you may do less, and you may also engage less with other people. This provides the exact landscape your anxiety needs to grow and thrive, which is what we don't want. To prevent this, it's crucial to maintain connections with the people in your life who have a positive impact on you. If you've lost touch, can you look at re-establishing a connection to those people? Get back in touch: send a simple message saying 'Hi, it's been so long, I've been thinking of you, how are you?' Sometimes people don't want to spend time with others because they don't want to share their problems with them. They don't want to burden them, or they feel ashamed, or there could also be other reasons such as a fear that they won't understand. If you feel this way, you don't have to talk about what you're going through, you can just say what feels comfortable. The key is to focus on the quality of the time spent, rather than feeling pressured to share everything.

*

The benefits of these basics improve as you sustain them over a longer period of time. These are not things to do for a short-term quick fix solution; think of them, rather, as lifestyle changes that will lay the groundwork for you to overcome your anxiety. Try to make them a habit, in whatever way works for you: don't strive for perfection, aim for good enough!

Chapter 1:
Understanding Your Anxiety

The foundation to overcoming your anxiety is understanding it, and understanding what sustains it. It might be tempting to skip over this section and jump straight into the strategies. Please don't do this; this knowledge is the basis for the effectiveness of the rest of the strategies in this book. Imagine you were trying to fix a car or an appliance. You wouldn't just start randomly tinkering without first identifying the actual problem, and making sure you understand how it affects the rest of the system. Similarly, you need to understand your anxiety and its effects on your system – your whole mind and body – before you can effectively deal with it. The more you can understand about your anxiety the better, and the easier it will be for you to overcome your problems. That's why this first skill of understanding your anxiety is so important. If you were coming to see me in my clinic, this is exactly where we'd be starting.

Why Do You Need to Understand Anxiety?

Some people are aware and acknowledge that they have a problem with anxiety. Others are taken aback upon realizing that their physical experiences are due to anxiety. It can be really perplexing to grasp that anxiety can cause such symptoms; have you ever felt this way? Part of this confusion stems from not fully understanding your anxiety. Once you grasp the nature of your anxiety, you'll realize that its presence is more logical than you might originally have thought.

Imagine walking through a forest on a foggy day, where the path is riddled with obstacles like rocks and fallen branches. You can only see a few feet ahead, and everything appears blurry and indistinct. This is what it's like when you lack knowledge and understanding of a situation, obstructed by hazy and unclear thoughts about anxiety. When the sun breaks through the fog, the path ahead is brilliantly lit, revealing all its intricate details. You can see clearly, and no longer stumble blindly. The same goes for gaining knowledge and understanding about how your anxiety operates. With knowledge and understanding of how your anxiety impacts you, the path ahead of you becomes illuminated, making it easier to navigate and overcome your struggles. The clarity gained from this information allows you to see what you're dealing with, and guides you towards recovery.

You're here because at some level you accept that you have a problem with anxiety. You might feel some doubt about this acceptance at times, but that's okay, it's part of how anxiety operates. Your problems with anxiety didn't just come out of the blue; there is a reason for them. Sometimes, something has happened to alter the way you think, feel and react to things. As you develop a better understanding of your anxiety, you'll be able to see the inextricable links between your thoughts, feelings and behaviours. You'll also gain insight into the working of your brain, and how this impacts both your physical and mental state. We'll look at causes of anxiety, so if you've ever asked yourself 'Why me?' then you might find the answer in this chapter. We will also discuss anxiety triggers, and you'll learn to identify those that are personal to you. In addition, this chapter covers the factors that contribute to the maintenance of your anxiety, keeping it going. This includes a detailed explanation of why you may have become trapped in what seems like a never-ending loop. We'll focus on these cycles that maintain anxiety to bring about significant changes. So, let's get started!

What Do I Mean by Anxiety?

Anxiety is a feeling, an emotional, psychological and physical experience. You don't need me to tell you that we all experience anxiety sometimes; it's a normal part of life. Anxiety is essential to our survival, and it enhances our performance when we need it to. We need anxiety to work for us, so it boosts our functioning, rather than impairing our ability.

When anxiety becomes a problem, it interferes with normal day-to-day life. This might be general anxiety, health anxiety, feelings of panic or social anxiety. Throughout this book, for ease, I'll mostly refer to these collectively as anxiety or anxiety-based problems unless a distinction is required for any tasks or case examples. Anxiety becomes a problem for many people when it's persistently present in the absence of immediate danger, and when there's no need to be primed for fear. Experiences like this can leave you feeling terrified without due cause. When there's too much anxiety, it's constant or it keeps kicking in when there's no need for it to do so, it's become a significant problem.

Your Brain and Anxiety

The fear pathway starts in your brain, which is wired to react instantly to danger. Fear is an absolutely essential function of the brain, keeping you alert, alive and well. Your brain reacts to suspected danger so it can ensure your safety and survival.

Part of understanding your anxiety is learning about what happens in your brain when threat strikes. Your brain has a number of regions that process fearful stimuli – this is the brain's fear network. The two important structures within your brain's fear network that we'll talk a little bit more about are the thalamus and the amygdala. In short, the thalamus receives sensory information, and the amygdala processes a fear response.

The thalamus has many vital roles in your body: it regulates consciousness and alertness, and relays sensory information, as well as motor signals. You can think of the thalamus as an information relay station. The sensory information your thalamus receives includes things like what you see, what you hear, physical sensation (touch), and what you taste. Basically, this means all your senses except smell, which goes somewhere else: the olfactory cortex.

The thalamus relays information to the amygdala to trigger a response. The amygdala plays a crucial role in regulating fearful emotions. It does this by processing emotions and memories that are associated with fear and anxiety. The amygdala is very sensitive to signals of threat, and it's also involved in attaching emotional meaning to your memories. It matches incoming information to past memories, and can process non-threatening events as threatening, based on memory associations that you may have made. This can happen unconsciously and outside your awareness.

If your amygdala perceives something as threatening it activates various pathways that lead to the production and release of stress hormones. The primary stress hormone in your body is cortisol. Adrenaline (also known as epinephrine) is another hormone released by your body in response to fear. Both these hormones lead to dramatic changes in your body, affecting your heart, your breathing and your muscles, and putting you

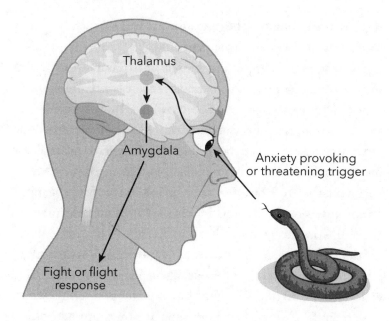

Thalamus

Amygdala

Anxiety provoking
or threatening trigger

Fight or flight
response

on guard. When this happens, there are literally hundreds of reactions that can take place in various parts of your body. These result in physical, mental and behavioural changes. This is the fight or flight response, also known as the stress response or fear response. This neurobiological response prepares your body and mind for action, whether that be fight or flight. Your brain will initiate this response regardless of whether you're in actual danger, and it will react even when the threat is not real, because its job is to ensure your safety and survival. When was the last time your body did this?

Simply contemplating the things that frighten you can be enough to initiate these responses. What thoughts or situations evoke such a reaction in you? Sometimes, even specific words can cause this fear response to kick in. On occasions some of my patients have even tried to ban me from using certain words in their presence, words like heart attack or cancer or vomit, because of how strongly associated these words are with their anxiety. Conquering avoidance behaviours like these is a crucial part of beating anxiety, and I'll show you how to do this in Chapter 8 (see page 266).

Horror movies are another excellent example of the fear response being triggered in the absence of actual danger or threat. During a suspense-filled movie scene, your palms can sweat, your heart rate can increase, and your muscles even tense up, despite there being no real danger to you. These intense sensations are not an indication that anything is wrong with you, they're a result of your brain's innate programming. In the case of a horror movie, once your brain has evaluated the situation and realized that you are not in danger, it turns off this fear response. These instantaneous reactions are essential to your survival. Dangerous situations usually need rapid action: they don't fit well with thinking and pondering, which would be a waste of valuable time if you were actually in danger. The stress response relaxes once the perceived danger has passed, and your body returns to a more balanced state. When people suffer with anxiety problems they experience prolonged feelings of threat, which don't fully subside. This can cause your body to remain in a heightened state of fear, and can keep the stress response going for longer periods.

Fight – Flight – Freeze
The three different reactions to the stress response are fight, flight and freeze.

- **Fight** is when you confront and manage the threat through necessary action.
- **Flight** is when you flee or escape from the situation to avoid the threat.
- **Freeze** is a response to fear that causes temporary paralysis, making you stay still and watchful.

Everybody responds differently to frightening situations: the response that your mind and body make is personal to you. It will be based on the situation, learned behaviour, personality factors and your thoughts at the time. Regardless of its specific make-up, the strategies in this book will help you feel calmer.

What Anxiety Does to Your Body and Mind

Anxiety creates hundreds of sensations and experiences, with each person having a unique occurrence of these, which may include bodily sensations, psychological experiences and behavioural changes. The bodily changes come in the form of physical sensations experienced in all parts of your body. You may experience sensations that are fairly constant, they may come and go, and they may also switch between different types. Fear-related sensations can come in waves of repeated attacks as well. Psychological changes relate to the way you think, perceive and how your emotions change. Behavioural changes refer to actions taken by you; the things you do.

As we've already learned, the fear response is supposed to be adaptive and helpful to you. All the changes associated with the fear response are supposed to enhance your performance and prime your body and mind to deal with potential threats. When the fear response is working as it's supposed to, the changes in your body and mind are sudden and intense, but short-lived, and everything is supposed to settle when the danger has passed. It's when these reactions don't switch off that the fear response leads to problematic anxiety. You're no longer at the peak of enhanced performance for threat management; instead your body and mind have become too stressed.

This type of stress can cause these changes to become more

consistent and unpleasant. Because the fear response has gone on too long, your mind and body are overstressed, and with this your ability to cope can deteriorate. Anxiety can cause your thoughts to become persistently negative, making you even more fearful, which in turn causes your sensations of anxiety to become more pronounced. Can you see how bodily changes and psychological changes fuel each other? You can get stuck in a vicious cycle of unbearable physical discomfort and psychological overload. This makes it difficult for you to stay calm and in control; even though you've tried to tell your-self to be sensible, it just doesn't work.

Many of the sensations brought on by anxiety can be alarming. Yes, they're uncomfortable and frightening, but you need to remind yourself that these are your body's reactions to stress. Understanding how your body can react when it's experiencing chronic or high levels of anxiety will help you take a different perspective. If you're worried about identify-ing typical symptoms and sensations of anxiety, it might help you to refer to the comprehensive list at the end of the book (see page 368). This list includes almost all the bodily, psycho-logical and behavioural changes that are commonly associated with anxiety, and all those that I've seen in my clinical practice. Please don't be alarmed by the sensations on the list. While some may appear unusual to you, remember that you're unlikely to experience all of them, and it is also unlikely that you'll develop completely new ones. If you've been struggling with anxiety for some time, your body has already established a personalized response to it. I hope this is reassuring to you.

So now for your first task. For each task, you will need to jot down your responses to the questions or instructions, so have either a notebook or digital device with a notes app handy. Your first task is pretty straightforward.

TASK 1
How does anxiety affect me?

You've learned that anxiety creates sensations in your body, and that psychological and behavioural changes occur alongside these. Your first task is to identify how anxiety affects you in these three areas. Consult the Common Symptoms and Sensations section on page 368 to help you with this task. By way of example, I've listed the symptoms experienced by my patient Margo.

Physical

Take note of the physical reactions you experience during anxiety. Margo experiences heart palpitations, breathlessness, and feeling hot and dizzy.

Psychological

How does anxiety affect your thoughts and mental state? What goes through your mind? Margo becomes fixated on catastrophic thoughts and she can't stop thinking in disastrous terms, believing that something bad is about to happen to her any minute.

Behavioural

Note down the behavioural actions taken by you, the things you do as a result of your anxiety, such as avoiding certain situations or seeking reassurance. In Margo's case she avoids going out alone, avoids exertion and asks for constant reassurance.

Things That Trigger Anxiety

So here we're talking about triggers, as distinct from causes, which we will get on to next. What do I mean by triggers? Something can happen to trigger an increase in the intensity of anxiety, a spike which may eventually go down, after which you're either free from anxiety – or you're back to your 'normal' or resting level of anxiety. Triggers can be internal, arising from within you – a thought, a sensation, an emotion, images that pop into your mind or reminders of past events. Triggers that are external are things that happen outside of you: situations, things other people say or do, things you see, hear and so on. It's important that you recognize and understand your triggers: you will need to know them in order to be able to do something about them. Getting a good grasp of them is crucial because it's your triggers that will often cause you to react in ways that maintain your problems with anxiety. Triggers are very different for each person, but there are some common ones listed in the table below.

Common Anxiety Triggers	
Body-based Triggers	◦ Physical sensations ◦ Being in pain ◦ Menopause ◦ Menstruation ◦ Pregnancy
Health Triggers	◦ Clinical environments ◦ Medical procedures ◦ A health issue (one's own or in others)

Online including Social Media / News Triggers	∘ News reports of people being unwell, coming to harm or dying ∘ Consuming too much anxiety-inducing material about illness, disease, catastrophe ∘ Adverts about life insurance, will writing, funerals, public health
Relational / Interpersonal Triggers	∘ Being alone ∘ Being around people ∘ Conflict or being mistreated ∘ Suffering bereavement or loss ∘ Becoming a parent
Cognitive Triggers	∘ Thinking about or remembering something frightening ∘ Trigger words such as cancer, death, disease, illness or Covid
Triggering Places / Situations	∘ Exposure to situations that feel risky, like germs or toxins ∘ Driving, and being stuck in traffic, in tunnels or on bridges ∘ Public transport, trains and planes ∘ Crowded situations

TASK 2
Identify your anxiety triggers
Have your notebook or digital notes handy.

Chronic anxiety can remain at a low-intensity resting level. Triggers, internal or external, can cause this anxiety to intensify. Understanding your triggers will help you see what you react to. Looking at the triggers in the table above, and considering other triggers that I may not have listed here, take a note of those that apply to you. We will be working on these reactions later.

Why Me?

Have you ever wondered why you are experiencing anxiety like this? This question might have crossed your mind numerous times and you might already have a clear understanding of the reason behind it. On the other hand, you may be puzzled about why this is happening to you. Countless factors contribute to the development of anxiety problems. The root cause can be related to an anxious temperament, your personality and psychological traits, or past experiences which have shaped your mind to function in a particular way. Your family history could also play a role. In some cases, something may have happened to make you more vulnerable to anxiety problems, such as a childhood experience or even a traumatic event. Situational factors can also be a cause, where you were doing fine until a particular life stressor disrupted your sense of safety and stability. The outbreak of the Coronavirus pandemic was one such stressor that affected many people.

Even though some causes are known, it can still be difficult to know exactly what causes anxiety problems. For some people it can seem like their problems have come out of the blue without any obvious cause. Some people develop problems with anxiety when life appears to be going pretty well, and there isn't a clearly identifiable cause. Whatever the cause of your anxiety problems, the strategies in this book will help you. I've learned from my clinical experience that while causes can give us great insight into why, it's the application of the various strategies that brings real progress. If you don't know the cause(s) of your anxiety, I caution against getting hooked on trying to find out, and suggest that you instead focus your resources on recovery and the application of the strategies in this book.

Based on my clinical experience, the known causes of anxiety typically fall under certain categories. However, it's uncommon to identify a single causal factor that independently contributes to the development of anxiety. Instead, multiple vulnerabilities can often interact with each other, leading to the anxiety problem. Let's explore some of these.

Temperament and personality

Your temperament and personality shape how you respond to things around you. If you have an anxious temperament, you may have an increased sensitivity and responsiveness to situations that seem uncomfortable. This heightened sensitivity may cause you to withdraw from these situations, leading to reduced self-confidence and negative perceptions about your coping abilities. This may compel you to avoid more things, which in turn worsens the problem. Avoidance is a common coping mechanism used by people with anxious or sensitive temperaments to navigate life; we'll see more of this in Chapter 8 (see page 266). People who have perfectionist tendencies can be at an increased risk of experiencing anxiety problems, as well as those who are easily overwhelmed by stressors. Additionally, people who desire control over their environment or personal circumstances can also be more vulnerable to developing anxiety problems.[1]

Adverse childhood experiences (ACEs)

Certain factors in your family life, childhood history and upbringing can be associated with an increased likelihood of developing anxiety problems. These might include things like:

- Growing up in an environment that felt unstable/uncertain
- Inconsistent parenting
- Attachment insecurities
- Family mental health difficulties
- Family substance misuse
- A disturbed or high-conflict home environment
- Having an unstable parent/carer who behaved in unpredictable, frightening or erratic ways
- Too much responsibility at a young age
- Being over-protected
- Being expected to cope alone with your problems
- Loss of a family member
- Physical illness or disability

Traumatic life experiences

Experiencing traumatic events during childhood, adolescence or adulthood can contribute to the development of anxiety problems too. What many of these experiences have in common is the sense of powerlessness and uncertainty they leave behind, creating a sense of unsafety and an inability to cope with everyday situations that trigger similar fears. Traumatic life events can affect an individual's beliefs, perception, emotions and reactions. The magnitude of the event does not determine the impact it can have on a person. Clinically we refer to traumas as 'big T' traumas and 'small t' traumas, and both can cause significant distress. While big T traumas are those that are widely acknowledged as traumatic and can lead to a diagnosis of post-traumatic stress disorder (PTSD), small t traumas are also distressing and may have a significant impact on your mental health. The terminology used to classify these traumas is meant to aid in treatment planning and does not diminish the severity of small t traumas. What truly matters is the impact that the trauma has left on you as a person.

Big T traumas that often lead to a PTSD diagnosis might be things like:

- Experiencing a situation where there was death, serious injury or harm, or other extreme threat to your physical integrity.

- Witnessing a situation where there was a threat of death, serious injury or harm, or other extreme threat to someone else's physical integrity.

- Events that are a serious threat to your existence and integrity can include sexual abuse, being affected by serious crime, violence, health-related incidents, accidents, or being in a war zone or natural disaster.

Small t traumas can be life events that don't usually involve a serious threat to your existence, violence or disaster, but they are traumatic for you at a personal level and create significant distress. Because small t traumas don't involve serious violence, disaster or death, sufferers can minimize their impact and overlook them. This might be because a person thinks these things are more common, therefore they might shame themselves for reacting to them when worse things could happen. Or maybe they don't recognize how much the event has actually affected them. Whatever the reason, whether it's minimization, avoidance or not knowing it can lead to bottling things up, it can in turn cause more suffering by worsening anxiety problems. Small t traumas can be things like:

- Non-life-threatening injuries
- Non-life-threatening health conditions
- Being bullied
- Interpersonal problems
- Relationship breakdown
- Medical intervention
- Phobic experiences
- Suffering pregnancy loss
- A stressful move
- Financial distress
- Job loss

People doing certain jobs can be at increased risk of traumatization and developing anxiety problems. Some of these have been documented in research studies, and I've also seen them in my own clinical practice.[2] These are:

- Military and war-zone personnel
- Firefighters
- Police officers
- Medical and healthcare workers

Non-traumatic causes of anxiety

Not all anxiety problems stem from a traumatic experience. I've had patients reporting to me that therapists have attributed their anxiety to trauma even where they do not recall a traumatic experience; these therapists have continued to search for, or even assume one, which can be frustrating and unproductive for the person suffering.

Sometimes people worry that they have experienced a hidden trauma and become frustrated when they cannot find evidence of it but, in some cases, such a trauma may not actually exist. Let's consider some of the non-traumatic factors that can contribute to anxiety problems:

- A life transition can trigger anxiety symptoms. Among the many examples of such transitions are getting married, becoming a parent, changes in your body, starting a new job and buying a house.

- Feeling anxious during a particular situation or scenario can create a preoccupation with that scenario and others like it. For instance, if you gave a presentation at work and it went wrong, you felt uncomfortable or stumbled over your words, it may lead to a preoccupation around performance in similar situations in the future. This results in a heightened self-focus which then triggers anxiety.

- Sometimes, past experiences can shape how much attention you give to a situation, event or physical sensation in your body. Traumatic events or illnesses can cause hyper-vigilance, and experiencing panic attacks can also heighten sensitivity to physical sensations. Difficult childhood experiences, including emotional suppression or critical parenting, can also contribute to the tendency to interpret physical sensations as threatening when they're not.

- Sometimes, something has happened that makes you feel uncertain and this causes you to worry about that particular thing. Even when the 'thing' is resolved you can remain anxious because you've become stuck in a cycle of overthinking and worrying about things. The anxiety-provoking situation has passed, but anxiety cycles have established themselves.

- Health anxiety can begin after a benign or minor health problem. This can cause sufferers to become over-aware, and over-prepared for health issues. This solution to managing health can seem reasonable at the start, but it ends up becoming a problem when anxiety is established and maintained.

- Sometimes, something has happened to firm up beliefs about health, death and disease, about how careful one should be. Public health campaigns, hearing a story or seeing something on the news can have this effect.

- Acquiring knowledge about diseases and illness can lead to the development of health anxiety when a person develops a preoccupation with that knowledge. As above, this knowledge might come from public health campaigns, advertisements, hearing about someone or seeing something on the news. Those working in medical professions can be affected by this.

- Sometimes, something has happened to affect a person's ability to tolerate doubt, following which they become hooked on certainty. This desire to know for certain how something will be leads to lots of control behaviours, and problematic anxiety quickly establishes itself.

What Keeps Anxiety Going?

Why won't this stop? How can I make it stop? I'm trying my best but it just seems to be getting worse and worse. Relatable? One of the main reasons that your anxiety isn't getting better is because you're stuck in a self-perpetuating cycle, based on how you've been responding to your problems. These responses could include:

- The way you think about your problems.
- How you focus on your problems.
- The sensations you feel.
- The way you use emotions to solve your problems.
- Having a low tolerance for distress.
- The actions you take in response to your anxiety.
- Avoidance and an intolerance of uncertainty.

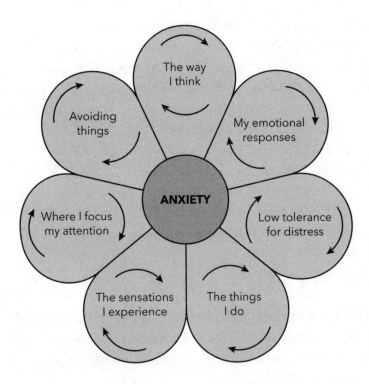

Imagine you come across a news story about a celebrity who developed throat cancer, which triggers an increase in your anxiety. This fear leads you to believe that you too could develop throat cancer, intensifying your anxiety. You start to focus your attention on your throat, which then starts to feel strange. You interpret these sensations as signs of throat cancer and respond by checking your throat and searching the internet, causing further fear and anxiety. As your fear and anxiety intensify, you start to experience bodily sensations that reinforce your belief that something is wrong. Seeking reassurance from others or medical professionals provides temporary relief, but when you experience another sensation in your throat, the cycle repeats itself and each time it intensifies. This feedback loop gives anxiety power as output from one loop feeds into the input of the next loop.

Anxiety cycles set in when you become trapped in a pattern that generates more stress, leading to a continuous need to manage this stress through various coping behaviours. To overcome anxiety, it is crucial to break free from these distressing cycles. Understanding the workings of these cycles is an important step towards beating anxiety. The positive aspect of a cycle is that it can be transformed from a negative pattern to a more helpful one. Think of a bicycle wheel spinning in one direction. You can change its direction by applying an opposing force, which will redirect its movement. Initially, this may need a lot of effort, but with perseverance, the wheel will start to gain momentum and keep moving in the new direction.

The way you think

The way you think about anxiety will either make you more scared, or less scared. If you interpret your thoughts as fact and agree with them that a catastrophe is about to take place, of course you're going to feel terrified. This terror will fuel your body's fear response. Remember, when the fear response is ramped up it becomes harder to think clearly, and you experience intrusive thoughts and scary images. These are coupled with intense emotional reactions, which can make your mind label them as a priority, and your mind will then bring these to your attention again and again, frightening you a bit more every time.

There are several ways in which you can take an unbalanced view of the situation, causing yourself more anxiety. Unbalanced views exaggerate the problem, they distort your thinking; and the more you engage with unbalanced thinking, the harder it becomes to hold a realistic perspective. Before you know it, your thoughts have become extreme and they fuel your anxiety by trapping you into a cycle like the one shown here:

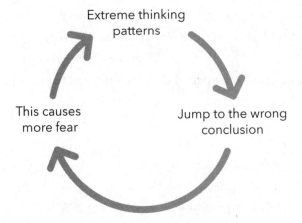

Extreme thinking patterns

Jump to the wrong conclusion

This causes more fear

Catastrophizer

This is the most frequent thinking pattern observed in my clinic. It involves assuming the worst possible outcome and convincing yourself that it will definitely happen, regardless of its actual probability. Catastrophizing often includes phrases like 'what if' and overestimating negative consequences.

Example: What if the plane crashes and we all die? What if my child's fever is really a fatal illness? What if this panic attack is a heart attack?

All-or-nothing thinker

You think in extremes: you're either completely safe and well, or you're dying of a heart attack. Things are either completely fine, or completely awful. When you think in this way, you're unable to see a middle ground where you tell yourself: 'Yes, this is hard, but it will pass.'

Example: I will never get better. This is not going to stop. Unless I'm free of all anxiety it's hopeless.

Over-generalizer

You take a bad experience, situation or event and project it into your future as a never-ending pattern. You've reached a conclusion based on one occurrence, and you go on applying that conclusion to every similar event or scenario.

Example: If it happened once, it will keep happening. I will *always* have panic attacks if I go out alone.

Fortune teller

Imagine having a crystal ball in which you can see your future, and all you tell yourself is that more pain and suffering are in store. In this thinking style you predict that future events will have a specific negative outcome for you or your loved ones.

Example: I know I'm doomed to die young, I can just tell, and it will be a horrible, painful end. If I come across someone who is sick, I'll be sure to catch what they have and become seriously unwell.

Mind reader

You make assumptions about what other people are thinking or doing in relation to you, and these assumptions are invariably negative.

Example: That person looked at me strangely because they know there's something wrong with me. The secretary at the doctor's surgery was looking at me funny because she's seen my test result and she knows it's bad news.

Mental filterer

You sieve out all the positives in a situation, leaving yourself to dwell on the negatives. You remove any reassuring facts from the information you have, and focus on the tiny thing that opposes them. This tendency to ignore positives in favour of negatives causes you considerable distress. Even when there might be positives, you steer well away from them.

Example: I know the doctor said my bloods were normal, but that one slightly elevated reading means I'm ill.

Labeller

You define yourself globally in a particularly extreme and negative way. This should really be known as 'mis-labelling' because that is what people are doing when they get stuck in this thinking pattern: taking a single attribute and turning it into an absolute.

Example: Because I felt dizzy in the car, I have a problem with fainting. Because I was anxious when driving, I should give it up.

Personalizer

You take things and apply them *too* personally to yourself. This can make you believe that you're responsible for bad things that happen, even if factually these are out of your control or aren't even that bad. You may also feel guilty if you don't do things to prevent the imagined catastrophe.

Example: Your child catches a stomach bug and you blame yourself for not being more careful.

Exaggerator

You believe that you're doomed, that everything always goes wrong for you and always will. If you note something concerning, you exaggerate the meaning of it.

Example: If you note a link between eating raw fish and parasitic infections, you assume that, because you've eaten sushi at one point in your life, you already have the parasite in your body. By exaggerating like this you don't pay attention to important details like the type of fish and how the fish is treated, stored or prepared as contributing factors.

Having positive beliefs about anxiety

Some of my patients have said they're low-key glad that they have anxiety in their lives. Perhaps you share this perspective? You believe that anxiety prompts readiness and vigilance, that anxiety helps you be prepared and alert. You view anxiety as a helpful strategy, a way of preparing for problems and a method of self-protection. You may also see anxiety as a valuable tool, a means of anticipating and safeguarding yourself and others against potential problems. However, rather than being helpful, this mindset causes you to get locked into a pattern of constant worry and it degrades your confidence and your coping ability.

Example: If I don't keep checking my blood pressure I'll miss something. If I try to get rid of my anxiety I might jinx myself into a catastrophe; I can't let go of it.

*

Let's dig into this last point a little more. Perhaps you're hesitant to let go of your anxiety because you fear that acknowledging your safety will invite disaster and you feel like it would be tempting fate. You don't want to do this because you believe that you will jinx yourself into a catastrophe. This trap of not wanting to tempt fate, or 'the jinxing' as I like to call it, makes you feel scared to admit you're safe. Here you're holding a positive belief that anxiety protects you from catastrophe occurring, when in fact it doesn't. The fear of letting go of this anxiety is so intense, it makes you believe that if, for one minute, you let go of it you'll end up with a catastrophe.

Let's say you have a fear of developing cancer or heart failure, even though you know rationally that you're healthy. You may resist admitting this to yourself, fearing that acknowledging your safety will somehow cause these catastrophes to occur. This resistance may stem from a belief that anxiety is a malevolent force waiting to punish you for being too confident. In reality, this idea of being jinxed is itself a symptom of anxiety: if you weren't suffering from anxiety, you wouldn't believe that you could jinx yourself into a catastrophe. Unfortunately, what typically happens is the person assumes their anxious thoughts are accurate, and therefore follows through with the actions demanded by their anxiety. By doing so they worsen the anxiety cycle and the wheel keeps spinning in a negative direction.

The way you focus your attention

The way you focus your attention when you're in a fearful state also keeps your problems going. Anxiety naturally increases hyper-vigilance and narrows your attention onto the thing you're scared of. This is what's supposed to happen in a situation where there's actual danger. If you're in a dangerous situation your mind and body will prime themselves to scan and attend to the risk. The purpose of this intense focusing is to help your mind examine, assess and deal with the potential threat. Of course, when you're experiencing unfounded fear you're not in any danger, but you still focus your attention as if you *are* in danger. When this happens, your attention becomes narrowly focused on the threat, and this is super scary. Let's say this threat is an internal sensation of anxiety: your attention will become narrowly focused on that, which in turn will amplify it, and you will get stuck in a cycle like the one shown here:

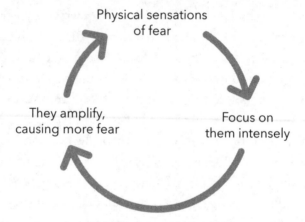

Physical sensations
of fear

They amplify,
causing more fear

Focus on
them intensely

Threats can be internal or external. Internal ones are often physical sensations of anxiety: you may have a scary thought which triggers a sensation, or the other way round where you have a sensation that triggers a scary thought. Regardless of which way round this happens, you then focus more attention on these internal processes. The interaction between them and your focused attention intensifies them, perpetuating another cycle of anxiety. External things might be events, situations or physical stimuli. Some examples from a seemingly endless list to help you get the idea are: confined spaces, news stories, videos, spiders, vomit, and having to go for medical procedures.

Over time, as you focus more and more on frightening things, your attention becomes biased in favour of those things. This is because your mind decides that these things pose a threat. Why? Well, because of the way you've interpreted them, the way you think about them, the emotional charge that goes with those thoughts, and any previous memory associations your mind has made of the 'thing' being frightening. When your attention is biased in favour of the things you're frightened of, you notice them in a different way. If this is a physical sensation of anxiety you become more aware of it, it becomes amplified, it feels peculiar, and you notice it all the time. When you notice it, you feel scared, it feels worse, you get more anxious, it worsens, leading to a further self-perpetuating cycle of anxiety.

When your attention is narrowed you also notice the 'thing' you're afraid of everywhere. This makes it seem much more common than it actually is. But the incidence of the 'thing' hasn't increased, you're just noticing it more because of the way your attention is focused. Because you notice it more, it seems scarier and more likely that it could impact you. This can also lead you to scan regularly for the things you're afraid of. When you're consistently scanning you increase the likelihood of noticing these things more, and when you do it brings more anxiety your way. And there goes another self-perpetuating cycle of anxiety.

Let me give you another example to illustrate how the way you focus your attention can feed anxiety. Suppose you discover a lump or bump on your skin, and you become fixated on it. Catastrophic thoughts flood your mind, and you begin to experience physical sensations of anxiety. Your attention becomes hyper-focused on the lump, causing you to constantly check and touch it, which eventually leads to soreness and inflammation, further intensifying the sensations in that area. Your worry and preoccupation only grow as the sensation becomes stronger, which fuels your desire to check it even more, ultimately resulting in more pain. As the pain worsens you become convinced that there's a serious physical problem, so you keep going with the pattern of focusing and reacting, leading to yet another anxiety cycle.

It can be very difficult to pull your attention away from the things you're afraid of, but this is something you will need to do. The good news is there is a whole chapter on how you can improve the way you focus your attention so that it doesn't feed your anxiety (see page 172).

The sensations you feel

Anxiety brings with it lots of unpleasant sensations. Viewing these sensations as evidence of a problem keeps you stuck in a cycle of fear. These sensations and your misinterpretation of them are huge factors in maintaining your anxiety.

Physical sensations of fear

View them as dangerous

This causes more fear

When you experience a sensation you don't like, a negative thought occurs with it. These sensations may be familiar, having been experienced for weeks, months or even years.

Let's say you get the sensation of air hunger and breathlessness and you interpret this as a sign of cardiac threat. This raises your anxiety level, and when your anxiety level rises the sensation intensifies, because that's how your body responds to threat. The result is an increased demand for oxygen because you're even more scared, which makes your body pump blood faster, and for this it needs more oxygen. As this gets worse your thoughts get worse too: 'I can't breathe, I'm going to suffocate and die, I feel light-headed. What if I collapse, am I having a heart attack, is this a stroke, what shall I do?'

The issue is that your body is reacting normally to the fear response in generating these bodily sensations. However, you interpret these sensations as alarming, which perpetuates a distress cycle. In some cases, the sensations can be so intense and unpleasant that you dread experiencing them again. This fear of the sensations themselves can heighten your sensitivity, making you feel activated even by the mere anticipation of their recurrence. This anticipation can then trigger anxiety, which can cause the sensation to then occur.

Blood pressure is another example. Anxiety naturally causes increases in blood pressure, which is part of priming your body for action. If you become fearful of this increase in blood pressure, you'll react by thinking about frightening possibilities, which in turn raises your anxiety and pushes your blood pressure up even more. You may then become so concerned about having a health problem due to the high blood pressure that you get caught in patterns of behaviour that only reinforce it.

Your emotions

There are a number of ways your emotions keep your anxiety problems going. To begin with, many anxiety sufferers turn their feelings into fact. They experience emotional distress, struggle to tolerate the distress, and assume this distress is a sure sign that something is wrong. Essentially, anxiety makes you react to how you're feeling, so you'll go with your feeling instead of weighing up the facts. Instead of dealing with whatever emotion has surfaced by regulating it, you unintentionally merge it with your anxiety problems. Suppose you are afraid of a specific sensation in your body. Your constant focus on it amplifies it and your reaction to it intensifies it further. This in turn makes you feel a certain way and reinforces your belief that there must be something wrong, and because you feel so scared it must be a sign that there is. The emotional trap of 'I feel it, so it must be true' then perpetuates your anxiety. Here, the emotion that needs regulating and calming is the feeling of being scared, but instead the emotion becomes viewed as proof that there's something wrong, or it influences another reaction that feeds anxiety further. Have you had unsubstantiated sensations of anxiety that, based on your emotional feeling, in your mind you've turned into fact? We can view this as a false emotional alarm that keeps being set off due to the habitual patterns your mind has gotten into.

TASK 3
Identify your false emotional alarms

Answer the questions below in your notebook or your digital notes.

- Looking back, have you experienced false emotional alarms?
- For how long have you been experiencing false emotional alarms?

- How often have you experienced false emotional alarms?
- Roughly how many false emotional alarms have you experienced?
- What patterns do you notice about the past false emotional alarms?
- What is the repeat message that you can take away from these past false emotional alarms?

Emotions can also impede your progress by creating a sense of hopelessness, making you feel stuck in a perpetual state of misery, as if nothing can change or be better. If you've been grappling with anxiety for a prolonged period, it can affect your mood, causing you to experience feelings of despair, sadness and frustration. This emotional state can be demoralizing, making it appear daunting to overcome anxiety. The fear that it may never cease can lead you to dread the future, making it challenging to persevere. The more you ruminate on these thoughts, the deeper you sink into a spiral of negativity, which further undermines your confidence, making it even more difficult to cope. This too is a self-perpetuating cycle.

Low tolerance for distress

I've worked with countless patients who have had a high sensitivity to anxiety, coupled with low tolerance for emotional distress. A complex mix, right? On the one hand you have a sensitivity to experiencing anxiety (with a fear of the consequences of anxiety itself), and on the other an intolerance of emotional distress. So what's the implication of this? Well, it means you react in the heat of the moment, you struggle to think before you react and you're therefore highly likely to take an unhelpful action. You may also react more intensely to the problems you experience: you want them gone quickly and can't tolerate the feelings they bring, so you go for ineffective quick fixes.

To effectively deal with anxiety, it's crucial to learn how to slow down your mind and develop a higher tolerance for emotional distress. This way, you'll be less likely to react impulsively and resort to unhelpful solutions to escape the discomfort. The good news is you can learn how to tolerate distress by establishing better emotional regulation skills, and I'm going to teach you how to do this in Chapter 6 (see page 196).

The things you do

The things you do in response to your anxiety can also maintain your problems. Many are avoidance-based, in that you try to avoid feeling a certain way or try to avoid certain events taking place by performing certain actions. These actions are primarily focused on evading unpleasant feelings or circumventing particular situations. This is the 'doing' part of your anxiety. Being in a state of high anxiety is horrible, so of course you want to relieve yourself of this by doing something, taking some kind of action to feel less afraid. I understand why you are doing this, but ultimately we will be trying to change this too, because it isn't helping your anxiety. The things that people do can include the following:

- Repeatedly asking for reassurance from loved ones.
- Repeatedly asking doctors for reassurance.
- Avoiding doctors because you believe there's something wrong with you.

- Searching for comfort, answers or certainty by conducting extensive internet research.

- Checking and monitoring parts of your body that have anxiety sensations within them.

- Using medical equipment, devices or trackers to monitor fear reactions in your body.

- Touching wood, or following other superstitions to ward off catastrophe.

It makes perfect sense to want to do something to alleviate anxiety. But it makes no sense when you've become reliant on doing things to relieve your anxiety, so reliant that you need to repeat these things again and again. Even when you repeat them your anxiety doesn't resolve. If they were effective at resolving your anxiety, you wouldn't need to keep doing them. The thing is, they give you short-term relief, so you have the illusion that they're helpful, but in the longer term they condition you into being unable to tell the difference between actual danger and harmless things. The more this happens, the less you trust your judgement, and the less you trust others. This is because your ability to discriminate between danger and harm has been degraded by your anxiety.

Asking for reassurance is a real biggie in maintaining anxiety problems. It's natural to want to seek comfort, and as a person without an anxiety disorder, when you do this occasionally it doesn't cause a problem. It's definitely not a bad thing to ask for reassurance; but it backfires on you when you do it too much. Seeking constant reassurance has the secondary effect of harming your relationships too. Family, friends and loved ones can feel frustrated and become tired of repeatedly trying to provide you with answers that simply don't seem to have a lasting effect on you. This can put a strain

Patient Example: Sarah's Reassurance Seeking

Sarah would ask her partner to check things for her, even though she'd already triple-checked herself, and he had already checked more than once. Her partner tried his best to help her, but no matter how often he checked things for her she quickly fell back to square one. This led to lots of frustration in their relationship, and ultimately the relationship broke down.

on your relationships, which in turn can cause more anxiety. The search for certainty above all else is at the heart of many anxiety questions, but the questions themselves can often be unanswerable. Unfortunately, it cannot be provided in the way that anxiety desires it. Seeking certainty from others is an elusive and unattainable goal that perpetuates anxiety.

In managing your anxiety, you may have initially tried to find logical and reasonable solutions to your problems. However, those very solutions may now have become a part of the problem. You may see these things that you *do* as the best way of coping with your anxiety, but you've unintentionally reinforced your anxiety by doing them. Doing them gives you the illusion that you have some control and certainty. It feels nice to have that certainty in the short term, and it feels like it works well, but ultimately it increases your preoccupation with fear, and in turn your distress continues to increase. Just remember, anything that you have to do again and again doesn't work: it's an ineffective solution. If it worked, you'd not be needing to do it so frequently. As you work through this book you'll come to see that there are much better ways for you to deal with your anxiety than the things you've been doing so far.

Avoidance

Just like seeking reassurance, and some of the other behaviours given in the bulleted list starting on page 50, avoidance provides you with immediate relief from anxiety, a quick fix, but it generates a whole host of other problems that make your anxiety worse. Avoidance seems helpful because it removes you from a scary situation, and who wants to feel worse than they already do? I get it, avoidance and escape are a natural reaction to distress. However, avoiding things or situations makes your mind internalize the message that you can't cope, and you never get to learn that you can cope, because you simply stay away. Let's say you've avoided driving on motorways because you once had a panic attack on one. By avoiding them you will never get the opportunity to re-learn that you are capable, that you can cope, you won't always have panic attacks and that you can get your confidence back.

Safety behaviours are another way people engage in avoidance. They act as a crutch to help you cope with anxiety-provoking situations. Crutches can be having a person with you at all times, never speaking in front of others or always sitting near an exit. Someone might go out of the house, but only if they have a certain person with them, or they only take a particular route or want to have specific items with them. This kind of prepping and reliance is a form of avoidance, because you are avoiding facing your fears by using other things to help you through. Again, you never learn that you can cope, but instead your belief in your coping ability erodes further.

Sometimes, people rely on drugs and alcohol to cope with their anxiety, by trying to numb themselves. Alcohol has a sedative effect; it depresses your nervous system. Sometimes people say they feel calmer after a drink or two and they feel that alcohol helps them forget about their fears for a little while. But you can get stuck in a trap of drinking, as your mind and body get used to the temporary crutch alcohol provides to help you feel calm. The problem is often the morning after, or even the whole of the next day, when there are withdrawal effects that increase anxiety. Alcohol reduces the amount of serotonin in your body, which acts as a neuro-transmitter to help you feel calm. So if you have less of this, over time you're going to feel more anxious. You may already have noticed that as the alcohol wears off you feel worse and the next day your hangover anxiety – or 'hangxiety' – is much higher. This feeling of elevated anxiety can last for hours, even a full day or two. When you're in this state of heightened anx-iety, you feel more fearful, your sleep is more disturbed and the tiredness is an additional factor in feeling unable to cope. Just like the other avoidance strategies, alcohol gets in the way of you being able to learn that you can cope with your anxiety. Not only that, if you get caught in this cycle of numbing your anxiety with substances or alcohol it can also lead to addic-tion. If you're worried about your drinking, or use of other substances, then please speak to your doctor about getting further support for this.

TASK 4
My reactions to anxiety
Your thinking patterns, how you focus your attention, how you interpret sensations, your emotions and the actions you take, including avoidance, and your tolerance for stress – especially if it is low, all maintain your anxiety. For this task I'd like

you to reflect on how each of these factors affects you, and what your reactions are to your anxiety. This will give you valuable insight into what's going on for you and how it is maintaining your problems with anxiety.

Looking at the way you think, let's take a few minutes to consider what might have kept you stuck. Again, use your notebook or digital notes to write these out.

- The more I've focused on the sensations of fear in my body, the more aware I've become and the more strange they've seemed: **Yes / No**
- Focusing on the sensations in my body amplifies their intensity: **Yes / No**
- When the sensations amplify I become more concerned about them: **Yes / No**
- When my concern about the sensations increases so does my desire to focus on them: **Yes / No**
- I can see that the way I focus my attention on sensations has trapped me in a vicious cycle: **Yes / No**
- I get caught in the emotional trap of 'I feel it, so it must be true' and assume that the distress I feel is a sure sign that something is wrong: **Yes / No**
- I have quick heat-of-the-moment reactions to my anxiety, where I don't think before I react: **Yes / No**
- Having quick impulsive reactions makes me take unhelpful actions that end up worsening my anxiety: **Yes / No**

- I react quickly to the problems I experience because I want them gone; I can't tolerate the feelings they bring: **Yes / No**

List the things you do to manage your anxiety. Consider noting how long you've been using these strategies, and reflect on their effectiveness in resolving your anxiety issues.

Ten Key Takeaways for Understanding Your Anxiety

1. Recognize the importance of understanding your anxiety as the foundation to overcoming it. Acknowledge that you cannot fix the problem until you understand what's going on and why you're stuck.

2. Start working towards understanding your anxiety as the first step towards feeling calmer.

3. Understand that anxiety is a normal experience that everyone goes through. Recognize that anxiety becomes problematic when you feel persistently anxious in the absence of actual danger, and when your anxiety is excessive or disproportionate.

4. Recognize that your fear pathway originates in your brain and is responsible for detecting potential danger. It can be highly sensitive to signs of threat and cross-references incoming information with past memories. Sometimes non-threatening events can be perceived as threatening based on memory associations that you may have made.

5. Understand the three different reactions to the stress response: fight, flight and freeze. Fight means confronting the threat through a specific action, flight means escaping from the situation, and freeze is fear-induced immobility.

6. Recognize that understanding the psychological and behavioural changes that come with anxiety is crucial for managing it effectively. Becoming aware of these changes will help you manage them better.

7. Understand that anxiety can create various uncomfortable and frightening physical sensations in your body. Recognize that these sensations are your body's natural response to stress, and learn to identify the physical sensations that are personal to you.

8. Recognize that anxiety can persist at a low or moderate intensity even when you're not facing an immediate threat. By identifying the specific internal and external triggers that cause your anxiety to intensify, you can become more aware of your reactions and respond to them more efficiently.

9. An anxious temperament, personality style, traumatic life experiences, family history, situational events and life stressors can all contribute to the development of anxiety. Sometimes the cause may be unknown. Regardless of the cause of anxiety, it is important to focus on developing strategies to manage it effectively.

10. Understand that your thinking style, attentional focus, interpretation of sensations, emotions and actions, including avoidance, all contribute to maintaining your anxiety. A low tolerance for stress can exacerbate anxiety symptoms.

Chew on this!

Chewing gum can be a great way to reduce anxiety! Not only does it help you feel calmer, but it can also boost your cognitive functioning. This can be especially helpful when it comes to managing anxious thoughts. When you chew gum, you give yourself a physical outlet for the nervous energy created by anxiety; this can also help relieve tension in your jaw, throat and neck. Plus, the increased blood flow to your brain can enhance your concentration, memory and recall. It's no wonder that students, athletes and military personnel have used chewing gum to improve their mental performance. If you want to try out chewing gum, be sure to opt for a sugar- and caffeine-free version, to avoid adding any unnecessary stimulants to your system when you're already feeling anxious.

Chapter 2:
How Can I Approach Anxiety Differently?

You should now have a thorough understanding of your anxiety. Let's move on to look at how you can do things differently. This chapter centres on skills to manage your anxiety in new ways, by using flexibility and acceptance. These are the first of many skills to help you overcome your anxiety. They will empower you to move away from fighting and suppressing your anxiety and instead shift your focus towards transforming your relationship with it. We can think of acceptance and flexibility as new ways of being with anxiety. Simply noticing it for what it is: a stream of thoughts, feelings and physical sensations. Most often it's the preoccupation and struggle against anxiety, the desire to control it, that is the primary cause of suffering, rather than the presence of anxiety itself. Changing your relationship with anxiety involves embracing flexibility in your approach towards it, but also in how you approach life in general, as well as cultivating a greater acceptance of challenging internal experiences.

If you keep doing the same things, you'll keep getting the same results. Embracing a new approach to managing anxiety may initially feel uncomfortable, unfamiliar, or even difficult. But with perseverance and willingness you can succeed. If you keep trying to untie a knot in your shoelace the same way every time, you're going to get the same result – a stubborn knot that won't budge. But if you take a different approach, like pulling the laces from a different angle or using a tool to help untangle the knot, you'll be able to loosen it up and eventually undo it. The same applies to managing your anxious thoughts and feelings – by trying new approaches, you can loosen the knot of anxiety and get the relief you want.

By the end of this chapter you'll know exactly what flexibility and acceptance are, why they're important in helping you with your anxiety, and most importantly how to 'do' them. This book is all about giving you the 'how to' for everything I tell you, because knowing is sometimes (well, often, actually) not enough: we need to be shown how.

What Is Flexibility?

Flexibility is rooted in your ability to adopt a new perspective, one that is more open and less fixed, rather than sticking to an unchanging path that yields no progress. When anxiety arises, you recognize that there are various ways to respond to it, and you can choose to act in a flexible manner. This means you're not controlled by your thoughts or feelings, and you persevere with flexibility towards the direction you desire. The goal is to move towards a life free from the struggles of anxiety, to reach a state of fulfilment and calm. Like many suffering from anxiety you might feel frustrated, fed up and disengaged with life, almost as if you've given up on doing anything helpful, because you believe it won't work. Or believing that you can't do anything because you have this debilitating problem. This is inflexibility, and this is exactly what we want to move away from.

Becoming flexible in how you do things is a vital part of building your toolkit for being ten times calmer. Many of the skills in this book will enable you to think of alternative actions or reactions that anxiety may previously have inhibited you from considering. When you can consider alternative ways of responding, you can take a different view and choose to act differently, acting in a more flexible way rather than a way that is fixed or dictated by your anxiety. Anxiety will often drive you towards actions that are unhelpful in overcoming your problems; developing skills that give you an alternative path to follow is your route out of this.

Flexibility is about your ability to accept and adjust to challenging experiences related to anxiety in more effective ways. It involves thinking in an adaptable manner rather than being rigid, and considering diverse and constructive actions instead of relying on fixed and unhelpful approaches. When you cultivate and apply flexibility in managing your anxiety, it can become a superpower that leads to significant improvement. Embracing different ways of approaching and coping with your anxiety can have transformative effects.

When you're not flexible, you're not exercising full awareness of what you're doing, and how what you're doing might make your anxiety worse. Conversely, practising flexibility when dealing with anxiety increases your conscious awareness of the impact of your reactions to anxious thoughts and feelings. This conscious awareness gives you choices: you can step back and think about what you're going to do about difficult thoughts and feelings, choosing either actions that move you away from the struggle with anxiety or towards more struggle with anxiety. Look at the following diagram, and notice how every triggering situation, thought and feeling presents an opportunity to make a choice on how to address your anxiety problems. You have the choice to take actions that bring you towards relief from anxiety and ending the struggle you have with it, or actions that take you away from this and lead to more distress and anxiety.

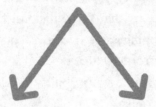

Faced with triggers, situations, thoughts or feelings that require me to make a choice

This choice moves me AWAY from my goal of overcoming anxiety, and worsens my anxiety

This choice moves me TOWARDS my goal of overcoming anxiety

When you develop the skill of flexibility it helps you avoid the pointless struggle you have with unwanted, unwelcome inner experiences, whether these are thoughts or feelings. This struggle gets you nowhere near where you want to go, and it keeps you stuck, making things worse for you. Are the things that you do to control or manage your anxiety working in moving you towards overcoming it? All the patients I've seen with anxiety problems have been doing things that have been ineffective in moving them in the direction they actually want to go. When I look at their situations this is clear. Because their anxiety problems have got worse and worse over time. If what you're doing and what you've tried so far is effective, then you should be feeling better, not worse. If things are getting worse, then you can be confident that you're making moves that pull you away from overcoming your struggle with anxiety.

Patient Example: Sophie's Fearful Sensations

Sophie is thirty-six years old and after her father suffered a heart attack she became extremely fearful. This heightened fear gave rise to lots of intense physiological sensations of anxiety in her body, especially her heart. Sophie became pre-occupied with heart-related sensations, and would notice a racing heart, pounding in her chest, tightness and skipped beats. Every day, Sophie believed that today she would have a heart attack; in fact she'd tell herself 'It's going to happen today, I can feel it, I can just tell.' Of course, she'd seen her doctor – in fact, she'd seen a few doctors – and they all said the same thing: there was nothing wrong with her heart and she was suffering with anxiety. Despite these reassurances Sophie remained preoccupied with these sensations. She regularly monitored herself with her smartwatch and she also purchased an oximeter (a device to check a person's oxygen levels) and a blood pressure monitor. Sophie couldn't stop checking herself and she couldn't stop thinking about her heart and the possibility of a heart attack striking any minute. Sophie stopped exercising, she stopped going out, became withdrawn and eventually found it hard even to leave the house.

Sophie's end goal

Sophie came to see me after her doctor told her that she needed help with her anxiety and not more cardiac investigations. I asked Sophie many questions, including:

1. Where do you want to get to?
2. What do you think is stopping you?

Sophie wanted these anxiety sensations to stop and she wanted to go back to where she was before her father had a heart attack. What do you think was stopping her from getting there?

The answer: inflexibility

These are the ways in which Sophie's inflexibility in dealing with her problem was stopping her from getting to where she wanted to be:

- Being blindly controlled by her thoughts without question.
- Treating her thoughts and feelings as literal truths.
- Not considering any alternatives.
- Doing things that made her anxiety worse, like checking, avoiding, withdrawal and deliberately self-focusing.
- Disconnecting from the present and projecting herself into an imagined future catastrophe.
- Stopping all meaningful and enjoyable activity.
- Not accepting her problem was anxiety but wanting to get rid of it nonetheless.
- Not being flexible, but responding in the same ways again and again, even though it brought her more pain.

Sophie's treatment plan included a focus on developing and practising the skill of flexibility. This involved making conscious choices towards the goal of reducing anxiety, and engaging in meaningful activities that supported this goal, despite the presence of discomfort.

Sophie's path to flexibility

These are the ways in which Sophie practised flexibility:

- Keeping an awareness that her end goal was to be calmer, and free from the struggle of anxiety.
- Making conscious choices every time she could that would take her towards her goal.
- Staying away from things that would feed anxiety and keep the problem going, like checking, avoidance withdrawal and so on.

- Staying in the present by re-engaging with activities and people, despite the presence of anxiety symptoms.
- Making room for difficult experiences to exist while still doing things that were meaningful and helpful.

I showed Sophie how to turn some of her inflexible behaviours into flexible ones and what the benefits were:

Inflexibility 'I can't do anything because of this problem. I can't even go out with my friend for a walk; all I'll think about is my anxiety, these heart palpitations are unbearable. I'm going to stay home.'

Flexibility 'I am experiencing these horrible sensations of anxiety. It feels hot and tight in my chest. I've experienced it before, I know it, it's familiar. I will go for a walk with my friend and see how I feel afterwards. Even if I stay at home, I'm still going to have the same problems, so I may as well go for a walk.'

Notice that both situations entail some level of distress, but the first one amplifies this distress by pushing Sophie towards more anxiety through avoidance. Meanwhile, the second one acknowledges the distress without intensifying it, or worsening her anxiety problem: she's effectively moved herself out of an anxiety cycle here. As well as that, Sophie gets to take part in an activity that is meaningful, which will move her away from the struggle with anxiety. By doing this she is staying present in the moment, which offers her an alternative experience to being overly preoccupied with her anxiety, and helps dilute her self-focused attention. Here are the two options again:

1. Does avoiding going out for a walk with my friend actually help solve my problem? No, it doesn't, it makes it worse, as I become even more controlled by my thoughts and feelings.

2. Does going out for a walk with my friend actually help solve my problem? The problem will still be there for now, but I will have lessened the impact of it by doing things differently. By acting more flexibly, I am moving away from what anxiety is telling me, not towards it.

I hope Sophie's story gives you some practical insight into how flexibility works. Can you see that when you're more flexible you're more self-aware and mindful of your actions? You're more able to keep your end goal in mind and make moves towards that, instead of using emotions and scary thoughts to guide what you should do. These will never take you in a meaningful direction. As you can see from Sophie's example, you have to be willing to experience or make room for difficult experiences in pursuit of your goal, and this means doing things that help even when distress is present, because it's going to be there anyway, at least for now.

Gaining a deeper understanding of how anxiety's inflexibility impacts you is essential: it is your first stride towards fostering greater flexibility. This understanding will guide your efforts in transforming it. To help you do this, here is a brief exercise.

TASK 5
How inflexible are you?
Use these questions to think about how your anxiety may be influencing you to respond in inflexible ways.

- I use distressing thoughts and feelings to guide my actions and the choices I make: **Yes / No**

- I mostly listen to what my anxiety tells me to do, and go along with that: **Yes / No**
- Looking back, the things I do to manage my anxiety have worsened my problems over time: **Yes / No**
- I react quickly and impulsively to my anxiety, doing something straight away because I want it gone: **Yes / No**
- I make day-to-day decisions based on imagining a future catastrophe: **Yes / No**
- I respond in the same fixed ways to my anxiety: **Yes / No**

Each 'yes' answer is a potential sign of inflexibility, and the more times you answer 'yes' the higher your level of inflexibility. Though this isn't a formal test, it gives us an idea of how much you might need to focus your efforts on acting with more flexibility.

Most people who struggle with anxiety tend to exhibit inflexible behaviour, which contributes to the maintenance of their anxiety problems. Don't worry if you you displayed a high level of inflexibility in Task 5; this is a common experience for those with anxiety problems. It's not possible to have a significant issue with anxiety while also being highly flexible, as the latter would prevent the problem in the first place. The purpose of Task 5 is to highlight rigid and inflexible patterns that may be present, so that we can work towards changing them. Nobody is born with the perfect response to their problems, and these skills are not always taught to us directly. We will focus on how you can learn the skill of transitioning from inflexibility to flexibility.

The table outlines examples of inflexible and flexible responses to anxiety. Its purpose is to encourage you to explore alternative approaches, allowing you to adopt a new perspective and choose different actions. I recommend that you review the examples and jot down your own experiences, making a note of what you could have done differently if you were acting more flexibly in anxious situations. This table can serve as a useful reference for generating ideas.

Inflexible Position	Flexible Counterpoint
Not being mindful of your end goal, of where you're trying to get to, therefore reacting in ways that don't help to achieve it.	Write out your end goal of becoming free from anxiety and read it every day to keep it in your awareness. You can stick it on the wall or save it as a daily calendar alert or reminder.
Dealing with anxious situations by using emotions to decide on the action you'll take. 'I feel so distressed and upset at the thought of being rejected it must mean I am a broken person.' 'There's something so wrong with me.'	Choosing to accept that social situations feel like they have such high stakes that this makes you uneasy and anxious. Remind yourself that just because you feel a certain way doesn't make it factually correct. Remember that what you choose to do helps move you towards your goal or away from it.
Using thoughts as your guide for choosing your actions, for example experiencing an anxious thought, then deciding to check your blood pressure again.	Your thoughts are not the literal truth. Remember that anxious thoughts will repeat the same things to you again and again. You don't need to go along with what they tell you to do. Choose not to take your blood pressure again, knowing that it pushes you further towards distress, not away.

Taking sudden impulsive actions when you're having thoughts, feelings or sensations that you don't like.	Instead of reacting impulsively, acknowledge the urge, and let time pass while you do something else, such as a breathing exercise, or staying in the present moment. After time has passed, check in with yourself and note how the intensity of the urge has changed.
'There's no point in trying any of this, it won't work. I just know I won't get better.'	'I'm learning about the things I need to do to help me get better. I can keep going in that direction, and keep taking actions that help me get there.'
'Something very bad is going to happen today, I can feel it, I can just tell. I'm doomed, there's no way out of this.'	'That's my mind playing the same story again, making me doubt myself. Right now, there's nothing wrong. I'm not doomed, but I am anxious. I can do things that help soothe my anxiety instead of scaring myself by talking to myself this way when I'm already frightened.'
'I need to keep an eye on these panic sensations, so I know what they're doing. I mustn't take my attention off them. I'll check them regularly.'	'Staying focused on these sensations will keep me preoccupied with panic, and it doesn't actually solve it. I will move my attention away onto something else, something absorbing and interesting; my mind deserves this.'
'I can't do any exercise, or activities, I can't go on a day trip, let alone a holiday, not when I'm anxious like this. I won't enjoy it, there's no point.'	'Whether I'm at home or away from home I'll experience this distress (for now). At least when I'm away from home, I'm not increasing it through avoidance and by continuing to be preoccupied with it.'

What Is Acceptance?

I'm sure you've heard phrases like 'You just have to accept it' or 'Acceptance is key', but what do these vague phrases actually mean, and how do you go about it? I'm going to tell you in simple terms what I mean by acceptance, why it's so important and how to actually do it.

Anxiety is like being in a tug of war with your anxious thoughts, feelings and sensations. You're pulling on one end of the rope, while they're pulling on the other. The more you pull, the more intense those thoughts, feelings and sensations become. It's like you're stuck in a battle that's hard to break free from. So here's the thing – trying to fight against these thoughts, feelings and sensations only reinforces them, making them even stronger. So their power over you continually grows, you try to pull even harder, and it's like a never-ending tug of war. Instead, you can learn to accept the presence of these anxious thoughts, feelings and sensations without letting them control you. You can choose not to engage in the tug of war and focus your energy on building your ability to handle anxious thoughts, feelings and sensations with more confidence.

Acceptance is about you consciously acknowledging what you're experiencing and allowing it to be what it is. Acceptance helps you learn how to make room for painful thoughts, feelings, sensations and inner experiences with the purpose of just allowing them to be there (for now – because they are). You can't just banish them; they're not going to disappear just like that. It seems like a good idea to try and get rid of negative feelings, because who wants to feel bad? I'm sure there've been times when you've tried to run away from anxiety, hide from it or argue with it. Have your efforts to eliminate or suppress anxious thoughts or experiences been helpful in achieving your outcome of overcoming anxiety? Or have these attempts proven to be ineffective, and you've seen that all these things just increase it?

Trying to get rid of anxiety is a type of avoidance, and acceptance is the opposite of avoidance. Where there's anxiety there's usually avoidance too. Avoidance means you're unwilling to stay in contact with uncomfortable thoughts, feelings and sensations, and you escape these in ways that have longer-term negative consequences for you. When you get fixated on doing this it keeps you stuck; you already learned in Chapter 1 that avoidance is a top reinforcer of anxiety. In my clinical experience it's the number one thing that maintains anxiety. Trying to rid yourself of distress only increases it, because it keeps you preoccupied in a struggle with it and turns it into something more problematic. You then have to grapple with this problematic thing, resulting in a constant back and forth, but with no improvement. The alternative is to accept it – but that doesn't mean giving up, being defeated or agreeing with suffering. Acceptance is an acknowledgement of your distress, and a willingness to allow these experiences to be there, because they *are*.

Acceptance doesn't mean you have to like what you're going through. Your willingness to accept your anxiety isn't about wanting to stay anxious or being okay with fear, it's more 'I'm willing to accept this anxiety because it's here'. Anxiety is a feeling, and feelings just *are*. When you can accept your feelings and your thoughts, you no longer have to be in a constant psychological tug of war with them. You're consciously choosing to see them and engage with them in a different way – because it serves your end goal. Acceptance can help you move away from struggling and fighting, into this open, accepting position. Acceptance is one of the best ways of practising flexibility; it's a move towards overcoming the struggle with anxiety. Acceptance will help you overcome your anxiety. Acceptance is necessary for healing, for acknowledging your pain, making room for that pain and processing it.

Allow yourself to simply experience your anxiety and let some time pass without attempting to control or eliminate it. How much time this will take varies from person to person, but it will not take an indefinite amount of time for things to improve. Some individuals may see progress within a few weeks, while for others it may take a few months, or longer. It's important to maintain a positive and hopeful attitude, and to actively engage in the strategies recommended throughout this book.

Key Principles of Acceptance and Anxiety

1. Accepting your distress is about learning to make room for it and allowing it to exist without efforts to control it.

2. Anxiety is a human emotion: accept it with understanding, kindness and an open attitude.

3. Acceptance is about accepting that you will have to live with your anxiety for now, instead of constantly trying to resist it, escape it, get rid of it.

4. Accept that your nervous system has got into the habit of reacting the way it does to stress.

5. Accept that your habitual nervous system reactivity has to be changed over time, not in an instant.

6. Accept that anxiety will be there while you work on your recovery.

7. Accept that there are no quick fixes, but there are fixes.

8. Accept that you are able and willing to let time pass as you work on yourself.

Sometimes quotes can be helpful in getting us thinking, in inspiring us to move from a place of struggling with anxiety to accepting its presence. One of my favourites is 'If you're not willing to have it, you will', meaning that if you resist or deny a difficult feeling or inner experience, it will persist or even worsen. You have to accept that difficult feelings and uncomfortable inner experiences are part of life. By accepting and acknowledging the presence of these feelings, you'll be more able to manage them effectively, and you'll feel less triggered by them. Accepting the inevitability and reality of difficult experiences allows you to shift your focus away from fighting them and onto finding ways to cope that move you forward. Acceptance is knowing that difficult feelings are inevitable, and sometimes the only way through is to ride out the discomfort they bring. A big part of riding them out is not reacting to them, not being controlled or dictated to by them. When you take on this approach of dealing with your problems the feelings will pass, and over time you will notice they pass more and more quickly.

TASK 6
My acceptance affirmation

Using the key principles of acceptance outlined above, write a short statement detailing an acceptance affirmation that is personal to you. Include things that you know might have shaped or contributed to your anxiety, what your anxiety makes you fearful of and what anxiety feels like for you. Note the things that haven't worked and accept that you'll get better with time.

Here's an example to help you:

Since my relationship broke down I've felt so different, life's been really hard. It makes sense to me that I'm so anxious and scared. This unexpected event derailed me, I'm only human, of course I'm going to hurt. I can make room for this pain. It's understandable that because of these things my mind and body find it hard to be at peace. I accept that I am anxious. I accept that my body reacts with fear to certain triggers now. I accept the sensations brought on by my fear. I accept that my nervous system needs time to heal, I accept that I can't just switch it all off in an instant. I accept that this will also leave me as I recover and my nervous system moves away from being in a state of fear to being in a state of calm again. I accept the situation before me.

The example I've given you here is fairly long, to help you see the range of things you might want to include. Yours might be shorter, similar or longer; all of these are fine. You can pick out one or two powerful sentences to memorize or note down so they're easy to recall at times when you might need them.

Once you have your affirmation, and any shorter powerful points from it, read it every single day if you can. Display it somewhere prominent or set an alert for it to pop up on your phone at different time intervals. Whenever you feel anxious, stuck or overwhelmed, come back to it: this will help practise acceptance, self-compassion, understanding of and openness to your experience. This acceptance also reduces the likelihood of impulsive reactions. You

can read this affirmation more than once a day if you
like. At times of doubt and stress you might want to
read it more often.

You can also make a video or audio recording of
yourself saying it out loud, so you can listen to it
instead of reading it. Many of my patients like this
idea, and it can be really nice to put your favourite
calming music on in the background. There's a real
power in hearing and seeing yourself speak back: try
it, and see how it works for you.

Accept the anxiety and be flexible – dedicate yourself to
pursuing meaningful aspects of your life, such as your interests,
relationships, work and personal growth. Even when you're
dealing with unsettling thoughts and feelings, it's important you stay involved in activities that hold value for you.
Remember that when you don't engage in these things your
distress is likely to persist or even worsen over time. Even if it
doesn't get worse, it can leave you stuck in the same anxious
state without any progress. Actively engaging in meaningful
activity, and in the things you value, may initially require more
effort, but it won't be making your anxiety any worse through
reinforcement.

What to Do If You Struggle

While understanding the principles of acceptance and flexibility is essential, simply having this knowledge may not always
be sufficient. I'm here to provide solutions for when these
principles don't seem to be working. Even when you're actively
practising acceptance and flexibility, your mind may still present you with the distressing thoughts, feelings, images and

scenarios that it's become accustomed to. In such situations, it's crucial to have a strategy for coping with these experiences as they arise.

At times, accepting anxious experiences can be challenging as we may be deeply invested in them and believe what anxiety is telling us. However, if we don't accept these experiences, it becomes difficult to act flexibly as anxiety then dictates our responses. In such situations you can use skills that help you detach from these anxious experiences and prevent you from over-identifying with them and viewing them as your absolute reality. One such skill is based on diffusing, creating distance and detaching, which enables you to recognize that you are not your thoughts, and nor are you what your mind is telling you.

Our minds have a tendency to present us with various stories and some come more frequently than others. These stories can be judgemental and inaccurate, taking us down the wrong path, and these are exactly the ones we want to detach ourselves from. While the mind helps us understand our experiences, at times it can be unreliable and fallacious, resulting in narratives that are disturbing for us. It's important to remember that the stories your mind tells you are often subjective and don't necessarily represent the objective truth. They're often our most personal and problematic narratives that we've become overly attached to. We repeat these narratives so many times in our minds that they seem to become part of our identity. Have you ever experienced this? Can you recall stories that you've told yourself repeatedly, to the point where it feels like they've become part of who you are?

Our minds repeat certain stories for various reasons, such as past experiences, over-attentiveness to anxious thoughts, heightened emotional reactions or habitual tendencies. Regardless of the reason, it's crucial to accept that this is a normal function of the mind. Often, the content of the thought itself is not problematic, but rather it's our relationship with it that causes problems.

'Thank your mind and name the story' is a diffusion task that helps you distance yourself from difficult inner experiences. Diffusion is the psychological process of separating yourself from these. It involves acknowledging difficult inner experiences without getting caught up in them, or letting them control your actions. By naming and acknowledging difficult stories or narratives you can also reduce their believability. Diffusion differs from separation or detachment, because it doesn't involve completely pushing away or suppressing your difficulties. Instead, it focuses on creating a more flexible relationship with your inner experiences. Diffusion helps you become more present; it can lead to greater psychological flexibility and more effective action towards the outcomes you want.

TASK 7
Thank your mind and name the story
When your mind presents you with a story about your anxiety and urges you to engage with it, follow these steps:

Start by thanking your mind for its contribution, and then label the story you're experiencing, like this:

'Thank you mind for reminding me of your opinion, this is the "you're going to faint again" story.'

I recommend that my patients say their phrase out loud if they can, but if they're in a public place, say it to themselves in their mind. Another option is to write it down; doing this can also help identify any repeat patterns of stories.

As more anxious stories appear, keep on acknowledging them as a product of your mind, thank your mind for its contribution, label each story, then let it go. If it keeps playing in the background, let it, while you shift your attention on to something you'd rather be doing. Here are some examples of more stories:

- Oh look, there's a replay of the 'You'll get sick' story.
- This is the 'There's something wrong with you' story.
- That's the 'Everybody is looking at you and judging you' story.
- That's the 'You'll have a heart attack' story again.

By incorporating the techniques discussed in this chapter, you can learn to manage your anxiety problems more flexibly and reduce your suffering. It may be challenging to accept anxious experiences when you are deeply invested in them and believe what anxiety is telling you. However, learning to detach from anxious experiences using these strategies can help you create distance from your thoughts, so you can see that they do not define you. It is crucial to commit to practising flexibility and acceptance regularly as you move forward. Even if it's challenging at first, keep trying. If you find yourself falling back into familiar anxiety traps, take a moment to reflect on what you could have approached differently from a perspective of flexibility and acceptance. Learn from the experience and give it another try. By doing this daily, you can reinforce and nurture your developing acceptance and become more comfortable with using flexible alternatives to managing anxiety.

Ten Key Takeaways for Approaching Anxiety Differently

1. Cultivate acceptance and flexibility by acknowledging your thoughts and feelings without judging them or taking them at face value. Take a step back and see them for what they are, so you can gain a better perspective and make more informed decisions about your actions.

2. Accept anxiety as a natural and understandable part of your experience. You can use acceptance to reduce the inner conflict and resistance that often intensifies anxiety symptoms.

3. Be more flexible in how you relate and react to your anxiety. Take a flexible, open approach to your anxious thoughts, feelings and physical sensations. By embracing flexibility, you can develop more effective coping strategies and learn to navigate the challenges posed by anxiety with greater ease.

4. Release the need to control or avoid anxiety to the best of your ability. Do this by working on letting go of any efforts you make to try and control or avoid experiencing anxiety.

5. Certain coping behaviours can actually reinforce your anxiety. Rather than relying on these for short-term relief, put your time and energy into developing long-lasting strategies, so you can learn to manage your anxiety in a more sustainable way.

6. Steer yourself away from using avoidance as a coping mechanism for your anxiety. Avoidance may reduce or eliminate contact with distressing experiences, providing you with short-term relief. But in the long term it actually maintains and even increases anxiety.

7. Notice your reactions to anxiety sensations, as well as the effect these reactions have on your anxiety and functioning as a whole. This will enable you to clearly see if your reactions are helping you or hindering you.

8. Re-engage in positive things you've avoided, even when unwanted anxiety is present.

9. Keep an awareness of what you ultimately want, and of the things that are stopping you from getting there.

10. Despite the presence of anxiety, it's important you continue engaging in activities that add value to your life. Anxiety may persist, but by focusing on meaningful activities, you can lessen the impact anxiety has on your life.

 Experience lavender!

Lavender is truly remarkable! Its beautiful aroma not only smells sensational, but it can also reduce anxiety, making it perfect for relaxation. Several research studies have explored the potential benefits of lavender in reducing anxiety. One randomized controlled trial found that lavender oil capsules reduced anxiety symptoms in patients with generalized anxiety disorder. Another analysis of 15 randomized controlled trials also found that lavender aromatherapy had a statistically significant effect on reducing anxiety levels. In another study, inhaling lavender oil for just 10 minutes was enough to significantly reduce anxiety levels. Lavender helps reduce anxiety by regulating your body's natural response to stress. Do you want to give lavender a try and see how it makes you feel? You can use it in a diffuser, as an essential oil for massage, or even spray it on your pillow for a peaceful night's sleep.

Chapter 3:
How Can I Calm My Stressed Nervous System?

Nervous system stress can be compared to a stormy sky with dark clouds and distant lightning as a thunderstorm builds. As stress levels increase, the clouds grow darker, and lightning strikes with fierce jagged bolts. To calm this storm you have to imagine yourself as a ray of sunlight breaking through the clouds, slowly shining brighter and brighter until the storm's dark clouds start to clear. You can do this by using the strategies in this section, and those in the rest of this book. As you focus on bringing out this light from within you, the storm will gradually begin to calm, the sky will clear, and eventually it will be bright and sunny once again.

Calming a stressed nervous system helps reduce the activation of your body's stress response, which can be frequently triggered when you suffer with persistent anxiety. Anxiety is triggered through exposure to unpleasant events, and this leads to physiological changes, emotional changes, changes in your thinking and perception, and behavioural changes. In this chapter we'll be focusing on these stress-based changes, which I'm going to refer to as physiological stress, and what you can do about them. Physiological stress takes place when you perceive a threat to your safety, security and well-being. This leads to the release of stress hormones adrenaline and cortisol, which are involved in your body's fight-or-flight response. This is your body's complex but very natural alarm system. Regardless of the type of anxiety you suffer from, you will experience an adrenaline surge when you're faced with a situation you fear. This could be a situation that causes or has caused panic attacks, while for social anxiety it will be specific social situations, and for health anxiety, coming across news about ill health can trigger the physiological stress. We're going to take a closer look at how both adrenaline and cortisol function in your body. I've then laid out four different practical skills you can integrate into your life to manage the stress caused by these hormones and bring it under control.

Adrenaline

Adrenaline plays a vital role in how your body responds to threat or perceived threat: it floods your body almost instantly when the stress response is triggered. This is to strengthen your physical performance and provide you with an energy boost, so you can do what you need to do. The human body is amazing, and thank goodness we have this built into our nervous system for when we need it. The problem is that often we don't need it; yes, it's great when you need that boost to do something scary like a bungee jump, but it's no good when it's persistently there due to unfounded threats. This surge of adrenaline creates many bodily changes, some of which can become problematic for the sufferer (see page 368 for a comprehensive list of these). Broadly speaking, these include an increased heart rate, redirection of blood towards larger muscle groups, an increased demand for oxygen, changes in breathing, dilated pupils, vision changes and dampened pain receptors. Have you ever come across stories of people who experience physical pain long after an injury has occurred? This intriguing phenomenon can be attributed to the body's stress response. Adrenaline can temporarily dull pain receptors, enabling us to act swiftly to ensure our safety. I recall a patient who shared his experience of being in a car accident and fracturing his leg. Remarkably, he was able to exit the vehicle, assist others to safety and walk away from the scene without experiencing any pain, thanks to an adrenaline rush in that moment. However, once he had reached a place of safety and the adrenaline subsided, he suddenly became acutely aware of the pain.

The changes brought on in the body by adrenaline usually settle after the stress has passed, though some can linger for several hours. Your body produces an adrenaline rush when your anxiety is high, or when it perceives some kind of danger. This rush creates a number of physical reactions which can themselves cause more fear, as you wonder what is going on and why you're feeling so odd and uncomfortable. You can then get caught in a cycle of feeling overcharged and anxious with more frightening thoughts, which in turn brings more adrenaline, and so the cycle of persistent stress goes on. When you're stressed and anxious for long periods of time, adrenaline levels can remain consistently elevated. This is problematic in many ways: the physical sensations remain constant, they trouble you, you feel scared of them, then more anxious thoughts come, trapping you in a cycle of self-perpetuating anxiety. For some people this might be experienced as constant heart palpitations; for others it might be red hot flashes, or even numbness and tingling. Given that adrenaline is produced by the body in response to stress and anxiety, it is logical to focus on reducing overall anxiety and stress levels to break free from this self-perpetuating cycle. To accomplish this, it's essential you consistently engage in activities that induce a state of relaxation, effectively countering the physiological stress your body has been experiencing. By prioritizing relaxation techniques and stress-reducing practices, you can diminish the impact of stress on your body and regain some balance. We'll get on to how you can do that in just a moment, but let's have a look at cortisol first.

Cortisol

Cortisol is a hormone that regulates a wide range of essential bodily processes, and it also plays a central role in helping your body respond to stress. Cortisol has many positive effects. Just like adrenaline, we need it and couldn't actually survive without it. It modulates your blood-sugar levels and has anti-inflammatory effects. Cortisol levels typically peak in the morning, to help promote wakefulness and alertness, and gradually decline throughout the day, preparing your body for rest. In a healthy stress response, cortisol is released when action is required and subsides once the stressor has been addressed.

> **Why is my anxiety so bad when I wake up?**
> Upon waking, your body experiences a natural surge in cortisol known as the 'cortisol awakening response' (CAR). It's supposed to promote wakefulness, alertness and reactivate your brain for the day ahead. However, this increase in cortisol can also contribute to feelings of anxiety. When combined with caffeine consumption, cortisol levels can be further elevated, resulting in still further heightened anxiety. If you already experience anxiety, your cortisol levels may already be higher than usual, which can be compounded by the CAR.

Cortisol also plays an important role in learning and memory formation, by consolidating memories of emotional events. When you recall an anxiety-provoking event, it can trigger a spike in cortisol levels, leading to the reconsolidation of that memory after every retrieval you make. Cortisol strengthens memories of fearful experiences because this supports survival and avoidance of future dangers. Cortisol spikes at the time of a fearful event, when a fear-based memory is being formed for the first time. Subsequently, when you re-experience the memory, cortisol levels rise again, further consolidating the fearful memory. This is why you may experience intense responses to memories associated with panic attacks, high-anxiety situations and phobic situations. The action of cortisol on memory consolidation helps explain why fear-based memories sometimes don't fade, but can instead become strengthened with each recall. However, it is possible to interrupt this process by reacting differently during the vulnerable recall stage, thereby preventing the memory from becoming further reinforced. Many of the strategies in this book are designed to help you do exactly this.

When anxiety is excessive and causes cortisol levels to remain elevated, it undermines the hormone's other helpful functions. Cortisol supply is being activated even when you don't need it to be. Too much cortisol, for too long, can also create longer-lasting symptoms of anxiety, leading to uncomfortable bodily sensations. Ideally the cortisol response should turn on when you're faced with a challenge and your body needs it, then turn off when the stress is gone. Prolonged and exaggerated physiological stress perpetuates cortisol dysfunction, which plays a significant role in anxiety disorders. When anxiety becomes problematic, your body tends to keep the stress response activated for longer periods of time and it becomes easier for the body to reactivate this response more quickly in the future. Therefore, even small amounts of stress can trigger a powerful and overwhelming stress response. This is like a fire alarm going off when there's no actual fire. Just like the fire alarm in your home is designed to warn you of danger, anxiety is your body's way of alerting you to possible threats. It is your body's alarm system. Sometimes this alarm can glitch and go off even when there's no real danger to you. When it does this it still causes your body to go into fight or flight mode, even though you might just be sitting on your couch, completely safe. Your heart races, your palms sweat, and your mind brings up thoughts of doom. Your response to these cues plays a crucial role in reducing anxiety levels. Using the strategies in this book you'll learn to regulate your body's response to anxiety, and reduce the occurrence of false alarms that activate your fight or flight response when it isn't needed.

It's great to have cortisol and adrenaline at your disposal so they can help you when the situation requires it, but it's equally important for you to learn how to turn the stress response off, so your body can return to a normal, relaxed state. You might be wondering how on earth you can get control over this, especially if you've been experiencing anxiety for a long time. Well, you can. There are some very effective strategies in this chapter that will help you calm your nervous system. With consistent practice you'll see that you're able to switch off the stress, and you can feel calmer.

The Snowball Effect

You can think of your anxiety as a snowball that started off small but has grown bigger and bigger over time. I'm not saying that whatever caused your anxiety in the first place was small or insignificant. Rather, as anxiety set in, it started to influence your thoughts, emotions and then actions in certain ways, causing the snowball to gain momentum and grow bigger and bigger. As it grew bigger, it exerted more stress on your nervous system and your body. Just like a snowball rolling down a hill, it accumulated more snow, becoming larger, heavier and more powerful. Despite your attempts to escape it, you found yourself becoming even more anxious, with this anxiety then fuelling the snowball's growth, creating more bodily stress. The good news is that by implementing the strategies outlined in this chapter, along with those found throughout the rest of the book, you can effectively tackle and overcome this snowball of anxiety. By approaching it from different angles, you can gradually diminish its impact. With persistent effort and commitment, you will have the ability to dismantle it piece by piece until it no longer poses a problem.

The snowball effect is a well-known psychological analogy that vividly captures the idea of a single situation gaining momentum and growing in influence, leading to a notable impact. By using this analogy, my intention is to show you how multiple factors have played a role in the development and continuation of your anxiety.

One essential skill you need to acquire is the ability to minimize your overall anxiety and stress, which in turn will reduce the production of adrenaline and cortisol in your body.

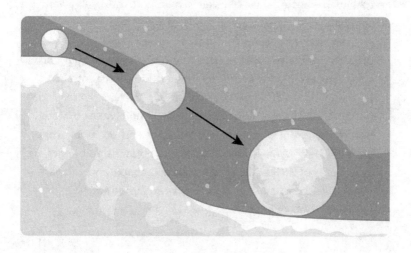

Since these hormones are released during periods of stress, the most effective approach to decreasing their production is by actively managing and mitigating stressors. In the next section, we will look at exactly how you can go about doing this. But first, let me introduce Mark, my patient, whose experience serves as an excellent illustration of how physiological stress can accumulate and become entrenched within the body's nervous system.

Patient Example: Mark's Sweating and Facial Flashes

My patient Mark found his facial blushing and sweaty palms to be his worst anxiety symptom, and he was so focused on making this stop he only wanted to do tasks that would directly impact these two things. Mark even bought an expensive cream, which he'd rub into his hands several times a day to stop the sweating, but much to his disappointment, the sweating persisted. These troubling symptoms were primarily a result of stress hormones causing the dilation of capillaries in Mark's face, making the blood vessels more visible and leading to a flushed, red face accompanied by a sensation of heat. I explained to Mark that these things were happening to him because he was socially anxious, overly self-aware, constantly telling himself all kinds of upsetting things, feeling terrified of talking in front of others, and his overall physiological stress was persistently high. In overcoming his social anxiety Mark needed to reduce this persistent stress, by doing things to lower adrenaline and cortisol, increasing the amount of time his body spent in a more relaxed state, before going on to manage his thoughts and do other work on his anxiety. We will follow in Mark's footsteps and engage in a range of strategies to effectively manage and regulate stress. By doing so, our goal is to reduce stress hormone levels as much as possible.

Reducing Stress Hormones

In this section, I will guide you through four approaches that can help diminish physiological stress on your body and calm your nervous system. You may find that all of the exercises resonate with you, or you may find certain ones to be more effective. Incorporate the exercises that work best for you into your anxiety toolkit. The most important thing is that you stick with them. Some of these exercises might not feel new to you, but that's because these are the things that work time and again. As you practise these exercises, remember that your objective is to reduce bodily stress and repeatedly activate your body's relaxation response, so that you can calm your nervous system.

Patient Example: Khloe's Breathwork Exercises

I prescribed my patient Khloe a set of breathing exercises a number of years ago. When Khloe came back to see me she said, 'I tried those breathing exercises, they didn't work, and actually I've tried things like that before, they're just not for me.' Fair enough, I thought, but I also asked how often she'd been practising, and for how many days. Khloe told me she tried every now and then over a period of one week. Khloe was surprised when I sent her away with the task of doing her exercises four to six times a day for at least thirty days before reducing the frequency. This frequency of practice might be a surprise. Khloe suffered with chronic anxiety, and for her particular situation she needed a more intensive approach. When Khloe came back to see me she could see clearly the benefits, her mind and body were more relaxed, there was less physiological stress, and she could get on with the rest of her treatment with less reactivity. Khloe learned several tools to use in response to physiological stress, so she could calm herself efficiently when her anxiety was retriggered.

The idea that a person themselves can create a more relaxed state of body and mind has been around for thousands of years. But the potential it has for people suffering from anxiety disorders is underrated.

It's unrealistic to expect your stressed nervous system to calm down immediately after trying a few techniques only sporadically. But, when you commit to consistent practice, you will see the benefits. The research supporting the exercises given here is truly astounding.[3] Achieving a state of deep physical relaxation can profoundly impact your emotional and physical response to stress. This state prompts the release of endorphins, which reduce anxiety and stress and improve heart rate and breathing, as well as enhancing overall well-being. By consistently practising exercises like these, you can significantly reduce physiological stress, alleviate anxiety, improve sleep, enhance mood and experience myriad other benefits. It's understandable that people often want a quick relief from anxiety, and they may not want to spend time practising various relaxation techniques. However, it is important to keep in mind that simple exercises, when utilized correctly and consistently, offer considerable long-term benefits.

I really encourage you to make a commitment to regularly practising these exercises. Reflect on Khloe's example, to consider how anxiety has significantly affected your life over the time it's been present, and invest the time that your mind and body need. I'm confident that by dedicating a small amount of time each day, you can calm your nervous system and achieve relief from some of the physiological stress you are under. While it's not essential to perform each exercise every time, I recommend trying each one to identify the ones that provide you with the best results. Trying an exercise only once is not enough to gauge its effectiveness. It's important to take the time to try it out on different occasions so you can properly evaluate its effect on you. Once you've determined your pre-ferred exercises, commit to doing them regularly to maximize their benefits. This personalized approach is what I use with my patients: each person responds differently to the different exercises. If you have any concerns about your mobility or physical health in relation to these exercises, please consult your doctor before starting.

1. Breathing exercises

Regular calming breathing exercises can help reduce adrenaline, calm your nervous system and improve anxiety symptoms. Studies also show that optimal breathing can reduce overall cortisol levels, which means there's less of this stress hormone circulating throughout your body.[4] Physiological stress can cause constriction in your airways, leading to breathlessness, rapid breathing, or what I often refer to as 'air hunger' – the feeling of not being able to take in enough air. Effective breath-ing techniques have been shown to reduce these problems, alleviate stress and lower the heart rate. Physiological stress can alter the rhythm and depth of your breathing, leading to shorter, shallower breaths or even hyperventilation. Hyperven-tilation may not always be overt or easily noticeable, as it can manifest more subtly. If you want to calm your nervous system, it's absolutely crucial to regain control over your breathing.

Don't be concerned if your breathing rate is currently outside the optimal range. Through practice of the simple exercise outlined here, you will gradually be able to achieve an improved breathing rate. It takes practice and commitment to get into the habit of improved breathing, so please stick with it, because this is such a simple but significant tool to reduce and control stress hormones. In my clinical experience, slow-paced, abdominal breathing, which combines a slow nasal inhale, with a slow but longer mouth exhale is most effective.

I really like this exercise because it's super simple, but there are also many others out there. Whichever breathing exercise you use, make sure you stick at it. In moments of heightened anxiety, breathing exercises can be especially beneficial, so

TASK 8
Simple breathing exercise

1. Find a comfortable spot, whether it's your bed, the floor, a chair or even somewhere outside – wherever feels right for you. Take a moment to loosen any tight clothing and settle into a soft, relaxed position.
2. Next, take a deep breath in through your nose, as deeply as you can, for as long as you can, filling your lungs to their fullest capacity. Count slowly to four or five as you inhale, gently push your stomach out to fully expand your breath. See the left-hand picture below.
3. Hold your breath for a count of four to five seconds. Then breathe out slowly, exhaling through pursed lips, counting four to five seconds again. For greater control, consider exhaling through a straw. Repeat this process at least five times in a row to feel the calming effects.

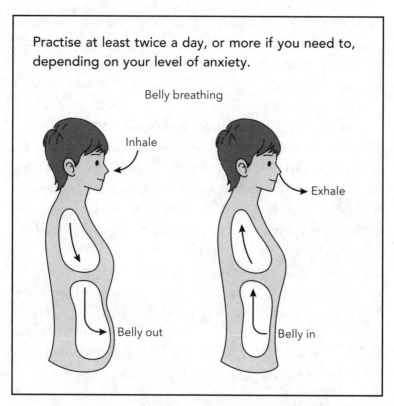

Practise at least twice a day, or more if you need to, depending on your level of anxiety.

Belly breathing

Inhale

Exhale

Belly out

Belly in

don't hesitate to practise more frequently during these times. To really establish your breathing technique, it's helpful to carve out some time twice a day when you can really focus on it. Consider integrating this into your daily routine – for instance, practising when you first wake up and before going to bed. Another method is to use specific prompts through-out the day, like before a meal or after visiting the bathroom. What prompts would work well for you? Setting reminders on your phone or calendar can also help keep you on track with regular practice. As you become more skilled, calm breathing will start to feel like second nature, and you'll be able to do it anywhere. If you start to feel dizzy during your breathing exercises, it could be a sign that you're breathing too quickly or heavily. Try slowing down your breaths and taking things more gently. Remember, when learning something new, it's natural to feel like you're not quite getting it at first. Be kind and patient with yourself and keep practising until you become more confident. Just like any skill, mastery comes with time, repetition and patience.

Some sufferers of anxiety experience a fear and heightened awareness of their breathing sensations. They can be over-focused on their breath, and may interpret certain normal sensations as signs of something serious. This heightened attention to breathing can create a cycle of fear and hyper-vigilance, where people become afraid of their own breathing and its potential implications. It's important to note that this fear of breathing sensations is a symptom of anxiety and can be addressed through the right strategies. If you have this prob-lem, then of course you may find these breathing exercises difficult. If this is the case, then you may need to work on the fear of these sensations first or even simultaneously by using the advice in Chapter 8 (page 277).

2. Progressive muscle relaxation (PMR)

PMR is a technique that involves slowly tensing and releasing each muscle group in the body, as outlined in the next exer-cise, and it is highly effective in calming the nervous system. PMR helps counteract the stress response by promoting relaxation and reducing muscle tension throughout the body. When you intentionally tense and then release each muscle group during PMR, it signals to your body that it is safe to relax. This process activates your body's relaxation response, which counteracts the effects of stress hormones.

Physiological stress can manifest as muscle tension, which can lead to a range of bodily aches and pains, as well as feel-ings of heaviness, weakness and fatigue. PMR is particularly effective for those who experience anxiety-related tension in their muscles. When we feel stressed or threatened, our muscles tense up as part of the fight or flight response. For people who experience long-term anxiety, this muscle tension can seem constant, as the body continually produces stress hormones, making it hard for the nervous system to calm. Anxiety-related muscle tension can affect the chest muscles, creating a sensation of tightness, and tension in the neck and throat can lead to the feeling of a prominent lump in the throat. The jaw can become tight from clenching, as can the neck and shoulders. I coined the term 'anxiety legs' to describe the various symptoms that my patients experience in their leg muscles, including weakness, jelly-legs, trembling, numbness or stiffness that makes it difficult to walk or stand.

TASK 9
Progressive muscle relaxation

To prepare your mind and body for this muscle relaxation exercise, find a comfortable surface to lie on, such as your bed, a thick mat or even somewhere outside. Before you begin, take three deep, slow breaths, inhaling through your nose and exhaling through your open mouth. Hold the tension in each step for ten seconds.

1. Starting with your hands, make fists and hold the tension before slowly releasing.
2. Then move on to your arms, folding them up towards your shoulders and holding the same tensing action before releasing.
3. Next, scrunch up your facial muscles, including your eyes, and release.

4. Open your mouth as if you're yawning, and then release.
5. Gently scrunch up your shoulders and neck towards your ears, and then release.
6. Continue to move through your body, pushing your shoulder blades together and downwards, and then releasing.
7. Scrunch your stomach muscles and then release.
8. Tense your thigh and buttock muscles, and then release.
9. Flex your toes upwards to tense your calf muscles, and then release.
10. Finally, scrunch your feet and release.

By the end of the exercise, you should feel a sense of relaxation and relief from muscle tension. With regular practice you'll gain increasing benefits.

3. Movement

It is quite common for people to unintentionally reduce their activity level precisely when they could benefit from more movement. I recommend incorporating physical movement as a response to feelings of anxiety and stress, particularly during acute episodes. Please note that I am not referring to a rigorous fitness regimen in this context; we will discuss that further in the next section.

Failing to move when you're feeling anxious prevents you from experiencing the positive effects that movement has on reducing physiological stress and calming your nervous system. Lack of movement keeps you stuck and keeps your nervous system in a state of stress. The benefits of regular movement in alleviating physiological stress on your nervous system improve in the long term, but the immediate effects are just as tangible. Ask yourself, 'How does my body feel like moving right now?' Listen to your body's signals and choose the type of movement that serves you best. Take a look at some of the ideas in the box: what do you like in this list? If you have any concerns regarding your mobility or physical activity, it is important to consult with your doctor before initiating any new routines.

Think of your nervous system as a glass of water filled with stress hormones. When you experience further physiological stress it fills up more, and the longer you go without dealing with the stress, the fuller the glass becomes. This glass has been so full, for so long, it's overflowing. This is where movement can help. By engaging in physical movement, you can start to drain the glass of excess stress, bringing you a sense of relief and calm. Over time, with regular movement, you can keep the glass from overflowing, preventing the accumulation of stress hormones and the negative effects they bring. It's a simple yet powerful approach to managing stress and anxiety.

Movement

Walking to work / the shop	Roller skating
Walking your dog	Trampolining
Cutting the grass	Vacuuming
Gardening	Deep cleaning an area
Doing DIY	Cleaning your car
Playing outdoors with children	Sweeping outdoors
Throwing frisbee	Riding a bike

4. Physical exercise

Exercising regularly has far-reaching benefits, with a significant positive impact on your overall well-being. Incorporating regular physical exercise into your routine is also a powerful tool for calming your nervous system. In addition to reducing cortisol and adrenaline levels, exercise triggers the release of endorphins, which can alleviate pain, improve your mood and boost your well-being. I encourage you to aim for at least thirty minutes of physical exercise a few times a week, or daily if that's possible. If you have any health concerns, again please consult with your doctor before starting any new exercise. I understand that starting to exercise can be challenging, especially when you're dealing with anxiety at the same time. If you're finding it hard, then I suggest starting small and gradually building up to thirty minutes. You can begin with five-minute walks and increase your time each day or week. In just a month, you'll be able to build up to thirty minutes a day.

Joining a gym or sports club is not feasible for everyone, and isn't necessary, unless of course you want to. There are many alternative ways to get your body moving and engage your muscles. The key is to find something that you enjoy and can commit to regularly. Here are some simple ideas to get you started, but feel free to explore more options that might fit with your interests.

Exercise	
Walking	Yoga
Cycling	Pilates
Rowing	Tennis
Skipping	Badminton

Running	Climbing
Swimming	Football
Dancing	Aerobics or HIIT

There are countless ways to adapt your exercise routine to suit your lifestyle. Break up your exercise into smaller segments if that's easier for you; it can be just as effective as doing a longer session. For example, take a brisk ten-minute walk three times a day: in the morning, at lunchtime and in the evening. Alternatively, you could do some cleaning in the morning and go for a walk in the early evening with a friend or neighbour, or listen to your favourite music or podcast while walking. You can also try free online yoga, dance or other exercise videos. If you're feeling resistant or lack the motivation to exercise, start by committing to just two weeks of exercise and notice the difference it makes in how you feel. The benefits of exercise are backed by science, and you might be surprised at how much better you feel after incorporating regular exercise into your routine.

Similar to the fixation on and fear of breathing sensations, some people can also develop apprehension towards the sensations brought on by exercise. Negative past experiences, such as previous panic attacks during exercise, can contribute to this fear or avoidance response as a protective mechanism against future distress. If there is a fear of having a panic attack, people can become vigilant and sensitive to any sensations that resemble it, even if these sensations are not an actual panic attack. During exercise, the natural increase in heart rate, sweating, shortness of breath and other physiological changes can trigger anxiety. These symptoms can be misinterpreted as signs of a panic attack or impending danger, evoking a fear response. Consequently, the perception of losing control due to these sensations during exertion can further drive exercise avoidance as a means of retaining a sense of control. If this is you, again you'll need to work on this avoidance using the strategies in Chapter 8 (see page 266).

Ten Key Takeaways for Calming Your Nervous System

1. Keep in mind that your body has a natural alarm system that triggers physiological responses when you're anxious. This mechanism releases hormones, namely adrenaline and cortisol, into your body.

2. Remember that adrenaline plays a key role in how your body responds to threatening situations. It serves to enhance your body's resources, enabling you to perform and manage situations more effectively.

3. Cortisol also plays a vital and advantageous role in your body. But extended periods of anxiety can lead to sustained high levels of cortisol, creating unwanted symptoms. To address this issue, it's important to consistently practise effective relaxation techniques.

4. Elevated levels of adrenaline and cortisol can lead to uncomfortable physical sensations, contributing to an increased sense of anxiety. This sets off a cycle where increasing anxiety intensifies the physical sensations and vice versa. Practising relaxation skills to trigger the relaxation response can break this cycle and prevent the reinforcement between anxiety and physical sensations.

5. Exposure to prolonged stress can lead to heightened sensitivity in the nervous system, causing even minor triggers to elicit intense anxious responses. This heightened sensitivity further amplifies the experience of anxiety. Regular practice of relaxation skills can calm this sensitivity.

6. Incorporate regular practice of these techniques into your daily routine. This can help activate the relaxation response

in your body, which helps counteract the effects of stress hormones.

7. Recognize that reducing nervous system stress takes time, patience, and a consistent commitment to practising relaxation exercises. To achieve lasting results, it's crucial that you remain dedicated to this process, and prioritize relaxation as a regular part of your daily routine.

8. Incorporate simple breathing exercises into your daily routine to help regulate your body's stress reactions.

9. Use progressive muscle relaxation to effectively reduce physiological stress and alleviate physical tension. By systematically tensing and relaxing various muscle groups, you can promote deep relaxation and a sense of calm.

10. Use physical movement, such as taking a short walk or doing an everyday chore, to respond to heightened anxiety. This can be a useful complement to your regular exercise routine, which is also vital in maintaining a calm nervous system.

 Icy goodness!

Holding ice can be a quick, helpful way to manage anxiety. You can hold an ice cube in your hand or try running it along the inside of your elbow or wrist. The intense cold sensation can be very grounding, bringing you into the present moment and taking you away from anxious thoughts. The sensory input from the ice can help shift your focus away from your nervous system's activity and onto your sensory system. Plus, ice can regulate your body temperature, which is especially helpful if you experience hot flashes due to anxiety. When your body temperature cools down, physical symptoms can also subside, making you feel less worried and anxious overall.

Chapter 4:
How Can I Address My Anxious Thoughts?

Now that we have a solid understanding of anxiety and how to manage the physiological stress it creates, it's time to shift our focus to dealing with anxious thoughts. An essential aspect of overcoming anxiety is to actively address and effectively manage the thoughts associated with it. This is the most extensive chapter in this book, and I've devoted more space to it because in my clinical practice I've seen the power of anxious thoughts. They are a significant factor in perpetuating anxiety problems, and many people struggle to know what to do about them, and how to free themselves of their grip.

I'm faced with an anxious thought again, which requires me to make a choice

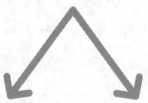

This choice moves me AWAY from my goal of overcoming anxiety, and worsens my anxiety

This choice moves me TOWARDS my goal of overcoming anxiety

Picture your thought processes as a flow diagram. The options you have in front of you will either make your problem better, worse or maintain it. When you have an anxious thought, you can either disagree with it (which I know isn't easy), you can simply accept it or you can agree with it. If you agree with it and go along with whatever your anxious thoughts have suggested to you, will you feel more or less anxious?

Patient Example: Joe's Silence

During my work with Joe, who struggled with social anxiety, we discovered a recurring thought: 'Everyone is looking at me, I'll say something stupid and make a fool of myself.' Joe believed this thought to be true and accepted it as such. Consequently, he opted to remain silent in social situations, prioritizing safety over potential embarrassment. Each time he validated this thought, the connection between the thought, his emotions and his actions grew stronger, inadvertently intensifying his anxiety. Although Joe experienced temporary relief from avoiding social embarrassment, this pattern unintentionally reinforced his anxiety and hindered his progress in challenging the thought's validity.

Patient Example: Maya's Multiple Choices

Maya was persistently anxious about a potential neurological condition, and this was her recurring thought: 'The twinge in my leg is a sign of a neurological problem.' Whenever this thought emerged, Maya experienced overwhelming anxiety. She bought into the thought, believing she needed to do something to control the situation and prevent the possibility of any bad outcome. Despite receiving confirmation from three different neurologists that there was no issue, Maya's relief was short-lived. Her response and belief in the anxious thoughts remained unchanged. The next time she experienced a similar twinge, just like Joe, she bought into the thought, unintentionally strengthening the pathway between it and her actions. Consequently, with each recurrence of the symptom, Maya found herself more and more inclined to follow the same path, inadvertently consolidating her anxiety.

Both of these are examples of exaggerated thought patterns, which have been coupled with exaggerated reactions. An exaggerated reaction from you towards your thought is a maladaptive response; it makes you buy into the threat and assume the worst. This can exacerbate cortisol levels in your body (see page 84), which not only kicks off the horrible physiological sensations you hate, but also facilitates the consolidation of more fear-based memories – keeping the problem going. Like Joe, Maya and many other anxiety sufferers, you've probably developed your own ways of managing and coping with troubling thoughts. Generally speaking, if these worked then your anxiety should have lessened over time; if they haven't worked then anxiety will have continued to worsen. Many of the ways people cope with troubling thoughts only add fuel to the fire, but often this is because they don't know what else to do.

When you become better equipped in managing your thoughts in an adaptive, helpful way you reduce cortisol secretion. If you agree with your thoughts that a catastrophe is about to take place, it's natural that you'll feel more anxious. This in turn will fuel your body's physiological anxiety response, making it harder to think clearly, and you will also experience more frightening thoughts and images. Anxious thoughts have the snowball effect we talked about in Chapter 3 (see page 86). The more you act on them, the bigger they grow, the faster they grow, the more powerful they become, and the more they're able to dictate your actions: 'Do this, do that, this will happen to you, you're not safe, you're this, you're that!'

The great news is there are numerous effective ways to deal with anxious thoughts, and I will guide you through the skills that can help you do this. Some of these skills are simple yet impactful and using them consistently can transform your perspective. While others might seem challenging at first, with practice you will become adept at using them. These skills are either thinking-based or practical, and I recommend taking notes when you first start out and then practising them mentally as they become more natural to your thinking style. Ultimately, the goal is for them to become second nature, so they can replace anxious thinking patterns, freeing your mind from the struggle with anxiety.

This chapter comprises three sections, each offering a set of skills that aims to help you overcome your anxious thoughts. We'll begin by looking at how you can get to grips with your anxious thoughts, then you'll learn how to effectively evaluate them, before we move on to transforming your anxious thinking style. I recommend you do not skip ahead but start with the first section, which lays the groundwork for success in transforming your thinking. These earlier skills are essential for building the strong foundation you'll need.

Once you've completed the full programme and become familiar with these skills, you can use them more flexibly. You can use as many or as few skills as you want. I recommend that you try all of them to determine which ones work best for you, and then use those ones as consistently as you can. You might find that you need to revisit different skills at different times, especially when your anxiety resurfaces or changes its presentation. Additionally, certain skills may work better for you in specific situations or at certain times. Over time, with consistent use of the skills, you will begin to notice a reduction in both the intensity and frequency of your anxious thoughts, as well as a decrease in your overall anxiety level. This transformation may happen quickly or may take some time, but remember that the more you use the skills, the quicker you will see these positive changes.

PART 1 – GETTING TO GRIPS WITH YOUR ANXIOUS THOUGHTS

Skill One – Identify Your Thoughts

Before we can do anything about anxious thoughts, we need to know what they are: this knowledge is our power. Being able to identify your thoughts will also help you see that your anxiety doesn't just come out of the blue, and this will really help you learn that it isn't as out of control as it may seem.

Identifying anxious thoughts is really simple. It requires you to tune into your thoughts so you can take note of them when you're experiencing anxiety. It's important to note them down as close to the episode of anxiety as possible, because when we feel calmer, often we can't remember exactly what we were thinking. Additionally, anxious thoughts occur so quickly and automatically we often don't notice them; instead we may notice that we feel anxious, or we may notice that we've jumped to reacting to our anxiety. There is always a thought there, you just have to find it and note it down. Some people's thoughts come in the form of an image: they might experience a flash image of themselves in a frightening situation. These should be noted in the same way: when you experience images like these, note down what they make you think. You can use the questions below as prompts to help you.

You may already know the kinds of thoughts that set off your anxiety. If you do then take note of these, either in your notebook or in your digital notes. You will come back to these thoughts time and again, because it is these recurrent thoughts that we are aiming to overcome. Once you start taking note of them, you will quickly notice a pattern, a recurring theme of some kind, so you won't need to keep using this skill (unless of course you start to experience new thoughts).

If you don't know what the content of your anxious thoughts is, don't worry; using this skill will give a new insight into identifying your anxious thoughts. Here are eight questions for you to ask yourself that will help you identify them:

1. When I feel anxious what is going through my mind?

2. What was I doing or noticing before I started to think this way?

3. What triggered this spike in anxiety, and what did that situation make me think about myself?

4. What is my worst fear, and why?

5. What do I worry about repeatedly?

6. What do I keep predicting will happen?

7. What types of conclusions is my mind jumping to?

8. What am I thinking about when I experience strong anxiety sensations?

Here are some general examples:

Maya: I'm terrified that I have a neurological illness
Jade: I think I'm going to die today
Joe: I'll say something stupid and everyone will hate me
Emily: A heart attack will strike me out of the blue

Based on Maya's response, here are answers for each of the questions:

1. When I feel anxious what is going through my mind?
   *That I will get a neurological disease, or that I
   already have one, and it just hasn't been detected by
   the doctors.*

2. What was I doing or noticing before I started to think
   this way?
   *I was looking at my calf muscle, paying close attention to
   it to see if I could notice any twitching.*

3. What triggered this spike in anxiety, and what did that
   situation make me think about myself?
   *I think I saw and felt a twitch in my leg, and it made
   me think I definitely have a neurological illness.*

4. What is my worst fear, and why?
   *That I will get a neurological illness, I will have a
   horribly long period of suffering before I eventually die.*

5. What do I worry about repeatedly?
   *Having a neurological illness that hasn't been detected,
   and that it will kill me.*

6. What do I keep predicting will happen?
   *That I already have a neurological illness or that I'll
   definitely get one. The so-called anxiety twitches in*

my body are not anxiety, they are a sign of a serious neurological condition.

7. What types of conclusions is my mind jumping to?
   That I have a neurological illness, which will kill me after lots of suffering.

8. What am I thinking about when I experience strong anxiety sensations?
   I picture myself being diagnosed with a neurological illness, and then dying, with my family crying by my side.

As you can see from Maya's case, the answers become repetitive. You don't need to have an answer for all eight questions, if you're coming up with the same thing each time. When this happens, use the questions again during a further anxious moment to see if you can discover more thoughts. The number of times you'll need to do this will vary. I ask some of my patients to record their thoughts over three days, some over a week, some for two weeks or even a month. It depends on how your anxiety presents itself, so be flexible and do what works best for you to get the information you need.

Once you've taken note of your anxious thoughts, it may also help to rank them from the most troubling to the least troubling. This ranking will help you prioritize which ones you want to address first as we work through this chapter.

Now that you've identified your anxious thoughts, let's move on to skill two where we will look at thought suppression.

Learning how to identify anxious thoughts helps you learn more about the content of your anxiety. This knowledge is power: it will provide you with the opportunity to directly target your troubling thoughts.

Skill Two – Stop Suppressing Anxious Thoughts

Thought suppression is a common coping strategy for people with anxiety. It involves you deliberately and actively trying not to think about the unpleasant thoughts you experience. Trying to suppress your thoughts ends up backfiring: the harder you try not to think of a pink elephant the more likely it is to come up in your mind. Thought suppression is counterproductive: it will give you the very thoughts and problems that you're hoping to avoid.

Imagine yourself standing in the sea, holding a beach ball beneath the water's surface with one hand. This beach ball symbolizes a thought that you would rather not have in your mind, so you try to suppress it by keeping it submerged. Take a moment to consider what thought might this be for you. As long as you successfully hold the ball underwater, the surface of the water remains calm and undisturbed. You may find some relief in keeping this thought suppressed, as it eases the discomfort it brings. But holding the ball with one hand limits your freedom of movement and your capabilities are restricted. Other situations may arise that need your action and attention, but you can't fully reach or engage with them because you're stuck, and they're out of your reach. You can't really hold that ball underwater forever either. Eventually, your grip will loosen, and the ball will propel to the surface, creating huge ripples, making a mess, soaking everything, with the surface water losing its temporary tranquillity. Panic stricken by this thought emerging again, you may desperately try to force the ball back underwater as quickly as possible, momentarily restoring the calm surface. But this perpetuates your anxiety, keeping you stuck in the same place, unable to move forward, as you remain trapped by your attempts to suppress this thought.

To release yourself from this, so you can be free to get on with other things, you have to learn to release this suppression.

You have to let go of the ball, let it rise to the surface of the water, set it free so it can float away. Of course, it might not completely disappear straight away, but when you release it, other things will influence its movement, like the wind and the waves. At times you might see the ball right back next to you, at other times it might float much further away, at times you'll only see it far in the distance. You have to accept that this ball is still there to varying degrees, but you are now able to move around more freely, to think, feel and act in ways that are full of possibility. You're no longer stuck in this impossible and unhealthy struggle of trying to force this thought down. You're free to understand the reasons why you might be thinking this way, and this understanding will make it easier for you to free yourself from the negative influences of this thought.

Patient Example: Jade's Mortality

Let me introduce you to Jade, one of my patients, and share her story with you. Jade grappled with an overwhelming fear of something fatal happening to her. The mere thought of her own mortality and the potential consequences for her children filled her with immense dread, so she suppressed this thought with all her energy. Jade believed that her absence would irreparably devastate her children's lives, beyond what they could possibly endure. As long as Jade held the ball underwater, the surface of the water appeared settled, and this avoidance made things seem easier in the short term. But because Jade was holding down this ball with one hand, just like you, she couldn't move freely. From time to time she'd lose her grip on the ball, and it would create huge ripples for her. Each time this happened she became more determined to suppress it as hard as she could. This temporarily settled things again, but it also made it certain that Jade would remain stuck where she was, unable to move. Jade learned that she really couldn't hold that ball underwater forever. She learned to release this pressure, letting the ball rise to the surface of the water, setting it free and watching it float. It didn't vanish at once, but it felt lighter and easier, and the struggle against it was gone. At times Jade would see the ball nearby, at other times it was further away, and sometimes she could barely see it. Jade was more free in her ability to think, feel and make choices to act in different ways. Stopping her attempts to suppress this thought released the power it held, and Jade felt less stuck. Once the negative influences of thought suppression lifted, there was more mental space to think through things, and work on her anxiety using other skills. I can empathize with Jade's desire to avoid contemplating her mortality. But, by suppressing this thought, she prevented herself from addressing it and finding a resolution, so her anxiety remained unresolved. Does Jade's story make you think of any thoughts that you have been suppressing?

This beach-ball metaphor highlights the futility of suppressing thoughts as a long-term solution to your anxiety problems, because it simply doesn't work. By trying to rid an unpleasant thought like this from your mind, you inadvertently give it power that it didn't have before. You have to let thoughts be there, understand why they're there and learn to let go of them. You have to learn how to develop a different relationship with your thoughts. I'll show you how to do this in the next skill – accepting your anxious thoughts.

Beach ball visualization

When you notice that you're suppressing an unpleasant thought, imagine yourself lifting your hand off the beach ball, imagine it floating by you, and visualize the freeness in your ability to move unencumbered.

Stop suppressing anxious thoughts. If you're not willing to have them, you will. Suppressing anxious thoughts can seem like a good idea, but it only feeds the problem, making anxiety worse.

Skill Three – Accept your Anxious Thoughts

Accepting your thoughts is the opposite of trying to control and suppress them. Cultivating flexibility in how you respond to thoughts is a key goal, and it starts with accepting them as they arise. By embracing acceptance, you open yourself up to considering alternatives, adopting different perspectives and choosing to act in ways that align with what you truly want rather than being dictated to solely by your thoughts. This shift in behaviour can lead you towards greater recovery and progress, even in the presence of persistent thoughts. As you continue to engage in meaningful actions aligned with our goal of overcoming anxiety, the power of these thoughts will gradually diminish. In this section you'll find five skills to help you practice acceptance of your anxious thoughts. Strive for consistency in practising these techniques, viewing them as a long-term approach to managing your thoughts rather than a temporary or quick fix. This process is about developing a new and evolving relationship with your anxious thoughts.

Your brain is constantly generating different thoughts to try and help you. Your reaction to these thoughts determines whether they gain power, or lose power and fade away. It can produce neutral thoughts such as 'it's pizza for dinner tonight' or more distressing ones like 'your heart palpitations are a heart attack'. When neutral thoughts arise, you typically don't react much to them, so they disappear on their own. But when a distressing thought like the heart attack example comes up, you're alarmed, and feel the urge to control it. It's similar to a small fire being ignited, causing you to go into emergency mode to extinguish it. This reaction makes your brain interpret your response as important, and the thought as something that needs prioritizing, so it sends more of these types of thoughts your way. The more you try to get rid of them, the more power and attention you give them, so the more they come, creating a vicious cycle. Rather than trying to push these thoughts away, you can choose to let them be there without reacting to them or trying to eliminate them. Over time, these thoughts will naturally lose their power and fade away. By doing this you're signalling to your brain that these thoughts are not significant, and as a result, you'll begin to have less of them and therefore feel less anxious.

Acceptance is about allowing thoughts to be there, recognizing that you can't just rid yourself of them. You also know that your attempts to eliminate or control unwanted thoughts has been counterproductive. It hasn't helped you overcome your anxiety. Non-acceptance of thoughts means you're regarding the thoughts as 'literal truths' and you are then acting accordingly. But my guess is that this hasn't worked for you either.

There is a thought-provoking poem 'The Guest House' by Rumi. It presents a powerful metaphor, beautifully capturing the concept of accepting thoughts. I use this poem to encourage patients to see themselves as a house where different thoughts come and go, just like guests visiting a guest house. Some thoughts bring joy and positivity, while others evoke fear, anxiety and sadness. The poem helps me emphasise the importance of welcoming and accepting all these thoughts because they have something valuable to offer. Instead of resisting or pushing away these thoughts, you can treat them with kindness and learn from them. By doing so, you can gain a deeper understanding of yourself. The poem is a reminder that each thought you experience holds significance and has the potential to contribute to your journey of finding inner calm. When you deny or reject thoughts, they persistently knock at the door of your mind demanding your attention. This resistance leads to inner conflict, increased anxiety and a greater struggle. Trying to keep them out becomes futile, because they continue to occupy your mind. Acceptance allows you to work with your thoughts with understanding and compassion, ultimately leading to a greater sense of calm.

Like this poem, there may be other sources of solace that can provide you with moments of reflection and that help you develop a healthier relationship with your thoughts. Songs, scenes from movies, and even certain parts of stories can offer opportunities to pause and contemplate your thoughts. Additionally, there may be specific words or phrases that others have shared with you that have resonated. Take a moment to consider what comes to mind and how you can keep those insights close at heart. Embracing these sources of comfort can help you nurture a mindset of acceptance.

Our next skill is a super simple way to practise accepting thoughts through an acceptance affirmation. Jade (see page 111) would affirm to herself countless times a day that she was suddenly going to die and that her children would be highly traumatized. When you tell yourself scary things with this kind of frequency, you are terrorizing yourself right at the moment in which you need calm, peace and relief. Jade affirming her anxiety like this brought no her relief; it did the exact opposite and frightened her even more, which then fed more anxiety. Once Jade was able to accept her thoughts, even if it was 'today I'm going to die', she was able to be more mindful of them, think about them before acting or reacting, and build up her ability to tolerate their presence without the need to do something. Look at this acceptance affirmation, and consider writing out your own personalized version.

TASK 10
Accepting your anxious thoughts affirmation

Here's a short and simple affirmation for acceptance that you can use or personalize according to your needs. Try to read this affirmation daily, as it provides your mind with the support it needs to facilitate change and embrace a path of increased acceptance.

'I'm going to be mindful of my thoughts as they occur. I'm deciding to accept them, instead of reacting to them in ways that make my anxiety worse. Accepting my thoughts means I will notice they are there, and just allow them to be there. I don't need to react to them or do what they tell me. I will gently shift my focus onto other things that I want or need to do.'

Now let's move on to a mindfulness exercise that can help you cultivate awareness and acceptance of your thoughts by simply observing them. This exercise is a powerful tool that can help you develop a non-judgemental attitude towards your inner experiences.

TASK 11
Accepting thoughts through mindful observation

Please read through steps 1–8 before you start the practice. I often suggest making a slowly spoken audio recording of this so you can listen to the instructions and follow along. If you don't like the sound of your own recorded voice (which many people don't), ask someone you know to make a recording for you, or try one of the apps available to convert text to audio in different voices. Find a quiet and comfortable place to sit with your back well supported, and your feet grounded on the floor. You can also use a cushion or mat on the floor if that feels more comfortable for you. Find a position that allows you to be present while also being physically comfortable.

Practise this skill as often as you need to; to begin with you might find more frequent practice beneficial and it can be helpful to integrate this into your daily routine. Of course, you can also practise this ad hoc whenever your mind feels noisy and full of thoughts.

1. Start by closing your eyes, and take a few slow deep breaths. Now notice any sounds you can hear around you.
2. Now, gently turn your attention to your thoughts; try to pinpoint their location – where does it feel like they sit? Notice where your thoughts are. Are they in your head, or in your stomach? Are they above you or below you? Are they behind you or in front of you? Are they to your left or to your right? Does it feel like your thoughts are inside your body or outside your body?
3. What form do your thoughts take. Are they words or are they pictures? What colours represent your different thoughts?
4. Do your thoughts move around or are they still? If they are still, where do they sit? If they move, what is their speed and in which direction do they move?

5. Notice how your thoughts are changing all the time as you observe them. What are the range of thoughts you're observing? What different topics come up?
6. Notice how some of your thoughts might be inviting you to analyse or argue with them. Notice how you're declining this invitation.
7. Notice how you are observing your thoughts: there's you, and then separate from you are your thoughts. You are not one.

Take a few slow deep breaths, in through your nose and out through your mouth. Notice the sounds around you. When you're ready, open your eyes and return to the present moment.

Accepting your thoughts can make it easier for you to hold a nuanced picture of your experiences, where you don't need to cling to one story or another about yourself. Things become less black and white, less this or that, more flexible. If we look at Jade's case again, she doesn't need to cling to the idea of death so strongly, nor does she need to cling to the idea that she needs to be free of all anxiety sensations at all times. When you accept your thoughts, you will also notice that you have many other thoughts, not just anxious thoughts. You will notice this because you've lessened the struggle with your anxious thoughts, meaning your mind will be less preoccupied with them, allowing you to see that there are many other thoughts in your mind too, both negative and positive.

You can recognize anxious thoughts are there, without taking them as literal truths. One way to do this is to reword your anxious thoughts; not only is it more accurate, it also helps with acceptance.

Now, let's explore a task that focuses on the practice of rewording your thoughts to make them more reflective of objective reality. Using this technique can positively transform your relationship with your thoughts. It helps you become more aware of the language and tone of your internal dialogue. This helps you create distance from anxious thoughts, fostering a more objective and compassionate perspective. Over time, as you continue to reframe your thoughts to be more accurate and constructive, your mind naturally begins to replace negative patterns with more helpful ones.

TASK 12
Rewording your thoughts
Instead of Joe thinking 'I'm such an embarrassment', he can reword his thought to 'Once again, I'm having the thought that I'm such an embarrassment'. This helps Joe effectively separate himself from the cognition, and when practised consistently it strips it of its negative influence.

Other examples:

Instead of: 'I'm going to die in my sleep tonight, I can feel it.'
Try this: 'Once again, I'm having the thought that I'm going to die in my sleep.'

Instead of: 'I will be rejected by everyone.'
Try this: 'Once again, I'm having the thought that I will be rejected.'

Instead of: 'I will vomit.'
Try this: 'Once again, I'm having the thought that I will vomit.'

Note down some of your own examples that are specific to your anxiety. Daily practice of this can really help; if you forget, at the end of the day try to think of three to five, and note them down in your journal or digital notes.

Remember, you are trying to change your relationship with your thoughts and this won't happen by rewording thoughts only every now and then. It will happen by you moving over to this as your new way of being with your thoughts. Consistency is key.

Explore your thoughts

Sometimes taking a closer look at your thoughts can help you accept their presence. More often than not, anxious thoughts are repetitive, following a particular theme and pattern. Here are some questions to help you explore your thoughts so you can accept their presence, instead of reacting to them by taking unhelpful actions.

- Is this thought an old story repeating itself?
- Have I heard this thought before?
- What do I get for buying into this thought?
- Has this thought ever helped me take effective action?
- Does this thought influence me to move towards ineffective action?

A further way to accept your thoughts is to thank your mind for its contribution to your mental health, and then label the thought. Let's look at this exercise and add it to your toolkit.

TASK 13
Thank your mind and label the thought

Thanking your mind and labelling the thought is a skill that helps you notice and accept your thoughts instead of you becoming absorbed and caught up in them. It also reduces the believability of thoughts by helping you break negative patterns and reduce how much influence your thoughts have on your behaviours.

When your mind presents you with an anxious thought and tries to get your engagement, do this:

Start by thanking your mind for its contribution, and then label the thought you're noticing: 'Thank you, mind, for reminding me of this, this is the "you're going to get a horrible disease" thought again.'

Say this out loud if you can. If you're in a public place and you can't say it out loud, just say it in your head. You can also note it down; soon enough you'll start to notice a pattern of repetitive thoughts.

As more thoughts appear, keep acknowledging them as a product of your mind, thank your mind for its replay and contribution, keep labelling the thought, then let it go. If it keeps playing in the background, let it, while you gently shift your attention on to something you'd rather be doing.
Here are some more examples:

- 'This is the "There's something stuck in your throat" thought.'
- 'Oh look, here's a replay of the "You'll get sick" thought.'

- 'That's the "Everybody is staring at you" thought.'
- 'That's the "You have a neurological disease" thought again.'

I've shown you some strategies to help you with acceptance. I encourage you to make a personal commitment to yourself to regularly practise these. Incorporating these techniques into your daily routine doesn't have to take up a lot of extra time since they can replace your current methods of managing your thoughts. Reflect on how much time you currently spend on these methods. Can you replace them with these new approaches? Consider the amount of time and energy you use to deal with anxious thoughts and think about substituting them with these alternative techniques.

Accepting the presence of anxious thoughts allows you to make room for them, make space for whatever they're about. This opens up the opportunity for you to work productively with them instead of fighting against them.

Skill Four – Understand Why Your Anxious Thought Is There

Anxiety triggers are almost always accompanied by an anxious thought, and it is this thought that often causes distress, so that you end up trying to do something to alleviate this distress. Your thought is there because something has probably happened to trigger its presence. In Chapter 1 we looked at anxiety triggers – having insight into these can help you understand your experience better and also help you work out when and how to do things differently.

When you develop an understanding of why the thought is there, looking at what triggered it, what has happened in the past to contribute to it and what reinforces it, you can manage it better. When you don't have this understanding, it's more likely that you'll have the horrible thought, immediately feel distressed, then react impulsively. This is exactly what we don't want; we want to slow down and take stock, instead of going around the same loop again: the anxiety–fear cycle. When you are back in this loop your anxiety is being reinforced and growing stronger.

Thoughts
I have a horrible thought

Feelings
I cannot stand how awful this thought makes me feel

Behaviour
I quickly and impulsively do something to get rid of this awful feeling

Patient Example: Amina's Travel Anxiety

My patient Amina struggled a great deal with anxiety triggered by any kind of travel away from home. Amina hated to be away from the safe zone of her home, especially overnight, and the further away she was, the worse her anxiety was. Amina would constantly think 'What if this happens?', 'What if that happens?' and she would also think 'I'll be trapped, I won't be able to get home immediately if my anxiety gets out of control.' The closer a proposed trip got, the more anxious Amina felt. She struggled to sleep, her stomach churned and she wasn't able to eat well. We can see here that Amina's anxiety was triggered by upcoming travel away from home. We know that Amina finds travelling highly distressing, so it makes sense that she would experience heightened anxiety at the prospect of travelling. Amina would misinterpret the experience of anxiety as a sign from the universe that something would go wrong on the trip. Of course, it was her anxiety that caused her to feel unusual and different in her body, but to Amina this unusual feeling felt like a premonition. It was very important for Amina to learn and understand her trigger in order to move away from these threatening predictions. Amina's travel anxiety began after she experienced a panic attack while on holiday, so it makes perfect sense that her mind would approach the prospect of travel with this kind of fear. What it doesn't mean is that something bad is inevitable just because Amina feels anxious.

The thoughts you have are not there without reason or cause, so it's worth taking the time to explore and understand them. There may be an event or experience that sheds light on why you're having these thoughts. Answering the questions in the following exercise can be helpful in gaining clarity and insight into your thought process.

Understanding why my anxious thought is there

- Did something happen externally (outside my body) that caused this thought to occur? What was it?
- Did something happen internally (inside my body or mind) that caused this thought to occur? What was it?

- What was I doing just before the thought appeared?
- Did the situation I'm in cause the thought – did I see or hear something?
- Did I remember something painful from the past? A memory, image or feeling that led to this thought?
- Why is it understandable that I am having this thought? What makes sense about its occurrence? It's no surprise that I'm having this thought, it makes perfect sense because . . .

Some sample answers:

- 'I'm remembering something bad and it's influenced my thinking.'
- 'I just saw something bad that made me apply that idea to myself.'
- 'I heard some bad news which set off this thought.'
- 'It makes sense that my mind would produce anxious thoughts out of habit.'
- 'I felt this feeling in my chest and it reminded me of a panic attack I once had, then it set off my anxious thought.'

When I have answered the questions and made sense of the presence of this thought, I don't need to respond to it, or take any actions as if it's a literal truth. Instead, I can soothe the anxiety caused in my body by using the skills in Chapter 3 (see pages 91–100).

Many things can trigger anxious thoughts; regardless of the trigger it doesn't make them literal truths. Something about their presence makes sense, and understanding this will help lessen the battle you have with them.

Skill Five – Stop Over-identifying with Your Thoughts

I want you to hold out your hands in front of you with open palms. Then, gently cover your face with your hands while keeping your eyes open. What do you see? Only your hands and perhaps a glimpse of light through tiny cracks, right? Now, gradually lower your hands to waist level. What can you see now? A lot more. This illustrates what it's like when you over-identify with your thoughts. You become so entangled with them that you lose sight of alternative views or perspectives. The following skill is aimed at transforming this pattern: remember that you are not your thoughts, even though anxiety may try to make you believe otherwise.

Anxiety can cause us to develop an intense attachment to negative beliefs about ourselves, life, others and certain situations. This attachment can result in significant distress and suffering. As you become more entrenched in these beliefs, you adopt all kinds of painful positions as you merge further and further with these strong beliefs, almost as if you've become them.

Patient Example: Ezra's Heart Anxiety

My patient Ezra suffered from anxiety relating to his heart, persistently fearing a sudden heart attack. Typical of many patients with heart-related anxiety, Ezra was overly preoccupied with the functioning of his heart, closely monitoring rate and rhythm changes. The content of Ezra's anxious thoughts included 'I have a heart condition that nobody can identify' and 'I need to be careful otherwise I will bring on a heart

---

attack'. Ezra over-identified with his anxious thoughts by changing how he behaved: he began acting as if he actually did have a heart problem. Ezra would avoid strenuous movement, he would not exercise and even going for a walk that caused changes in his heart rate resulted in him returning home, walking very slowly. Ezra would move carefully and rest a great deal so as not to aggravate the heart condition that his anxiety convinced him that he had. We can see clearly how Ezra became the content of his thoughts: he acted as if they were true, and took on a persona that matched their content.

Over-identifying with your thoughts stops you from seeing that *you* are you, and these are just your thoughts. Instead, you think *they* are you, they are your reality, but they are not. On occasions, particularly when you're busy, and less aware of your over-identification with your anxious thoughts, you may have moments of relief.

It's so easy to get lost in the drama of your thoughts, and it doesn't take long before thought pathways in your mind become deeply ingrained. In this section, you'll find three more tools to help you learn how to distance yourself from your thoughts, so you can prevent or reduce your over-attachment to them. With consistent practice, these tools can help you develop a more observational relationship with your anxious thoughts.

These tools are about changing your relationship to your thoughts. By changing the way they're expressed you can step back and view them from a different perspective, rather than being trapped in them.

TASK 14
Stop over-identifying with your thoughts

A) Use your voice to detach from your thoughts

Occasionally, I've shared this exercise on my social media stories, much to the delight of my followers. It's a wonderful technique to create distance between yourself and the troubling thoughts. You can transform your thoughts into a song, using a tune you know or a rhythm that resonates with you. Begin your song with the lyrics, 'My thoughts are telling me . . .' followed by whatever they're conveying to you. Repeat this a few times.

Another option is to express your thoughts in a different voice or accent. When you notice the thought, vocalize it out loud in a playful voice, starting with, 'So this time, my thoughts are telling me . . .' followed by whatever they're conveying to you.

Here's an example based on Ezra whose anxiety was about his heart:

'My thoughts are telling me that I have a heart problem, and it will make me afraid I'll die of a heart attack today.'

Ezra repeated this out loud several times in a row.

Ezra also used a Scouse accent to voice his thoughts out loud, saying:

'So, here we go again, my thoughts are trying to tell me that I'm going to drop dead of that heart condition that I don't even have.'

You can also sing or say the thoughts to a loved one, a friend, or even perform them in front of a mirror. Consider recording yourself on your phone and watching it back when the same thoughts resurface. Add gestures and movements to make it more theatrical and engaging. The more different it appears from your usual self, the greater the distance you can create between yourself and the thoughts. Give this technique a try and see how it works for you. Regular practice will enhance your ability to observe your thoughts. By altering the way you express them, they sound different, and this prevents automatic identification with them as undeniable facts, which allows you to establish an objective distance from them.

B) Give your thoughts an identity
Creating an identity for your anxious thoughts, or even for your anxiety as a whole, can be a helpful method for distancing yourself from those thoughts. You can think of anxiety as a bully or a dictator that thrives on spreading propaganda. Some of my patients find it helpful to select a person they would despise taking orders from and assign that person's identity to their anxiety symptoms. When anxiety tells them something, they imagine that person as saying the exact same thing. Then they respond to that person: 'I refuse to let you dictate or bully me. How dare you try to tell me what to do? You have no power over me, and I won't entertain your nonsensical demands.'

To keep the use of this tool simple and straightforward, be sure not to choose a person you are afraid of, or someone who may have a strong emotional influence on you.

C) Change how you behave in response to your thoughts

If your thoughts tell you that you have a heart problem, and you start acting as if you actually do, then those thoughts will become more consolidated. The stronger they get, the more often they will appear, and the more likely you are to continue identifying with them. To stop yourself from taking on the persona that is consistent with the content of your thoughts, you need to change how you behave in response to them. You have to reduce and ultimately stop behaving in accordance with your thoughts. If you don't want the anxiety problem you have, then don't act in supportive ways towards it.

Changing how to react to thoughts can be hard, so it's important to start small and be realistic. Here are some simple ways to begin:

1. What thing do I do that is supportive of the content of my thought?
2. How often do I do this thing?
3. What duration does it take me each time I do this thing?

Once you have this information, gently work at reducing the reactions you have to your thoughts. Let's take Ezra as an example again:

1. What thing do I do that is supportive of the content of my thought?
   When I am walking and my heart rate changes too much, I immediately stop and sit down.
2. How often do I do this thing?
   Every time I walk, in fact I've reduced how much I walk.
3. What duration does it take me each time I do this thing?
   Well, I walk for about six minutes before I check my heart rate, then I stop to rest for about fifteen minutes, before I very slowly walk back home.

Use the information you have to make some manageable changes. In Ezra's case, these were as follows:

1. I will not check my heart rate when I'm walking; if I really have to, I will only check it after ten minutes, and add two minutes to this on each subsequent walk. I will have eventually built up to thirty minutes.
2. If I stop to rest, I will shorten my rest period by halving the time from fifteen minutes, then halving it again when that becomes doable.
3. If I walk back home, I will keep a steady pace, not too slow, and not too fast.

Take note of the changes that you can make based on your situation, and put these in your notebook or into your digital notes.

You are not your thoughts, you are you, and your thoughts are separate. You can practise different skills to help detach yourself, and keep a healthy distance between yourself and your anxious thoughts.

PART 2 – EVALUATE YOUR ANXIOUS THOUGHTS

Skill One – Monitor Your Anxious Thoughts. What Happened Next?

Anxious thoughts often fall into repetitive patterns. Even though you have been impacted by these threatening thoughts for a significant period of time without them actually materializing, you still cling to them. Is this right? This is what an anxious mind does, and you need to help your mind filter through these repetitive thoughts. This skill will show you how you can do that, and when done with regularity anxious thoughts will diminish.

For this simple skill, look at the table below and make your own version, either in your journal or digital notes. Note

Date	What threat did your anxious thought make to you?	Did that threat come true, yes or no?	If that threat didn't become reality, what happened instead?
1st April	You're going to pass out.	No	I felt anxious but I didn't pass out.
20th April	You're going to pass out.	No	I carried on with what I was doing.
5th May	You're going to pass out.	No	Nothing happened, I was fine.

down the date, the threat your anxious thought presented you with, if that threat came true, and if it didn't, what happened instead.

Once you've made a table like this, keep adding thoughts, keep recording a 'yes/no' response and the actual reality of the situation. You'll soon notice that there is a very clear distortion between your anxious perception and the reality. I also suggest counting the number of 'no' responses you have each time you add another thought, and say out loud to yourself, for example: 'That's fourteen noes so far'. This will help your mind in processing the actual facts of the situations you encounter. It enhances your understanding and allows you to recognize the distortion that exists between your perceptions and objective reality. By doing so, it facilitates a natural restructuring of your thinking processes.

To further help you, here are some examples of thoughts associated with various anxiety problems. For each thought, we aim to determine whether the anxious prediction actually came true or not. As you can see, for this skill, the focus is on predictive thoughts that anticipate specific outcomes.

General Anxiety	I'll be late.
	I'm going to mess up at work today.
	My academic work will be a disaster, I'll fail this project.
Health Anxiety	My heart feels weird, I'm going to have a heart attack.
Social Anxiety	I will totally humiliate myself at the meeting today, people will laugh.
Panic Disorder	I will have a panic attack on my commute, I could even lose my mind.

Anxiety makes frightening predictions all the time. You can monitor these threats carefully and objectively. Doing so will help your mind adjust its approach to distorted perception.

Skill Two – Consider Things that Go Against Your Anxious Thoughts

Anxiety thoughts are biased in favour of fear, and this bias means that you're likely to dismiss anything that goes against them. Disqualifying all the neutrals, or even positives, in a situation leaves you absorbed with the negatives. This tendency also causes people to discount any reassuring facts from the information they have. Because of the biased way in which anxiety works you can become hyper-fixated on the bad stuff, even when there's a multitude of reasons to believe otherwise. This propensity to ignore positives in favour of negatives causes much more distress.

Patient Example: Reese's Reality

My patient Reese had a persistent and disturbing anxiety that he was losing his mind and losing touch with reality. Reese often felt anxious that he may go 'crazy' or that he was developing dementia at the age of twenty-eight. When Reese was in a higher state of anxiousness he would forget words or find it hard to find the right word, and he considered this proof that he was suffering with an unusual presentation of dementia. Reese's thoughts would race at a level that he felt was uncontrollable, which is what happens when people become very anxious. Like many sufferers, Reese's anxiety was biased in favour of his fears, which meant he only considered things that supported these fears. Reese had to learn to widen his

---

perspective and consider everything before him, not just the frightening stuff that so easily grabbed his attention. In considering other possibilities Reese was able to accept that his persistent lack of quality sleep was part of the explanation. There were also hundreds of things Reese did on a daily and weekly basis that he simply wouldn't be able to do if he really had lost his mind, and these needed to be noticed and taken into account. There were also things that simply didn't fit with his thought that he was losing his mind, and his insight into himself was considerable. I asked Reese how he'd respond to his best friend if he had the same fear and he told me he'd list all the things they can do, how they are, how they converse, all their capabilities to help them see it's simply not correct. Reese was also able to see that when his stress levels at work were low and he slept better, he wouldn't have the same types of thoughts. Finally, Reese could see that having had these thoughts since his late teens and nothing actually changing in his day-to-day ability that he was probably doing okay, and not losing his mind.

I have listed some questions below that you can use to help you take a fuller view into consideration. Considering things that go against your anxiety will guide you further away from anxious thoughts. Again, the more you practise using these, the more skilled you'll become, the easier it will be for your mind to consider a wider viewpoint, and a wider viewpoint means you will feel less anxious.

1. What other possibilities are there that I just haven't considered?
2. What things do I know that disagree with my anxious thoughts?

3. What goes totally against, or even somewhat against, the thought I'm having?
4. What things have happened that just don't fit with this anxious thought?
5. If someone else told me they were thinking this way, what would I point out to them?
6. When this has happened in the past and my thoughts have been wrong, what do I think afterwards?
7. Is there a recurring pattern in this thought, and what has this pattern taught me so far?

Anxiety is biased in favour of fear, meaning your mind only takes distressing things into account. You can question these views to widen your thinking. This will help train your mind into considering other possibilities, particularly things that go against your anxiety.

Skill Three – Is it Theory A or Theory B?

Let's explore the skill of using two theories in relation to your anxiety. Theory A suggests that your anxiety is accurate, that its thoughts and suggestions are correct. Theory B, on the other hand, posits that anxiety is the problem, causing you to believe things that are not true. Have you ever questioned whether what you fear is truly the case, or if it's actually the influence of anxiety? I find the Theory A vs Theory B approach to be impactful with my patients, as it allows them to discover the truth through their own experiences rather than relying solely on my words. Seeking reassurance from others often falls short in convincing your mind. However, by engaging in the process of examining these theories for yourself, by using a strategy like Theory A vs Theory B, you're likely to achieve better results.

Just as certain raw ingredients need to be carefully cooked and combined to create a flavorful dish, information needs to be thoughtfully processed and analyzed to develop accurate knowledge. Incomplete, inaccurate ideas are like half-baked ingredients, which can be unpleasant and even harmful to your health. When it comes to your anxious thoughts, there are two competing theories. Theory A is that your anxious thoughts are correct, while Theory B is that your anxiety is the problem, making you believe things that are simply not true. Just as incomplete dishes have gaps and holes, incomplete theories have shortcomings that need to be identified. Comparing these two theories helps you cover all aspects, so you can decide which one is best for you to follow. Anxious thoughts are half-baked ideas that haven't been fully analysed yet. Just as cooking requires time, effort and attention to detail, analysis of these two competing theories needs the same. The great news is, it helps you self-reflect and choose the theory that aligns with your factual reality, and also moves you towards the goal of beating anxiety.

Keep an open mind as you embark on discovering which theory holds true for you. It's not about favouring one theory over the other, but rather investigating and evaluating the evidence to make an informed decision. The goal is to determine which position is supported by more substantial evidence and which one lacks supporting evidence. This process empowers you to gather the necessary information and make a well-informed judgement about the validity of each theory.

Patient Example: Jenny's Dual Theories

My patient Jenny and I worked through this skill together in clinic. Her two theories were:

Theory A – The heart palpitations I'm having are the sign of a heart attack.

Theory B – The heart palpitations I'm having are due to the harmless physical changes in my body brought on by anxiety.

Next Jenny was asked to keep a record of all the situations she encountered, over a two-week period, where she experienced heart palpitations. She used a table to record her experiences:

Date	The situation and outcome	Was it Theory A or Theory B?
11th April	Went for a walk with my friend, felt anxious and over-aware of my heartbeat, noticed thudding in my chest.	I didn't have a heart attack so it's Theory B.
20th April	Did an online exercise class, my heart rate increased, I was super anxious.	I didn't have a heart attack so it's Theory B.
26th April	At a large family gathering indoors, I felt hot and trapped with heart palpitations.	I didn't have a heart attack so it's Theory B.
27th April	Had a work medical, super scared that the doctor was going to tell me I have a heart problem. My heart was racing.	I didn't have a heart attack so it's Theory B, and the doctor also said it was anxiety.

I'd like you to use Jenny's example to help you formulate and experiment with two distinct theories of your own. Spend two weeks recording situations where you experienced your physical symptom, and noting whether what happened fits with your Theory A or Theory B. After this two-week period, review which theory gained more support through the experiences you had. I'd like you to keep using this technique with any number of situations. It works really well when you have an 'is it this or is it that?' thought problem.

In Jenny's case you can see that Theory B was proven. Though Jenny has anxiety symptoms, she doesn't have a medical problem with her heart. From this, Jenny learned that her anxiety symptoms are the problem, not a heart problem. This reduced her level of fear, the intensity of her symptoms and the frequency of her troubling thoughts. Jenny also learned that it's normal for her heart to race and for her to react when her body is under physiological stress.

Either your anxious thought is correct, or your anxiety is causing you to believe something that isn't true. You can test out which one it is by carrying out a two-week evaluation of the symptom you're concerned about.

PART 3 – TRANSFORM YOUR ANXIOUS THOUGHT

Skill One – Considering Alternative Explanations

By now, you are well aware of the influence anxiety has on distorting your perspective. You know that anxiety tends to favour fear and amplifies thoughts to an extreme level. When anxiety takes hold, individuals often succumb to its suggestions due to the overwhelming fright it instills. This prevents you from considering alternative explanations and possibilities for your experiences. These alternatives often provide a more accurate and realistic understanding compared to the distorted narratives anxiety presents.

Imagine anxiety is the worst housemate you could ever have. A roommate who won't stop talking about your worst fears, that's all you hear from them, nothing else. This roommate is constantly in your ear, reminding you of these fears; their mission is to make it difficult for you to think about anything else. It's as if this annoying roommate has moved into your head and won't leave you alone, no matter how hard you try to ignore them. They continuously make it hard for you to focus on anything else, making sure your mind is constantly preoccupied with fear. Their voice is always playing in the background, telling you about all the things that scare you, even when they're not talking to you. It leaves you exhausted and overwhelmed, feeling drained and helpless. The way out of this helplessness and overwhelm is to open yourself up to alternative voices, and not just listen to this worst ever housemate.

Patient Example: Emily's Troubling Thoughts

Emily consistently grappled with anxious thoughts, almost on a daily basis, convinced that she was on the verge of experiencing a heart attack. Contrary to her anxious predictions, Emily did not have any underlying heart condition. This discrepancy demonstrated that her anxiety-driven beliefs were inaccurately perceived by her. If her beliefs were indeed valid, we would expect the heart attack to have occurred. Emily endured this distressing struggle for a period of three years.

One of the things Emily worked on was considering alternative explanations for her troubling thoughts. These were most often triggered by her becoming anxious, and she would then experience heart palpitations as one of the physical symptoms of anxiety. The heart palpitations would always take her to the thought of a heart attack. All the time Emily was cemented to this one view, her anxiety did not get better. In fact, it got progressively worse, and as it did, so did the intensity of her physical sensations. This felt very reinforcing for Emily: the worsening intensity and frequency of her anxiety symptoms led her to believe it must be a cardiac problem. In considering an alternative explanation for her experience, Emily came up with these more accurate and much less frightening possibilities:

- 'I'm anxious about my heart but there's nothing wrong, it's anxiety that's causing me to feel this way.'
- 'My heart rate and rhythm has definitely changed, I can feel the pounding. I have just been vacuuming so it's probably that, I know it's not a heart condition, because I don't have one.'
- 'My heart palpitations today were due to feeling super anxious when I had to talk in front of everyone at work. I was nervous, that's what my body does when I feel like that.'

I asked Emily to come up with an alternative for every single time she felt triggered into assuming she was having a heart attack. In the beginning this was a lot, but it lessened pretty swiftly. It didn't matter that Emily's anxiety wouldn't fully allow her to believe these alternatives; what was more important was to practise presenting alternative viewpoints to the mind.

Just like Emily did with me, I want you to be able to consider helpful, constructive, less frightening, more realistic and accurate alternative explanations for your anxiety experience. Commonly it's anxiety symptoms themselves that are misinterpreted as something else, which is understandable given how powerful they can feel. We're looking for less anxiety-provoking interpretations of your experience, ones that are more probable than the exaggerated view that comes from fear. In the table you can see two more examples of Emily's thoughts using this skill.

Anxiety has a way of making you think that disaster is imminent. Imagine a bucket half-filled with water as a representation of this feeling. When you focus solely on the negative thoughts and actions put to you by anxiety, and you give in to them, it's like dropping a heavy stone into the bucket, causing the water level to rise. Each time you give in to avoidance or dismiss factual evidence that contradicts your fears, it's like adding more stones to the bucket, causing the water level and your anxiety to rise even further. Eventually, the bucket overflows with anxiety, and you're completely overwhelmed. To reduce the suffering caused by anxiety, it's essential to change the way you react to these negative thoughts. Instead of taking them as a sign of factual reality, treat them as a symptom of anxiety. This is like removing a heavy stone from the bucket, causing the water level to decrease. Consider alternative neutral or positive possibilities instead of only negative outcomes, which is like removing more heavy stones from the bucket, causing the water level and your anxiety to decrease even more. When you observe these thoughts without immediately buying into them, allowing them to be present without judgement, it's like taking more heavy stones out of the bucket, further reducing the water level and your anxiety. By consistently practising these

What anxiety made me think	Alternative explanation 1	Alternative explanation 2	Where possible, note down which view was found to be correct
My heart is racing; I will have a heart attack.	Anxiety naturally increases heart rate; because I'm thinking anxiously, that's what's happened. I'm safe.	My heart is racing because I just ran up two flights of stairs.	It wasn't a heart attack; I didn't have one. It was because I ran up the stairs and then felt frightened of my racing heart.
Sophie's not here yet, she's probably had a car accident.	Sophie might be running late because of traffic.	Sophie got held up at work.	Sophie told me there was lots of traffic due to a broken-down vehicle.

skills, you can reduce the power of anxious thoughts as well as the actions that go with them.

So now it's over to you. You can either make a similar table, or you can practise this in your mind. To start with I'd suggest writing it out, or using digital notes, and once you've become proficient in this skill you can switch to practising it in your mind. Here are three questions to help you further with this skill:

1. Has my anxiety predicted this before and if so what was the outcome?

2. If I could be misinterpreting physical sensations, what other explanations might there be for the sensations I'm experiencing?

For example; it's an anxiety symptom, I've been sitting in a fixed position for too long, I haven't eaten/drunk enough.

3. Have I considered every possible alternative factor?

Anxiety skews thinking. It's important to come up with alternative explanations that account for the situation you are experiencing. There's a high likelihood that one of these alternatives is more factually correct.

Skill Two – Dealing with Problematic Thinking Patterns

Taking a closer look at your thoughts to examine problematic thinking patterns is another management strategy for anxious thoughts. Remember the thinking patterns from Chapter 1 (see page 39)? Take another look at them if you need a reminder. When you can identify that you've got stuck with a problematic thinking pattern it can take away some of the negative charge in your thought, allowing you to take a step back and gain more perspective. So how can you do this in practical terms? It's quite simple, just write out the thought, and next to it note down the type of problematic thinking pattern it is. For example: 'Even though the doctors have told me otherwise, this lump I can feel is cancer and it's terminal.' That's catastrophizing.

You can also make a simple table like the one following, where you record your thoughts in one column, and then note down the problematic thinking pattern next to it. In the third very important column you note down what you would think if you weren't using that particular thinking pattern.

Your anxiety thoughts are biased in favour of your fear, so this is your opportunity to train your mind into becoming less biased. Imagine yourself in a supermarket, manoeuvring a shopping trolley that constantly pulls to one side due to its half-filled state. What would you do in such a situation? You would adjust your grip and handling of the trolley to correct its bias. Similarly, in this skill, our aim is to do something similar with our thoughts. When you become aware of your thoughts being biased in a particular direction, make an effort to correct that bias by considering an alternative perspective. You can counterbalance the bias by taking note of how you would think in the absence of this pattern of thought, for example, how someone who doesn't catastrophize might think. I'm not asking you to immediately adopt this alternative view as your own belief. Initially, I'm simply encouraging you to contemplate this alternative viewpoint. With practice and time, this process will become more natural, and your thoughts will gradually lose more of their negative charge.

Thought	Thinking error	Thought without the error
This lump I can feel is cancer, and it's terminal.	Catastrophizing	I can't know it's cancer, and there's nothing to suggest it is.
I'm a failure unless I'm on time every day.	All-or-nothing thinking	Other people aren't always on time; they're not failures.
I know I'll be sick if I go out.	Fortune telling	I can't know this; the last five times I predicted this I was wrong.
I know they're judging, everybody does.	Mind reading	I can't know what people think.

I'm so weak, other people don't do this.	Labelling	Lots of people are anxious, but I don't see them as weak.
If that happened to them, it will happen to me.	Personalizing	That's not how problems work; knowing something doesn't make it more likely.
I feel warm, oh my, I'm going to faint.	Exaggerating	My mind thinks this every time. I've been wrong every single one of them.
I'm always making mistakes, now here I go again, I've messed up.	Mental filtering	I am filtering out all the things that show I don't always make mistakes, and focusing only on this mistake that makes me anxious.
It's a good job I overthink; if I didn't, I'd be less prepared.	Having positive beliefs about anxiety	Overthinking takes more time than it would to actually deal with a problem if/when it happened. It also sucks the joy out of my life.

Always take a close look at your thoughts to identify any problematic thinking patterns. Correct this by restructuring and rewording your thoughts to remove the bias present in favour of anxiety.

Skill Three – Dealing With Worst-case Scenario Thinking

How often do you have an anxious thought that transports you to the absolute worst possible outcome? This tendency to assume something catastrophic will happen in the future is worst-case scenario thinking. This particular type of thinking is remarkably prevalent in anxiety disorders. In my clinical experience, it is the most commonly observed pattern.

Worst-case scenario thinking possesses the extraordinary ability to transform a simple headache into a dreaded brain tumour, cancelled plans into personal rejection, or a routine flight into a catastrophic plane crash. It seems that your mind is inclined to persuade you that the absolute worst outcome is not only possible but highly probable.

Your mind's ability to imagine vividly is so powerful that simply by imagining things that haven't happened you can emotionally and physically feel as if they're happening right now. This ability to imagine the worst has an adaptive advantage for our survival, but we rarely need to use this function nowadays. It's when you experience this level of disturbance in your thoughts constantly that you can easily feel overwhelmed. We're all capable of imagining all sorts of scary, weird, wonderful and exciting things. Because an anxious brain is biased in favour of fear it readily grabs onto things that fit with that, usually doom and catastrophe. Worst-case thinking creates high-level psychological threats, leading to even more physiological stress in the body. Worst-case scenario thoughts will keep you very attached to whatever the high-level threat is about and your mind will be preoccupied with this catastrophe, so much so that it can lead to paralysing levels of fear.

When you envision these terrible situations, it's more than likely that you'll experience an emotional reaction proportionate to that imagined scenario. If you imagine something catastrophic, your emotions are going to be very intense. People often view these emotionally intense responses as a further sign that something bad will happen. Here you fall into predicting the future based on an imagined catastrophe and coupling that catastrophe with intense emotions. In reality your thoughts and your feelings have no predictive effect on the outcome of any such future event.

Many of my patients describe this as a sort of 'sign' from

the universe, 'I'm feeling this for a reason, it means it's true', as if it's some kind of message, when in fact this is simply another anxiety symptom. One that is experienced by millions of people.

Worst-case scenarios are a product and symptom of anxiety, they are not realistic facts, and your best way of dealing with them is to treat them as if they're a symptom of anxiety. Maybe you've come across this quote by Mark Twain: 'I've had a lot of worries in my life, most of which never happened.' The beliefs you hold about the future have a big impact on your mental health and well-being. If you keep telling yourself that your future is full of doom and catastrophe you won't feel good at all. It is much better to hold a more balanced view of the future – it doesn't even have to be overly optimistic, just more realistic: 'Life has its ups and downs, there are good times ahead, and there may be some challenges too.'

Anxiety is like a GPS that only gives you directions to the worst-case scenarios. If you keep listening to this GPS, blindly following it, you'll end up at a place you don't want to be. To get to somewhere different, you have to change the input into the GPS. You have to choose a different route. A GPS can only take you where you tell it to go, just like your thoughts can only take you where you allow them to take you. You have the power to influence this. It's important that you carefully and consciously choose which of your thoughts you're going to go with, so it leads you to a more helpful and productive path.

Worst-case scenario thinking gets in the way of you doing so many things because your mind will be highly adept at thinking of everything that could go wrong in the worst possible way. This gets in the way of your everyday life because it leads to avoidance: if you're constantly imagining the worst, then you won't want to do anything or go anywhere. The problem with dwelling on worst-case scenarios is that your mind defaults to these options, leaving very little room for alternative considerations. Is having just this stuff in your head likely to make you feel more or less anxious? Is thinking in just this way going to help you overcome anxiety, or is it going to push you towards more suffering? Have a think about what your experience has shown you so far.

Below are three different techniques you can use to help you with worst-case scenario thinking. Take your time to work through each one.

TASK 15
Expand the options you present to your mind

Help your mind see that the worst-case scenario isn't the only plausible outcome, and help your mind shift away from this as its default mode.

- *My worst-case scenario is:*
- *Other possible outcomes are:*

Either in your notebook, or your digital notes, write down what else could happen, or could not happen. Consider what else is even remotely possible. Try to note two or three alternative outcomes here.

Come back to this skill a week, two weeks or a month later to circle the outcome that became reality. Was that worst-case thought rational or not rational? Noting these outcomes can help boost your mind's ability to see things through a less catastrophic lens.

Patient Example: Nico's Scary Thoughts

Let's go through another clinical example of this skill. My patient Nico struggled a great deal with worst-case scenario thinking, and the content of these thoughts would jump from one thing to another. One of his worst-case scenario predictions came about while he waited for a routine blood test as part of his employment medical. During the waiting period Nico repeatedly told himself he was dying, and they were certain to find evidence of this in his blood sample. Nico experienced scary thoughts and images relating to this outcome. Looking at the technique described above, he noted down these other possible outcomes:

- There will be nothing wrong, and all my bloods will be normal.
- There may be something minor elevated, which requires no further action.
- There may be some minor deficiency that I can alter my diet for.

Question the validity of your worst-case scenario

Here are some helpful questions to help you look at the validity of worst-case thoughts. I suggest doing this as often as you can. The more you use this, the better it will work.

1. Did things end up happening in the worst way you predicted they would?
2. If not, what happened instead?
3. Would you say the worst-case scenario thought was a realistic prediction?
4. Have you had this thought before?

5. If so, for how long, and how many times has it become a reality?
6. Looking back, would you say the thought was more rooted in your feelings or in reality?
7. Given what you know, what's the best way to respond to this thought if/when it happens again?

Let's go through the above technique using Nico's experience of anxiety to illustrate:

1. Did things end up happening in the worst way you predicted they would?
   No, they did not.

2. If not, what happened instead?
   My bloods were actually all normal.

3. Would you say the worst-case scenario thought was a realistic prediction?
   Absolutely not, no.

4. Have you had this thought before?
   Yes, when I've had other medical tests, I've assumed the absolute worst every time.

5. If so, for how long, and how many times has it become a reality?
   For about eight years, and no, it's never come to reality.

6. Looking back, would you say the thought was more rooted in your feelings or in reality?
   I was more scared than the thought being factually right, and my fear just kept pushing me to think the worst. I felt so bad, so assumed it must be bad.

7. Given what you know, what's the best way to respond to this thought if/when it happens again?

   To not buy into it straight away, to be more critical, and think it through, as well as trying to have a bigger range in my thinking.

TASK 16
Worst-case scenario vs best-case scenario

I love this powerful technique, and so do my patients. An anxious mind exists in the company of worst-case scenarios from day to day and moment to moment. Often these worst-case scenarios never materialize, and when they don't they can be replaced by a different worst-case scenario, or by the thought 'well if it didn't happen this time, it definitely will next time.'

So in this exercise I'd like you to come up with the absolute best-case scenario, and consider what it would be like if that happened. When you do this, first write out your worst-case scenario. Then ask yourself if this turned out to be the best it could, what would that best case be?

In noting these details, really immerse yourself in the best-case scenario by imaging what it looks like visually. Where are you, what are you doing? Who else is there? Use your senses to help you build the picture: what sounds are there? Are there any scents? What can you touch and taste to immerse yourself in the texture of something?

Try to take your time over this, spending a few minutes. You can do this with your eyes closed too, as this often helps create a stronger visualization.

In doing this exercise, Nico was able to construct a wonderful best-case scenario in his mind, incorporating vivid imagery and sensory experiences. He envisioned himself comfortably working from home, with his favourite music softly playing in the background and his dog resting by his side. As he immersed himself in this mental scene, his phone rang and it was his doctor delivering the news that his blood test results were normal. A wave of happiness and relief washed over Nico. Taking a well-deserved break from his desk, he prepared a cup of coffee, savouring its aroma and relishing the taste in every sip. Notice how Nico engaged all his senses in this visualization. I'd like you to do the same, by diving into intricate details. You can revisit and use this visualization whenever you need it to help alleviate your worst-case scenario anxious thoughts.

Night-time worst-case scenarios

Through my clinical experience, I've observed that many individuals become more susceptible to worst-case scenarios at night-time, with a susceptibility to perceiving threats in a more frightening light. If you find yourself in this situation, it's understandable that this can induce a significant sense of fear just as you're attempting to, and wanting to unwind and relax. This night-time occurrence of worst-case thinking often steers your attention towards the negatives, and potential catastrophes. Consequently, it activates your nervous system, keeping you alert and impeding your ability to fall asleep. It's crucial to recognize that night-time thoughts are not as rational as those during the day, and fatigue diminishes your problem-solving capabilities too. One strategy to address this issue is to jot down the irrational and frightening thoughts that arise at night, and then re-evaluate them in the morning when your mind is more rested. If you can't switch off and get to sleep, then go back and read the section on sleep in Getting the Basics Right, page 12.

Deal with worst-case scenario thoughts using any of the techniques in this chapter. It might not make the thoughts stop immediately, but they will eventually fade and disappear when you work on helping yourself consistently. Once you've worked through the thought as best you can, and as I advised in Chapter 1 (see page 54), accept how it is, then move your attention onto other things. If the thought is still there, let it be: you now understand why it's not going to go in an instant; it makes sense that it could linger. Let it linger and get on with what you want to or need to do.

Worst-case scenario thinking is a very common symptom of anxiety. It keeps you focused on the absolute worst, feeding physiological stress and maintaining anxiety. You can use various skills to support your mind to move away from this kind of narrow-range thinking.

Skill Four – Dealing with 'What Ifs' and Question-Based Thoughts

In addition to worst-case scenario thoughts, the persistent presence of 'what ifs' and question-based thoughts is another prominent symptom of anxiety. If you didn't experience anxiety, you wouldn't find yourself consistently immersed in this type of thinking pattern. While it's natural to have occasional question-based thoughts when your mind anticipates future situations, they typically don't dominate your thinking to the same extent as anxiety does. At certain points in our lives 'what if' thinking can be useful, as it can help us with our decision making. Sometimes we need to be conscious of 'what if' possibilities and working our way through them can be a problem-solving exercise. For example, if you're out on a long journey you might think 'What if my phone loses power? I'll take a charger and a power bank', or 'What if the train is cancelled again? I'll plan another route'. It's when the 'what ifs' happen persistently that they become a major problem. I've met many patients whose only way of thinking was 'what if' or question-based anxiety thoughts.

An anxious brain will not only find the worst, it will present endless questions, overestimating the range and likelihood of bad things happening to you. If you are someone who feels almost 'allergic' (as many patients have put it) to uncertainty, then it's likely that your desire for control and predictability is high. This can make it more likely that you will engage in 'what ifs', because you want to cover all bases. This type of thinking does not offer a solution to your anxiety. If you believe otherwise, I encourage you to reflect on how long you have been engaging in this pattern of thinking and assess the outcomes it has yielded. Have you noticed any improvements or reductions in your anxiety as a result? If you haven't, then this thinking is not a solution for your anxiety; it is in fact a problem which may have been disguised as a solution at an earlier point.

The good news is you can deal with these question-based thoughts using the following skills. These will reduce the intensity of 'what ifs' and lessen their power over you. It is important to note that there are different types of question-based thoughts.

Okay, so now I'm going to show you what to do with these kinds of thoughts by taking you through some examples.

TASK 17
Dealing with 'what ifs' and question-based thoughts

Step one is to write down your thoughts, noting that anxious thoughts that follow this pattern will usually be in the form of a question:

- What if this headache is a tumour?
- What if he doesn't like me?
- What if everybody laughs at me?
- What if I get sick?
- What if I faint?
- What if I lose my job?
- What if I have a panic attack?
- What if they're thinking something bad about me?

We can't do anything with these 'what if' or question-based thoughts because they're not real. How can we come to any certainty about something that is uncertain because it doesn't exist? We can't. But what you can do is change how these thoughts are worded and then put them to the test.

Step two is to reword the thoughts. Look at these examples, reworded from step one, to give you the idea:

- I'm anxious that my headache is a brain tumour.
- I'm worried that he won't like me.
- I'm anxious that people will laugh at me.
- I'm worried that I'll get sick.
- I'm worried I'll faint.
- I'm anxious that I'll lose my job.

- I'm worried about having a panic attack.
- I'm anxious that they will think something bad about me.

Then, **step three** is to fact-check the thought and whether it happened:

Thought: I'm worried that he won't like me.
Did it happen? No, not as far as I could notice. I didn't see anything that would confirm this.
Thought: I'm worried that I'll get sick.
Did it happen? No, I didn't get sick.
Thought: I'm worried I'll faint.
Did it happen? No, I didn't faint.
Thought: I'm anxious that they will think something bad about me.
Did it happen? There was nothing to confirm this, so no, it didn't happen.

Questioning every possible outcome without being able to provide an answer, because you can't answer something that is in the future, will wear you down and strip you of your confidence. When you don't have an answer, an anxious mind will create its own imagined scenarios, picturing things that could happen. There's no doubt that an anxious mind conjures up the most troubling of scenarios. The 'what if' questions are created by anxiety, and the imagined outcomes are also created by anxiety. This feeds the build-up of more and more anxiety, causing your thought processes to feel like they're spinning out of control. Your thoughts have spun far away from objective reality, and anxious perception has taken over.

Here's another technique to help you deal with these types of thoughts.

Practise 'even if' and 'so what'

Another way to deal with 'what ifs' is to work through what you could do if they did end up happening. This skill can be used for non-tragic 'what ifs'. First note down the 'what if' or the question-based thought like this:

What if I can't get my words out when I'm talking to them?

Then answer yourself from a place of compassion and understanding, with an explanation of 'even if/so what' included. Here's an example:

I might feel anxious and I do worry about getting my words out. Even if that does happen, and it might be silent for a little while, they'll wait for me to speak.

Or

I might feel anxious and I do worry about getting my words out. So what if I can't speak? Nobody is going to do anything, and there won't be a disaster. I might feel awkward, but I've never gone permanently silent.

Here are some more examples to help you:

What if I faint? I'm often worried about fainting, no wonder I feel anxious about it again.
Even if I did faint, someone would get help and I'll be fine.

What if I have a panic attack?
Since that one panic attack I've felt worried about having one again; it hasn't happened. Even if it does, I'll get through it. I'm still here, it'll come to an end, and I can do things to help soothe myself and feel safer.

> **What if I'm told I need to have some medical tests?**
> Even if I am told that, that it doesn't mean I'm doomed;
> people have tests all the time, it's good to find out. My
> doctor and my family/friends are there to support me.

*Be aware of 'what ifs' and anxious thoughts that come
in the form of a question. When you notice these, ask
yourself 'Is this factual reality talking or is this anxiety
talking?' Practise problem solving these, so you stay
in the here and now, as opposed to an imagined
catastrophe.*

Skill Five – Anxiety About Jinxing Yourself or Tempting Fate

Are you scared to stop being anxious in case it jinxes you, or somehow tempts fate? This is something I've worked with a lot in my clinical practice, particularly in people who are anxious about health, illness and disease. For these patients their reason for worrying was superstitious, and by superstitious I mean beliefs that are irrational or false. They didn't want to tempt fate by letting go of their anxious thoughts or even consider anything positive. They also believed that remaining anxious and worried was a good way of dealing with potential threats. Of course this then led to a strong desire to hold onto their anxiety. Many people who suffer with anxiety rely on superstitious beliefs as a coping mechanism. It's another attempt to control for uncertainty, and it gives them the illusion that they have some sort of influence, when in fact they don't. But they feel too scared to accept that they don't, so just to be on the safe side they continue as they are.

Whether you are inclined to think in this way or not, it doesn't affect real outcomes, though it is symptomatic of anxiety to make you think it does. You might see this as a way to cope with life's uncontrollability, but thinking in this way doesn't give you any personal control over the likelihood of future events. Does having these jinxing and superstitious

---

Patient Example: Kerry's Anxiety Jinxing

My patient Kerry, who suffered with health anxiety and generalized anxiety, had a huge fear of jinxing herself. Look at some of her thoughts and ask yourself if you have had similar ones:

- 'If I don't remain anxious about my health and scared of getting a disease I will get it.'
- 'If I don't remain focused on my anxiety it will be bad luck.'
- 'If I dare to become less frightened it will be as though I've tempted fate, and I'll be punished for my arrogance.'
- 'I have to dismiss any positives that go against my anxiety; otherwise I'll jinx myself into a disease.'

Kerry and I looked at how we could turn this around to an almost opposite position, so she could work from a different perspective, and we came up with these questions:

- Will staying focused on thoughts of winning the lottery make it more likely I'll win?
- Will telling a loved one I'm proud of their achievements jinx their success?
- Will fixating on the weather make it beautiful and sunny?

Kerry's response was always a 'no' to these questions. My guess is you'll say no to all these too; is that right?

---

beliefs about your fear create a feeling of control for you? You thinking a certain way doesn't influence the outcome of a future event. Also, you being less scared of a future catastrophe doesn't make it more or less likely to occur; it has no bearing on the outcome.

When you suffer from anxiety, negative outcomes are much more accessible for your mind. They're much easier to come up with, because they fit with the things you're afraid of. Remember in Chapter 3 where you learned about the role cortisol plays in consolidating fear-based experiences (see page 85)? When you experience these projections about the future they can really embed themselves. Then, when you recall them, they bring a further spike in cortisol, which reinforces their presence and association, and so the cycle goes on.

It's very easy for these types of superstitious thoughts to set in. You may even have associations between your superstitious thoughts and coincidental past events. Let's say you know someone who was diagnosed with an illness on a particular date; you may remain vigilant of the numbers associated with that date and this might mean that you notice those numbers in other places, which in turn will reinforce the jinxing thought, because you'll assume that these coincidental events fit some kind of pattern that affirms your doom. At the same time, you'll have dismissed all the things that did happen that didn't fit with your belief.

Rationally, you know it is no more likely that you'll become ill with a disease if you think about it or stop thinking about it, but your mind can't help reminding you how terrible it will be if you tempted fate in this way. This keeps you trapped in another cycle of fear, which can be illustrated thus:

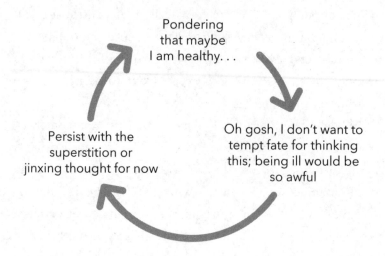

Pondering
that maybe
I am healthy. . .

Oh gosh, I don't want to
tempt fate for thinking
this; being ill would be
so awful

Persist with the
superstition or
jinxing thought for now

Anxiety places a significant cognitive burden on its sufferers, and research suggests this makes people even more likely to behave as though tempting fate leads to negative outcomes.[5] An anxious state limits your ability to think rationally, and you are more likely to quickly jump to these superstitious or jinxing beliefs. You're also more likely to jump to the conclusion of a jinxing thought when you think and react impulsively. The more logical and rational part of your brain works slower than this: it requires you to deliberately think things through and process thoughts by taking a more objective look. When you don't do this, you're more likely to keep jumping to the same distressing conclusions.

Actively and consciously addressing your jinxing beliefs is an important step in overcoming your anxiety. It will take you towards recovery, whereas holding on to them will take you towards more anxiety. Here's an exercise to help you become more conscious of these beliefs and practise using more of your rational mind. Over time, as you keep using this skill, you will notice how your brain will adapt to how it reacts to these messages.

TASK 18
Dealing with the fear of jinxing yourself (and others)

Remember that these types of beliefs only exist because they make you feel like you have power over an outcome.

- Can you find any evidence to support your jinxing thought, either from your own life or from someone else's?
- What evidence do you have that simply doesn't support this kind of thinking?
- Keep a note of the belief that regularly appears. Try to do this over a two-week period. Write them all down, then look at any patterns. What are they mostly about?
- For each jinxing thought you have, note down a rational perspective, even if you don't want to believe it just yet. Keep doing this, and aim for at least three thoughts a day, especially if you're prone to jinxing-type thoughts. Over time you can reduce the frequency as the power of these thoughts fades.
- You can't control the outcome of future events based on how you think or react to thoughts. Test this out by selecting one positive thing each week to give your time and mental effort to, like winning the lottery for example. Think about this event with the same attention and intensity that you give your anxious jinxing thoughts. Then wait and see if it becomes a reality. Were you able to think it into existence?

An anxious, stressed mind is vulnerable to developing superstitious and jinxing beliefs. These can set in very quickly and are reinforced by quick, impulsive reactions. Working on actively and consciously processing these can alleviate anxiety.

Skill Six – Problem Solving Your Thoughts

Redirecting your attention towards actively problem solving anxious thoughts and addressing anxious questions can significantly reduce anxiety and weaken unproductive thinking patterns. When people suffer from anxiety, whether their anxiety is specific to, say, health or social triggers, or more general, their ability to problem solve is impacted. When anxiety sufferers are faced with a problem (or a problem thought) they feel more anxious and are more likely to react with fear or panic. This increases anxiety, the problem is still there and it feels increasingly challenging to face it. At times there might be legitimate external problems that you have to deal with, and at other times your thoughts may present a problem to you. Regardless of which one it is, learning how to tackle these will help you reduce your anxiety, while at the same time giving you a solution for your problem. I use these six steps with my patients when helping them learn effective problem-solving skills:

- Step 1: Identify and define your problem; write it out.
- Step 2: List possible solutions, brainstorm ways to deal with the issue; try to come up with at least three.
- Step 3: Look at the pros and cons of each solution.
- Step 4: Consider your strengths and resources.
- Step 5: Put your best solution into action.
- Step 6: Evaluate the outcome: how did it work out?

Patient Example: Jess's Blood Test

Jess, who suffered from health anxiety, didn't have any medical issues, but constantly feared being diagnosed with a life-threatening disease. Jess had to confront a real-life problem when her doctor suggested she have a blood test following a consultation where she reported symptoms of fatigue and twitching. This is how Jess dealt with this problem before she learned more effective problem-solving skills:

1. Jess identified the problem as 'OMG I can't believe it. It's happening, I'm going to die, I have a condition, that's why he's sending me for tests.'
2. Jess saw absolutely no solutions to this problem.
3. There was no need for her to look at the pros and cons of each solution, because she said there weren't any solutions.
4. Jess felt like she had no strengths or resources to help her with this problem.
5. Jess couldn't put anything into action.
6. Jess continued to feel highly anxious and very distressed.

Jess was confronted with a real problem, which led to a never-ending spiral of problematic thoughts: she told herself there was no way out, all was doom. This panic in the face of her problems not only made her feel worse, it prevented her from moving away from this very distressed position. This is why making attempts to problem solve situations and anxious thoughts is so important. This is how Jess used effective problem-solving skills:

1. Defining the problem: I have to have a blood test, and I don't want to have it because I think the doctor will find something wrong with me, but I also want to have it to be on the safe side. I need to be able to do this. Can you see that there are two problems here, not one? Problem one is

having to have the blood test. Problem two is finding out the results. Each of these problems needs to have its own separate action plan, so for now we will look at problem one, the actual blood test.

2. Brainstorming possible solutions: Jess came up with these ideas as possible ways of dealing with her problem:

- Don't go to my blood test; ignore it.
- Never go back to see the doctor again.
- Drink lots of wine before going for my blood test.
- Ask my mum and my husband to come with me.
- Try to do something relaxing before the blood test appointment.
- Plan some interesting activities for after my blood test, so I'm not obsessing over it.
- Take into consideration how I've managed blood tests in the past.
- Go for the blood test but leave if I can't go ahead with it.
- Listen to something on my headphones to distract myself.
- Talk to my friends and family about how scared I feel, ask them what they do in a similar situation.

3. Looking at the pros and cons of each solution, Jess eliminated solutions that would not fit with the overall goal of overcoming her anxiety problems. Not only would these be unhelpful solutions, they would actually lead to an overall worsening and reinforcement of her existing anxiety:

- Don't go to my blood test; ignore it.
- Never go back to see the doctor.
- Drink lots of wine before going for my blood test.
- Go for the blood test, but leave if I can't go ahead with it.

4. Considering her strengths and resources: Jess had the support of her husband, her mother and a few close friends. Jess could talk to them, and also ask for their support on the day of the blood test. Jess also recognized that she had the ability and strength to overcome challenges, which she'd already done in her life so many times. Reflecting on these strengths helped Jess see that she could cope far better than her anxious mind would have her believe.

5. Putting the best solution into action: Jess decided to face her blood test by planning the day and taking time to soothe her anxiety before and after. Her solution looked like this:

- Eat my favourite breakfast, drink enough fluids and avoid caffeine.
- Do something relaxing before the blood test appointment, maybe go for a nature walk with my mum.
- My husband can come with me to my appointment, but wait in the car.
- Listen to my favourite uplifting music while I'm in the waiting room, and during the test.
- Meet a friend for tea after my blood test, and ask my friend's perspective.

6. Evaluating the outcome and how it worked out: Jess recognized that she was anxious and accepted that this would be the case. Jess accepted that she was doing something that she was really scared of, so it made sense that she was anxious. Planning out the appointment carefully helped Jess soothe her anxiety symptoms, and she was able to have her blood test. Jess saw this as a huge achievement given her initial fear and panic.

Just as Jess used the six steps, I'd like you to do the same. You can employ this skill to problem solve in real time when an issue arises, or you may already have an upcoming situation that is causing anxiety and can apply the steps to address that.

Look at this image. I imagine that you've been going downwards and not upwards when you've been confronted with a problem, is that right? Can you see how going downwards reinforces the same patterns of thinking and behaving that we are trying to move away from? We always want to try to get up the stairs, to be heading up, not down. Even if that means we're slower to begin with, or that we only get halfway, we're still going up. Problem solve your way up these stairs, and stay above ground!

Anxiety can impact upon your confidence and problem-solving ability. In overcoming anxiety, it's important to consciously work through solving problems that actually exist, and the thoughts that go with them. This will provide productive solutions and prevent you from reinforcing your anxiety.

Ten Key Takeaways for Addressing Anxious Thoughts

1. The way in which you deal with your anxious thoughts can either alleviate or intensify your anxiety. If you want to overcome your anxiety it's crucial that you change the way you interact with anxious thoughts.

2. To address your anxious thoughts, make use of the comprehensive set of strategies presented in this chapter. Begin by identifying your anxious thoughts, then proceed to evaluating them, before you work towards transforming your thinking patterns.

3. Remember that suppressing or trying to avoid anxious thoughts is counterproductive, but accepting and learning to manage them is vital to making progress.

4. Anxious thoughts often contain inaccuracies and are expressed in language that is biased towards fear. Work on this basis to rephrase these thoughts in a more accurate way that reflects your reality. This will give you a clearer perspective and reduce the impact of anxious thoughts.

5. Monitor your anxious thoughts, so you can identify where you need to adjust your thinking. Through monitoring you can gain valuable insights into the triggers and patterns of your anxious thoughts, which then allows you to make more informed decisions.

6. Remember that anxious thoughts reflect a negative perspective, and an anxious mind often dismisses many other viewpoints. Use the strategies described to broaden your perspective, so you can open your mind up to new possibilities.

7. Anxiety often leads to worst-case scenario thinking, where disaster and catastrophe are the primary focus. This pattern of thinking can become habitual for anxiety sufferers. Remember that the worst-case scenario is just one of many potential outcomes, and its occurrence or likelihood is often overestimated.

8. Keep in mind that experiencing 'what if' thoughts and engaging in question-based thinking are common symptoms of anxiety. These patterns of thought project you into the future, making it impossible to reason and rationalize with something that doesn't exist.

9. Anxiety leads to hasty and irrational thinking, which in turn makes it easier for false beliefs like superstitions and jinxing to take hold. Remember that these beliefs have no actual power over factual outcomes. Make efforts to consciously and deliberately process them, so you can cultivate a more realistic perspective.

10. Use active problem-solving strategies to deal with relevant anxious thoughts. This can weaken unhelpful patterns of thinking and lead you to constructive solutions.

 Let the beat drop!

Listening to music can stimulate the release of neurotransmitters like dopamine, which can reduce your anxiety and boost your mood. Music can activate neural pathways involved in mood regulation, memory and emotional processing, which all helps with anxiety reduction. Music also gives you a distraction from anxious thoughts by shifting your focus onto the music instead of what's going on in your mind and body. This is especially helpful if you tend to be overly self-focused when your anxiety is high. Certain types of music, like calming instrumental sounds or nature sounds, can also promote feelings of relaxation. So if you don't already have a favourite playlist, get creating!

Chapter 5:
How Can I Stop Over-focusing on My Anxiety?

The way you direct your attention towards your anxiety and its symptoms can exacerbate the problems you have. It's like wearing glasses that only show you the things that scare you. These glasses make you see the world in a way that supports your anxious beliefs, reinforcing everything you're terrified of. This can make you feel overly self-conscious and hyper-sensitive to things that might confirm your fears, like the physical sensations in your body. The tools in this section will help you take those glasses off. As you learn to widen the scope of your attention you'll be able to see through a different lens, even multiple lenses of different colours, and with more clarity. With practice, you'll train your brain to focus on these other perspectives and let go of anxiety.

Patient Example: Maddie's Breathing Battle

Maddie suffered a panic attack two years before she came to see me. Her visit to me was precipitated by her increasing anxiety about her breathing. This started after she ran to catch the bus after work: once she sat down on the bus she noticed her breathing was different, which was to be expected given

---

she'd just been running. Maddie paid more and more attention to how her breathing felt; she then remembered that it felt similar to when she had the panic attack. This made her feel more anxious, and the more anxious she got the more her attention became focused on her breathing, and anxious thoughts naturally followed: 'What if I'm about to have another panic attack on this bus!' Thereafter Maddie continued to focus a great deal on her breathing. She said some days it was 'non-stop' and she'd have to call into work sick. Maddie was anxious that she wasn't getting enough oxygen in her body, so she would compensate by opening her mouth to catch air and trying to take deep yawns. Hyper-aware of every breath, she was so sick of it, but Maddie just couldn't stop focusing her attention on her breathing. Her anxiety about her breathing caused her to over-attend to it, and this attention was reinforced each time she did this. Before long, her attention was narrowly focused on her breathing. This gave her brain the message: 'Maddie is anxious about her breathing, she is trying to monitor each breath she takes, this must be important, let's highlight this and keep it at the forefront of her mind.' Because it was more in her awareness, she gave it more attention, which reinforced its presence in her mind.

In our work together, Maddie and I got to a point where she was able to widen the scope of her attention. By doing so her brain received this message: 'Maddie is less focused on her breathing, she doesn't seem to be controlling it as much, it's not really a problem so we can relax the focus on it.'

Maddie's case gives an example of what we'll be doing in this chapter: learning how to reduce the anxiety bias in your attention. You will learn how to widen the scope of your attention so it is less focused on fear. It's natural for anxiety to make people self-conscious, overly aware, biased and hyper-vigilant to things that support their anxious beliefs, including physiological sensations. This is especially the case in people with social anxiety, health anxiety, and those who suffer with panic attacks.

Is this something you've noticed about yourself? You may focus on your breathing, how hot you feel, how red your face is, twinges in your body, twitching or shaking – there are endless possibilities. Your hyper-vigilance may cause you to be on the lookout for things that fit with your fears: tight spaces, overcrowding, or news of disease and illness. Anxiety then causes your mind to narrow its attention onto these threats. It's natural for the brain to develop a more narrowed focus when there is a perception of threat. This is adaptive and helpful for our survival. If you were out in the jungle and there was a threat of harm from wild animals, your mind would narrowly observe this threat. In situations like this, it's helpful of course that we have this inbuilt mechanism, but when it isn't working as it should, it can become a significant problem that maintains your anxiety. Remaining focused on things that don't help you is in itself an anxiety symptom. We have to learn to let go of this focus, and gently make changes that take us away from this place and towards more freedom. Learning how to redirect your attention and changing the way you focus can move you away from this.

Let's move on to look at the diverse ways in which attention and anxiety can interact to worsen anxiety problems: the role that self-focus plays, as well as hyper-vigilance, and the biased way in which your mind connects with threat. Then we'll look at the crucial part: what to do about these problems and how to adjust your attention so you're not overly tuned into anxiety and the bias it presents.

How Anxiety Affects Attention

As humans, our attention can be fragile, and this is particularly true when anxiety hijacks the mind. There is substantial research evidence supporting the notion that anxiety impairs people's performance due to the impact it has on a person's ability to expand the scope of their attention.[6] Anxiety impairs your attentional control in a number of ways. One is inhibitory control, one of your brain's executive functions. It involves you being able to control your attention to override a strong internal or external pull. The second one is set-shifting, or task shifting, also one of your brain's executive functions. It relates to your ability to shift attention between one thing and another. These two factors combine to create a range of problems for anxiety sufferers. Clinically, my patients often have low attentional control, making it harder for them to override the strong urges that come with anxiety. They struggle to shift their attention onto other things, so they remain preoccupied with their anxiety, which ends up worsening their problems. This preoccupation can take various forms, such as overfocusing on yourself, on sensations, or on specific thoughts, and being hyper-vigilant. People with poor attentional control tend to exhibit biased attention, leaning towards negative information that reinforces their anxious thoughts. They are more likely to quickly notice things that align with their fears and anxieties, while disregarding potential counter-evidence that goes against their anxiety. In the following section we will look at four specific areas of attentional bias in anxiety: biased attention, self-focused attention, selective and narrowed attention, and hypervigilance.

Biased attention

Biased attention is when you focus on certain factors while ignoring others. Have you noticed that when you really take note of something with a higher degree of attention you start to notice it more often? This then makes you believe that 'thing' has a higher occurrence than it actually does. If you've noted someone you know has a certain breed of dog, suddenly it seems like that same breed of dog is everywhere. In terms of anxiety-provoking triggers there can be an attentional bias towards threat-related stimuli. If you hear of someone developing a certain type of illness, let's say a celebrity being reported in the news, you start to notice this illness and things that relate to it more frequently. You may then become hyper-vigilant (see page 180) towards any sensations that could relate to that particular illness, as well as being hyper-vigilant to external factors that could fit with your fear. Have you ever done this?

Self-focused attention

Self-focused attention is the tendency to excessively focus on yourself, your internal experiences and your anxieties. This self-focused attention causes you to become overly aware of your own bodily sensations, thoughts and behaviours. As a result, you may have difficulty shifting your attention away from these things, and redirecting it towards the external environment. This self-focused attention can intensify anxiety symptoms, by contributing to a heightened sense of self-consciousness and distress. Self-focused attention diverts focus from other important factors that could contribute to your recovery from anxiety too. In the case of social anxiety, being overly self-focused on your own words, actions and how you

An anxiety trigger presents itself

You focus your attention on anxiety and its sensations

The sensations of anxiety get worse, or they feel amplified

You then notice them even more

This leads you to making misinterpretations about what's going on

You feel even more anxious now

think you're being perceived hinders your ability to accurately interpret social situations. This can lead to misreading cues and missing out on genuine engagement with others. When you're absorbed in your own thoughts, important information goes unnoticed, resulting in a limited understanding of what is truly happening around you, and this is true regardless of the type of anxiety problem you have. If you have health anxiety about a particular condition, let's say a heart problem, self-focus means you'll attend to internal sensations more, and notice any sensations or triggers that could be heart-related. This in turn will make you more anxious, which will naturally increase your heart rate, amplifying your experience of the sensations. As you become more anxious, your anxiety thoughts will feel scarier and scarier. Inevitably, when you follow this pathway, you get stuck in another self-perpetuating cycle of anxiety.

This brings us onto our first important task of this chapter. This task is all about helping you understand more about the ways in which you focus your attention.

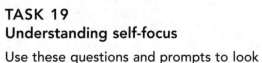

TASK 19
Understanding self-focus
Use these questions and prompts to look at your attentional patterns and self-focus when experiencing anxiety. By doing so, you can gain insights into any recurring patterns in your attentional bias. Note down your responses in your notebook or your digital notes.

- When I'm self-focused I pay attention, or get caught up with these physical sensations . . .
- How do I self-focus? Do I think and analyse, or do I use objects or monitoring devices such as a smartwatch to help me with this?
- When I'm self-focused I pay more attention to these kinds of thoughts . . .
- When I'm self-focused I experience images that show . . .
- These physical sensations, thoughts and images leave me feeling . . .
- Being self-focused has distracted me, and taken me away from meaningful things like . . .
- Being self-focused has made me feel more anxious/ scared: **Yes / No**
- What misinterpretations have I made due to being self-focused?
- Looking back at past situations, how has being self-focused stopped me from taking account of information that could have eased my anxiety?

- Think of a time when I was self-focused, and later learned that I didn't need to be. What information did I not take account of?
- What are the benefits to me of being self-focused? How does it help me? If it doesn't help me, what is my reason for doing it? Is that reason being met?

Selective and narrowed attention

Sometimes people selectively narrow their attention onto threatening triggers, usually in an attempt to ensure they are properly prioritized. This narrowing of attention leads to an increased level of engagement with threat and a reduced ability to engage with non-threatening stimuli. As an example, a person with social anxiety may selectively focus on facial expressions that seem negative towards them. This was exactly the case for Alice, who I worked with to help her overcome her social anxiety. Alice said, 'I just hone in on those things, I need to know what's going on, that's why I do it.' For Alice this didn't produce any helpful information; instead her narrowed focus made things seem more problematic than they actually were and she was misreading lots of information. Because this then made her feel worse she became increasingly hyper-vigilant (see below) and on the lookout for more things that fitted with her anxiety.

Have you noticed that there are things that you also get narrowly focused on, that make you more anxious?

Hyper-vigilance

Hyper-vigilance is a state in which people constantly monitor themselves and their environment for potential threats. This scanning process widens attention in order to enhance the detection of potential threats. However, a heightened focus on threat can also lead to distractions from non-threatening stimuli, causing you to become stuck, and fixated on perceived threats. Hyper-vigilance will often cause you to scan much more widely, but when you locate a threat, real or not, you will narrow in on it. Your hyper-vigilance will also cause you to misconstrue things, such as the words people say, a facial expression, a visual object and so on.

How Does Anxiety Affect Your Attention?

Do you relate to some of the difficulties I've described? When anxiety affects your ability to control your attention, it can lead to inefficient mental functioning, making it harder for you to cope and more likely that you'll get caught up in cycles of anxiety. Learning how to widen the scope of your attention can help you direct it towards what is relevant and away from what is not. Over-focusing on problematic sensations can hinder recovery goals by fuelling anxious thoughts: it's like providing them with a nourishing meal to grow even stronger!

Before we dive into the strategies for improving your attention to anxiety, it's essential to understand how this is currently playing out. You can gain insight by tracking your attention patterns over a couple of weeks and identifying anything notable. Keeping a journal or log can provide rich data, but taking general notes can also work if that's more your style.

TASK 20

Learn about how you focus your attention on anxiety

Look at the example table. I'd like you to make a similar one, noting the date and what you were doing, then how self-focused you were on that particular occasion, and how distressed and anxious you felt at that time.

Use this table over a couple of weeks, keeping a note of anxious things that take up your attention.

As well as the example table, here are some more prompts to help you:

- Keep a note of the things that you focus on a lot more than other things. These will always be anxiety-provoking stimuli.
- Keep a note of things that your mind seems biased towards, and the things it discounts, or pays less attention to.
- Next to each thing you record, note the length of time you spend giving it attention. Whether that's monitoring a physical feeling in your body, paying attention to people or following up on news stories.

Be sure to include the following as well:

- Anxious thoughts that you are over-aware of
- Anxious information you are over-aware of
- Anxious images you are over-aware of
- Anxious things about others that you are over-aware of

Date and main activity	Focus of negative attention	Intensity of negatively focused attention: Low, Medium or High	Level of anxiety and distress: Low, Medium or High
14th May At home doing nothing, trying to watch a movie.	I couldn't stop thinking about what I said in the team meeting at work, and how badly I must've come across. Then felt dizzy again.	High	High
16th May Out for the day shopping with my mum, and a meal afterwards.	Nothing today.	Low	Low
18th May Saw a news story about a footballer becoming unwell. Spent my breaks researching the condition to see if I might have it.	I was so focused on myself, checking if I was feeling faint or not, then felt dizzy too.	High	High
22nd May	I woke up feeling off, I thought it's going to be a bad day with the dizziness, then couldn't stop focusing on it.	High	High

As you can see from the example, dizziness is what is being paid attention to, and it is worsening anxiety.

When you do the exercise, it's important to note down anything you over-attend to, whether just one thing or, as often the case, multiple things. This information will show you what you need to target when we get onto the practical skills of improving attention.

How to Widen the Scope of Your Attention

What you've read so far will have helped you understand the important role attention plays in worsening your anxiety. As I've seen in my years of clinical practice, getting greater control over your attention is linked with a reduction in anxiety symptoms and has positive implications for your everyday life. It gives you more flexibility in your thinking and improves your concentration, which in turn reduces the propensity for becoming distracted or absorbed in anxiety sensations and thoughts.

You can train your brain to improve your attentional control, which in turn can lead to a reduction in anxiety. I've set out eight ways to widen and improve the scope of your attention. The aim of these tools is to:

- reduce hyper-vigilance
- reduce how self-focused you are
- increase how easily and diversely you can switch your attention onto other things apart from anxiety
- build your ability to stay focused on the task at hand.

I suggest you use these tools in two ways. First, think of them as a form of regular exercise that will lead to general attentional improvement with daily practice. If you wanted to learn how to do the splits for example, you'd practise a bit of stretching every day to improve your overall flexibility. Over time your muscles will get better and better at stretching because of the frequency with which you've practised. You can think of your attention in a similar way: you want it to get better, easier to shift, more diverse, and more flexible. The more you practise these skills, the better you will become at them, so when you need to utilize them further at times of anxiety it will be easier for you to do that.

The second approach, especially useful for dealing with acute attention-anxiety problems as they arise, involves redirecting your attention persistently and repeatedly to other things whenever you notice that anxiety is beginning to take over, causing you to become self-focused.

Eight skills to improve the scope of your attention

Having eight skills to practise may seem overwhelming at first, but don't worry, you don't have to do all of them. Experiment with the different exercises and find the ones that work best for you. Whichever ones you choose, it's important to practise them regularly. If the way you focus your attention is a big problem, then you'll need to practise more, perhaps several times a day to begin with. If your attention is affected only moderately then a couple of times a day may be enough. If you struggle a lot with attention bias, then don't vary the frequency until you've done a few weeks of practice; I find that this works best. It's also important to continue practising the skill that works best for you even after you've noticed improvements. This can be done in just a few minutes each day, and it will help keep your attention muscle strong, safeguarding you from any setbacks and reducing your future vulnerability.

We don't focus a hundred per cent on any one thing, so

don't try to aim for that – that's impossible for anyone. We accept attention naturally drifts, but we can notice that and bring it back. I'd like you to aim to consistently catch your attention when it drifts and bring it to the task at hand. Your job is to notice it's happening and redirect it. It really doesn't matter how many times you have to do this; in the beginning when you start to work on your attention it might be more, but it will lessen as you continue. Try not to be harsh on yourself if it feels difficult to begin with – it's normal for your mind to want to go back to anxiety because that's what it's used to. Every time your mind places its attention on anxiety, see it as another opportunity to practise improving your attention muscle.

The first two skills involve training yourself to notice when your attention is becoming fixated on anxiety-inducing stimuli, so that you can then redirect your focus towards other things in your environment or situation.

Skill 1: Switch from worst to best

This skill is about moving your attention from what feels like the worst thing right now, to what the best thing is right now. This is about the present moment.

What is the absolute worst thing your mind is focusing on in the present moment? For example – *a pounding heart.*

In this very moment where you are right now, whatever it is that you're doing, what is the best thing about being here? For example – *I'm sitting safe and comfortable in my home, having a warm tasty drink.*

Here you're shifting your attention from an anxious heated state to something that represents a calmer, cooler state. You're moving from a negative bias towards a positive bias.

Over time, when you consistently use this tool alongside other tools to shift your attention away from the negative to the positive it will help reduce your anxiety.

Skill 2: Redirecting Your Attention

Situational refocusing is a cognitive behavioural technique used to refocus attention away from anxiety. The goal of situational refocusing is to deliberately shift your attention onto something else in your current situation. This could be a task, an object, your surroundings, things that are available to you in your environment, or an activity. Use this method to redirect your attention away from anxiety and its symptoms. By doing so, you can intentionally interrupt the cycle of over-focusing.

Whenever you become aware that your attention is excessively focused on anxiety, you can consciously acknowledge this by saying:

'I am over-focusing on . . .'

and then say out loud:

'I'm going to refocus my attention on . . .'

Then shift your focus to the task or activity you've chosen.

Try to do this every time you notice that your focus is getting caught up in anxiety. Initially, you may need to repeat this process frequently, but with consistent practice, the frequency will decrease. Even if it feels challenging at first, don't be discouraged; the effort required will lessen over time, so keep going.

The following exercises are based on using your sensory system as deeply as you can to help train your attentional ability. Your sensory system presents so many possibilities for you, the things you can see, the sounds you can hear, what you can smell, the texture of things on your skin, and the taste of things in your mouth. You can use all your senses to your full advantage to help you refocus your attention away from anxiety-maintaining reactions. You can keep your eyes open for these exercises where applicable or close them if you don't need to use your vision. Do whatever works best for you.

Skill 3: Use sounds to improve the scope of attention

For this skill you will need to set a timer, and then focus on simply listening to sounds as closely as you can for one to two minutes to start with, increasing this over time to five minutes. Repeat this exercise several times a day.

Close your eyes and notice what sounds you can hear in the space you're in. Count and list the different sounds mentally. You may be able to hear the sound of people talking, the hum of a machine, the wind or rain, maybe there's a clock ticking or a tap dripping: you get the idea.

Skill 4: Use textures to improve the scope of attention

Exercise 1

Move around the space you're in and touch as many different textures as you can find. Say them out loud, describing each one, like this, for example:

- 'This is wood, it feels smooth, hard and cold'
- 'This is a blanket, it's soft and slightly scratchy'
- 'This is a nail file, it feels gritty, with some smooth patches'

Exercise 2

Fill up two bowls of water, one as warm as you can handle, and the other one as cold as you can handle. Place your hands in the cold-water bowl, close your eyes, and focus on the water's temperature, how it feels on your skin when you gently move your fingers. Use a timer, then after a minute, move your hands to the warm-water bowl, notice how different it feels. Again, after a minute move your hands back to the cold-water bowl. Notice how it feels when you switch between the two bowls. You can do this exercise for as long as is helpful to you; try to aim for five minutes so you can really get into it.

Skill 5: Use your body to improve the scope of attention

For this exercise you will focus on the sensations you feel on your bare skin. Again, use a timer and aim for three to five minutes. To begin with, take off some of your clothing, like your socks, or wear a short-sleeved T-shirt, a vest top or shorts, so some of your skin is exposed. Then lie down on a cold surface like your kitchen or bathroom floor, or even outside if that works for you. Take a small pillow or cushion to place under your head and neck if that would make you more comfortable. Then focus your attention on the sensations you feel on your bare skin from the surface they are in contact with. If you do this exercise outdoors, you can try it in different weather conditions too. Not only will you be able to notice the sensations on your skin, but also sounds, and the feeling of warmth from the sun, the wind, the cold, or even rain. Standing barefoot on a clean surface also works well.

However you go about practising this skill, the aim is to deeply connect with the sensory experiences on your skin and body.

Skill 6: Use your vision to improve the scope of attention

Utilize your vision in redirecting your attention in any of the following ways:

Colour

Pick a colour, for instance blue. Then look for different blue objects you can see in the space that you're in. How many are there? Move around the entire space you're in and say them out loud. Again, try to focus your attention on this exercise for at least a few minutes, switching to different colours if you need to.

Objects

In this exercise, you will identify and name objects based on specific categories. Begin by exploring your surroundings and moving throughout the entire space you are in. For instance, you can focus on naming all the objects made from wood and vocalize them aloud. You can utilize other categories as well, such as electronic objects, glass objects, plastic items, fabrics and more.

People

If you're in a space where there are other people present, redirect your attention towards them. Select a specific characteristic or pattern to observe. For example, you can count the number of people with long hair, short hair, black hair, blonde hair, or focus on the clothing they are wearing, such as sweaters, T-shirts, trousers, dresses, or specific colours. The key is to shift your focus away from yourself and onto something external, by searching for frequencies or patterns. It is not necessary to stare at people intently; rather, the goal is to shift your attention away from yourself.

Vehicles

If you're out and about, or can see vehicles nearby, focus your attention on them. Set a timer for two to three minutes and count how many red cars you can spot. You can switch to other colours too, or how many makes there are starting with a particular letter of the alphabet, or the number of vans, buses, lorries, and so on.

Street and Road

When you are outdoors, you can make an effort to refocus your attention by reading and acknowledging street or road names as you pass by. By doing so, you are directing your attention towards external stimuli that are unrelated to your anxiety.

Trees or Flowers

Expand your knowledge by learning to identify various types of trees or flowers during your outdoor walks. Instead of spending time browsing the internet for catastrophic news, challenge yourself to recognize and name as many tree or flower species as you can. You can also observe and learn about seasonal changes in plants. This practice not only helps improve your attentional skills but also provides a restorative experience, as being surrounded by nature can have therapeutic effects. Studies suggest that exposure to natural and green environments can boost positive emotions, increase feelings of well-being and reduce negative anxiety.[7]

Skill 7: Noticing breathing sensations

Expand your focus of attention by immersing yourself in the soothing sensory sensations of your breath. Find a comfortable spot to sit or lie down and turn your attention to your breathing. Feel the cool air gently flowing in through your nostrils, tickling the tiny hairs inside as it passes through. Follow the trail of your breath as it cascades down your throat and notice the subtle sensations along the way. As the air fills your lungs, observe the gentle expansion of your stomach and chest, noticing changes in the feeling of your clothing against your skin. Then, slowly release your breath through your mouth and feel the warmth of the air as it exits your body. Notice the sensations created by the trickle of air as it passes through your lips. Feel your body and mind becoming more calm and centred.

Skill 8: Use smells to improve the scope of attention

Throughout your day, purposefully take notice of any smells that come your way and strive to engage with them as deeply as you can. If you encounter an unpleasant odour, there is no need to linger. You can either mentally remember the scents you've experienced or, if you prefer, keep a written note of them. This practice helps broaden your attention by expanding your sensory awareness for scent.

As well as the skills I've detailed here, you might have ideas of your own. Lots of everyday tasks can be used to practise improving the scope of your attention too. If you find something else that works for you, then please add that to your toolkit. Regardless of what you use, the aim is to focus as fully and broadly as you can on the target.

To finish, here are additional suggestions for everyday activities that can help in redirecting attention:

- Using a brain training games or apps
- Practise recalling times tables that you may have forgotten

- Deliberately pay deeper attention to the texture, taste, temperature and aroma of your food and drinks
- Take note of the sensations produced by water on your body while swimming, being in the rain, doing dishes or cleaning
- Pay attention to the tactile sensations and textures experienced during activities like showering, hand washing, toothbrushing, cooking or doing laundry
- When travelling as a passenger, observe and appreciate the sensory aspects, visuals and sounds surrounding you

Remember, it doesn't matter if you experience thoughts that distract you away from your practice. That might happen, and if it does gently go back to your attentional task. Over time, as you work on developing more flexibility in your attention, the distractions will diminish and their pull will also be less intense. Keep attentional practice as part of your daily routine and it will ensure your attentional 'muscles' are getting stronger. This strength can reduce future vulnerability to anxiety, as well as being good for your mind. So if you want to keep your attention abilities strong and healthy, keep this brain fitness going.

Ten Key Takeaways for Over-focusing on Anxiety

1. Recognize that anxiety can hijack your focus. It can make you self-conscious, hyper-vigilant, and biased towards things that feed your fear.

2. Try to identify when your anxiety is causing you to become too focused on symptoms, and on your bodily sensations.

3. Remain aware of the attentional problems anxiety creates, and how these can make you more likely to lean towards negative information, which in turn can cause you to react impulsively.

4. Anxiety focuses your attention in such a way that it can make you ignore things that don't fit with your fears. Try to notice when this is happening; it usually peaks when anxiety peaks.

5. Develop an understanding of how you focus your attention when you're anxious. This understanding will help you move forward in changing this.

6. Flex your attention muscle with simple exercises that help you focus on things beyond anxiety. The more you train this muscle the better it will get, and the wider your scope of attention will become.

7. Incorporate attention-improving techniques into your daily routine to enhance your ability to focus on a broader range of material. Consistent practice will strengthen your attentional skills and facilitate greater flexibility in your thinking.

8. Use the diverse range of strategies provided in this chapter to engage your senses, practise situational refocusing, and use your cognitive skills to improve and widen your attention.

9. Think of attention exercises as a way to build and maintain mental strength. The more you practise, the better you'll get, which will give you much better attentional control when you need it most.

10. Practice of attention skills is crucial in overcoming anxiety problems, especially during times of heightened attentional bias. By dedicating time to this practice, you can not only improve your current anxiety symptoms but also reduce your susceptibility to future anxiety.

Unleash your voice!

Tap into the healing power of your own voice to calm your anxiety. You can sing or hum for a quick hack to help manage your anxiety. When you sing or hum, you breathe in a rhythmic and controlled way, regulating your breathing and reducing hyperventilation. Singing or humming can also stimulate the release of feel-good neurotransmitters like endorphins, promoting relaxation and reducing anxiety. As an added bonus when you sing or hum mindfully, by paying attention to the sounds and sensations of your voice you can be in the present moment much more, instead of being stuck in your head with anxious thoughts. As well as being a great distraction from anxious thoughts or feelings, singing or humming is a wonderful method of self-expression that can help you process and release your emotions.

Chapter 6:
How Can I Manage My
Intense Emotions?

How you manage your emotions can contribute to the maintenance of your anxiety problems. Anxiety creates lots of emotional distress, which can be challenging to tolerate. You may mistakenly interpret this emotional distress as a definitive sign of an actual problem, rather than recognizing it as the charged emotion associated with your experience of an anxious thought or sensation. This misinterpretation frequently leads to reactive responses that favour anxiety, trapping you in a cycle of more anxious thoughts and feelings. By establishing and cultivating effective strategies to regulate the distressing emotions that anxiety triggers, you can overcome this pattern of responding.

Strong heated emotions are like a huge wave in the ocean. At first, it seems like this wave is going to consume you: it towers over you, threatening to pull you under. But just like a wave, emotional distress comes and goes. If you try to fight against it, you'll just exhaust yourself, you'll feel like you're drowning, and it'll only make things worse. Instead, try to imagine yourself as a surfer. You're riding the waves, accepting them and allowing them to carry you forward. The wave will eventually subside as its energy dissipates, and you will find yourself back on solid ground.

In this chapter, our focus will be on exploring how emotions come into play as you navigate your anxiety problems. We will explore the tendency to misinterpret the emotional distress that accompanies anxiety, how this is often perceived as evidence of a genuine problem rather than being recognized as the heightened emotional response associated with anxiety. Our aim is to gain a deeper understanding of these processes and their potential to perpetuate your anxiety. Most importantly, you will learn a range of strategies aimed at changing these patterns, equipping you with additional tools to enhance your progress in overcoming your anxiety problems.

Emotional Regulation

Emotional regulation is something every single one of us does, every single day, with each of us having our own unique style of managing our emotions. It includes how we express and communicate emotions to ourselves and others, how we interpret our emotional state, how we respond to it and how we learn from it. This learning, in turn, shapes our future approach to emotional management. People who struggle with anxiety often face challenges in effectively regulating their distressing emotions, particularly when they are triggered by something frightening.

Patient Example: Khadija's Intense Emotions

In my work with Khadija, who suffered with generalized anxiety, health anxiety and death anxiety, we focused a great deal on emotional regulation. Khadija struggled to cope with the emotions that came with her anxious thoughts and images.

Khadija's problem would often start when she was triggered by hearing about death or coming across something bad. This would lead her to believe that the same thing could happen to her, and she would experience visual images in her mind of terrible situations. Her emotional distress at these imagined scenarios felt out of control, and she didn't know what to do with these strong feelings. Khadija would also take these intense emotions as a further sign that things were really bad, that doom was about to strike. She would say 'I shouldn't feel this way, it must mean something bad is about to happen.' This pattern of responding convinced her brain that intense emotions are a threat, adding a further layer of suffering to her anxiety. Khadija had not only her anxiety problems, but also the accompanying problem of these intense intolerable emotions. The more distressed she was, the more she sought an escape, which makes perfect sense. But it meant that she reacted by using unhealthy coping strategies, and though this led to some very short-term relief, in the longer term Khadija's ability to feel, experience and manage her emotions was no better. As part of Khadija's recovery, she had to learn how to manage these intense emotions, and how to tolerate increasing levels of distress in ways that felt safe and achievable.

Do you recognize anything from Khadija's experience with disturbing emotions in yourself? Ineffective emotional regulation creates heightened distress, compelling you to resort to unhealthy coping mechanisms as a way to swiftly escape the intensity of your troubling feelings. While you might gain some temporary relief, this kind of coping doesn't enhance your ability to manage troubling emotions or develop a greater tolerance for distress in the long run. This cycle of poor emotional regulation and decreased distress tolerance exacerbates anxiety issues. My clinical experience has shown me how mental health is inextricably linked to a person's ability to be adaptive and flexible in managing their emotions and increasing their ability to tolerate distress. The clinical research supporting this is enormous, not just for anxiety problems but for every single mental health issue.[8]

Nobody likes to feel anxious or distressed. Just like all other emotions, the distressing emotions brought on by anxiety are an inevitable part of being human. You can't escape distress, but you can learn to manage it better so it's less disturbing to you. Trying to escape distress is exactly what makes it more disturbing. If you view feelings as intolerable, you'll try hard to get rid of them, and these attempts will inadvertently worsen your problem. It's okay to feel what you feel, whenever you feel it, because feelings just *are*.

How Anxiety Hinders Emotional Regulation

Problems with emotional regulation are linked to increased symptom severity in anxiety disorders, as well as many other mental health problems. High-level anxiety creates difficulties in emotional regulation, including dysfunctional, inflexible and unhelpful reactions to your feelings. In this section we'll explore four key ways in which anxiety can hinder the regulation of emotions: emotional distress reinforcing anxious thoughts, emotional suppression, avoidance of emotion and impulsive reactions to emotional distress.

Emotional distress reinforces anxious thoughts

The intense emotions that accompany anxious thoughts and sensations can make you believe that what your anxious thought is telling you is true. These intense emotions are not an indication that your anxious thoughts are true. But because anxiety distorts your perception of reality, it becomes really hard to tell the difference between actual threats and perceived dangers, and this can be so much harder when you experience intense emotion. You may use the turmoil of your emotions to unintentionally strengthen and validate your anxious thoughts, which then makes them seem more legitimate. Have you had thoughts that you've assumed are factually correct based on the associated emotions you experience with them? Thoughts like this can trigger intense fear, which can be challenging to manage. In response, you may resort to unproductive coping mechanisms, further perpetuating the cycle of anxiety and keeping you trapped in its grip.

Suppression of emotions

Another common strategy that anxiety sufferers use to manage their emotions is suppression. Do you find yourself attempting to suppress the troubling feelings you experience? As if you have a strong aversion to experiencing them, having them be present or expressing them, whether through words or in any visible physical sense. Trying to suppress emotions does not reduce their negative charge; it actually tends to increase distress, particularly in the longer term. Long-term suppression of emotions can have unintended consequences, particularly when it comes to anxiety. Continuously suppressing your emotions over an extended period of time can lead to heightened physiological reactivity in your body, which manifests as an increase in anxiety symptoms. Interestingly, the irony lies in the fact that the initial physiological disturbance that prompted you to suppress your emotions is now perpetuated by the very act of suppression. It creates a cycle where suppressed emotions continue to impact your body, exacerbating the symptoms of anxiety.

Anxiety can make you more emotionally vulnerable, and fear triggered by bodily sensations prompts avoidance, which is an attempt to suppress, not accept emotional distress. This non-acceptance creates a lack of emotional clarity and increased distress, and as there has been no opportunity to manage the emotion, your confidence in dealing with emotional distress remains low. This in turn results in heightened anxiety, and you find yourself stuck looping through another anxiety cycle like the one shown here.

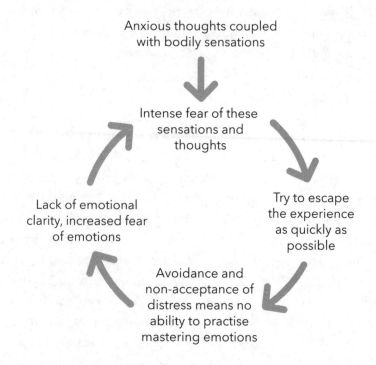

Anxious thoughts coupled with bodily sensations

Intense fear of these sensations and thoughts

Try to escape the experience as quickly as possible

Avoidance and non-acceptance of distress means no ability to practise mastering emotions

Lack of emotional clarity, increased fear of emotions

Avoidance of emotions

Avoidance is a common and counterproductive approach to dealing with emotions, and its significance in anxiety recovery cannot be overstated. In fact, a subsequent chapter will be entirely dedicated to exploring the concept of avoidance and its impact on anxiety. Avoidance can take many different forms. There's emotional avoidance and there's behavioural avoidance; emotional avoidance usually leads to behavioural avoidance. You don't want to feel distressed, so you do something to dampen that feeling, like removing yourself immediately from a situation, or performing an immediate action. It's not uncommon for people to use substances, alcohol and food to create distance or temporary detachment from distressing feelings too. Distraction can be a healthy and helpful activity to engage in after emotional processing, but sometimes it is used in an unhealthy way, as a means of avoiding feelings altogether. Later in this chapter, in How to Manage Your Emotional Distress, we'll look at how to process emotions more effectively, including the use of healthy distraction.

Reacting impulsively to emotions

The way you deal with challenging emotions arising from your anxiety can often involve impulsive reactions that then hinder your progress in overcoming anxiety. Defensive reactions and behaviours are triggered in response to perceived threat. Of course, when you're fearful and upset you may experience the desire to try and get rid of those horrible feelings as quickly as you can. These impulsive attempts to reduce unwanted emotions have a high cost that truly outweighs the short-term relief you might get from taking an action to ease the emotional intensity. For instance avoiding speaking up in a group or social situation might make you feel better in the short term, but with that comes the long-term cost of you having unintentionally consolidated your anxious beliefs. These counterproductive strategies are seen across various anxiety problems. In health anxiety, for example, the cost of short-term relief through repeated impulsive checking leads to an overall sense of unsafety, because you only feel safe if you check, so you need to keep on checking, and this becomes an additional source of distress that then perpetuates anxiety too.

Having read through the four ways in which anxiety can interfere with emotional regulation, are you able to see which ones apply to you? Awareness of these patterns can help you see where you might need to make changes, so keep these in mind or take a quick note of the ones that apply to you.

Understanding Your Emotional Experience

It's essential to understand your emotions because it helps you recognize how they affect your thoughts and actions. So, before we delve into strategies to enhance your capacity to cope with emotional distress, it's important to gain a deeper understanding of your emotions, and how they may be dictating your actions. This will lay the groundwork for the exercises that will follow. When you're aware of these patterns you can make smarter choices about what you do. It also guides you in selecting the right strategies to manage how you feel. To gain insight into your emotional distress, it is important to look at the connections between triggers, anxious thoughts, emotional distress, and the subsequent actions they drive. By identifying these connections, you can better comprehend the mechanisms underlying your distress and make informed choices about how to respond.

The diagram helps us with this understanding, as it illustrates how triggers can spark anxious thoughts, which lead to emotional distress. In an attempt to alleviate this distress, people often take actions that inadvertently reinforce the original anxious belief. Consequently, this cycle gains strength, becomes more ingrained, and is easily activated in subsequent instances, resulting in a downward spiral of worsening anxiety.

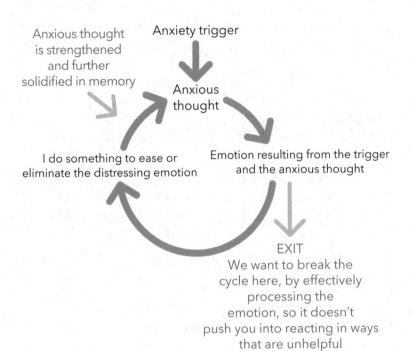

Anxious thought
is strengthened
and further
solidified in memory

Anxiety trigger

Anxious
thought

I do something to ease or
eliminate the distressing emotion

Emotion resulting from the trigger
and the anxious thought

EXIT
We want to break the
cycle here, by effectively
processing the
emotion, so it doesn't
push you into reacting in ways
that are unhelpful

As I said earlier, in many cases triggers ignite anxious thoughts that subsequently give rise to emotional distress. In an effort to alleviate this distress people often engage in actions that inadvertently reinforce their initial anxious beliefs. However, there are instances where the stage on the diagram representing emotions seems to be bypassed. This typically occurs due to the urgency to react and quickly eliminate the distress of being triggered. Acting hastily leaves little room for stepping back and reflecting on your feelings, and this inhibits the processing of your emotions which could allow an exit from this cycle. To demonstrate this, let's look at the case of my patient, Olivia. You may relate to Olivia's tendency to be so quickly triggered by anxiety that it leads to a lack of awareness regarding underlying emotions, so you resort to reactive responses as a way to control the situation you're in.

Patient Example: Olivia's Emotional Skipping

My patient, Olivia, had a tendency to skip the emotional stage altogether. She would move from trigger to reaction without even recognizing what she was feeling or understanding why. As a result, she felt powerless to address her distress and was left with no option but to respond defensively, which only exacerbated her anxiety. Olivia's case highlights how anxiety can rapidly generate emotions, creating a sense of urgency for an immediate response. This urgency sometimes occurs so swiftly and intensely that the accompanying feelings can go unnoticed or unacknowledged. Through our work together Olivia learned that her emotions largely centred around feeling insecure, apprehensive, uncertain and unsafe. It makes sense that she used to react in ways that made her feel secure, less apprehensive, and reduced uncertainty, so she could have a sense of safety – even though it was only temporary. Once we discovered that these were the feelings she was trying to escape from we were able to do something about them. To begin with Olivia developed an improved understanding of why she would feel insecure, apprehensive, uncertain and unsafe. It was understandable that Olivia's emotions would align with and correspond to the content of her anxious thoughts. She also recognized the role her difficult past experiences played in shaping her current emotional state. Acknowledging this connection allowed Olivia to distinguish between the influence of the past and the present moment. This awareness helped reduce the intensity of her emotional distress. Olivia also worked on monitoring the patterns her thoughts and feelings would follow, including situations that would trigger them. Importantly, Olivia had to keep track of the things she did to try to escape these feelings, because this is where she needed to make changes. Following this, Olivia used a mixture of strategies to build her confidence in dealing with her difficult feelings, including acceptance, labelling and observing emotions, practising self-compassion, cognitive distraction, and soothing her feelings. These skills, all set out later in this chapter, helped Olivia exit this cycle.

Now, let's move on to the next task, designed to help you gain a deeper understanding of your emotional reactions. This exercise will shed light on your triggers and the subsequent pathway your emotions direct you towards, and the potential purpose or function behind the emotions you experience. This enhanced emotional clarity serves as a solid foundation for the additional tools and techniques I'm providing for you later in this chapter.

TASK 21
Understanding your emotional reactions

Think of a recent situation during which you experienced heightened anxiety and emotional distress. Based on that situation, work through these questions.

1. What was the situation?
2. What did the situation make you think about yourself?
3. What emotions did you experience? Refer to the word cloud on page 213 for help with identifying these.

4. How intense were these emotions on a scale of 0–10, with 10 being the highest level of intensity?
5. Is there anything from your past that feels similar to the emotional distress you experienced in this recent situation? If so, what?
6. Did your emotions influence you to act in a particular way? If so, how did you react?
7. Why do you think that was your reaction? What positive or neutral emotion resulted from your reaction?
8. What was the conclusion of the situation?
9. Looking back, did your emotions influence you to react in ways that you didn't need to?
10. Do you believe that your reactions have fed into your anxiety problems, making them worse? If so, do you know how or why?

Take a look at the experience of my patient Ava, who struggled with panic attacks. Her experience is an illustrative example of the task I'm asking you to explore too.

Patient Example: Ava's Panic Attacks

To help you with this exercise, let's consider the experience of my patient Ava, who suffers from panic attacks:

1. **What was the situation that triggered your panic attack?** I encountered a situation that felt overwhelming or threatening.

2. **What thoughts did the situation make you think about yourself?** I thought, 'This is it, something bad is going to happen. I can't handle this.'

3. **What emotions did you experience during the situation?** I felt intense fear, a sense of unsafety, and overwhelming panic.

4. **How intense were these emotions on a scale of 0–10, with 10 being the highest level of intensity?** The intensity of these emotions was around 8/10.

5. **Is there anything from your past that feels similar to the emotional distress you experienced in this recent situation? If so, what?** Yes, it reminded me of past instances where I felt terrified and alone, facing overwhelming challenges. It brings back those feelings of fear and helplessness.

6. **Did your emotions influence you to act in a particular way? If so, how did you react?** Yes, I engaged in behaviours aimed at seeking safety and control. I might have avoided certain situations, engaged in repetitive behaviours or sought reassurance from others.

7. **Why did you choose to react like that, and what positive or neutral emotion resulted from your reaction?** I reacted this way because it provided a temporary sense of relief and security. It gave me a feeling of being in control and reduced the immediate anxiety I was experiencing.

8. **What was the conclusion of the situation?** In the end, nothing bad happened and the situation resolved without any negative consequences.

9. **Looking back, did your emotions influence you to react in ways that you didn't need to?** Yes, my emotions led me to engage in behaviours that were unnecessary or excessive for the situation.

10. **Do you believe that your reactions have fed into your anxiety problems, making them worse? If so, do you know how or why?** Yes, by giving in to avoidance and seeking constant reassurance, I've reinforced the anxiety response. This pattern of behaviour has perpetuated my anxiety and made it more challenging to break free from its grip. I understand that it's important to find healthier ways to cope and face my fears, but I'm unsure of how to do so at the moment.

Keep using the exercise above as as many times as you find helpful. You can use it for different emotions and triggers, continuing to explore until you gain a clearer understanding of the emotional patterns surrounding your anxiety. This understanding in itself can help alleviate some of the fear, and can also help slow down the very quick emotional reactions you experience. When your reactions are slower, you're more able to notice them and do something about them.

Incidentally, it's worth noting that there are other factors besides anxiety that can impact the level of emotional distress you experience. You're more likely to feel more distressed when you're physically tired or haven't slept well. Perhaps you haven't eaten enough – hunger can lead to changes in the hormones that help regulate mood, so you'll always feel worse when you are hungry. It's important that you keep track of your basic needs as well, especially when you're going through a distressing period (for a review of these basics see page 12).

How to Manage Your Emotional Distress

Now, let's step into the how-to section of this chapter, where we'll explore some practical strategies to deal with emotional distress. These skills are designed to help you manage your emotions more effectively. They may take some practice, but over time, they can become second nature if you stick with them. Once they become part of your everyday life, you'll find that they require less effort and conscious thinking, making things a whole lot easier. Whenever you find yourself facing challenging emotions, see it as an opportunity to put one of these skills into practice and strengthen your mastery of them.

The skills in this chapter have one main thing in common: they're about you learning to notice but not act on your feelings in unproductive ways. Essentially these skills are about you identifying your emotional distress, paying attention to your emotional distress, allowing it to exist, then creating distance between yourself and the distress, noting that you are not your feelings. Responding to yourself with compassion and soothing your difficult feelings is what follows. We cover all these steps in turn below so you have the tools you need for each one. You might notice familiar themes here that we've already covered in previous chapters, such as acceptance (see page 70) and attention (see page 175). Many of the skills you're learning serve multiple purposes in overcoming anxiety: they often intertwine and complement each other, building upon the foundations we've established in earlier chapters.

Skill One – Accepting and Observing Your Emotions

All feelings are transient, and we don't experience a particular emotion indefinitely. Emotions are ever-changing, even though they may seem permanent when we're experiencing them. Practise cultivating acceptance of your emotional distress by observing your experience, without trying to change, control or resist the emotions you have. This skill is about trying to receive the emotions as they arrive, with an open and welcoming attitude towards them, without judgement or resistance. By taking this open and accepting attitude towards your emotions, you can gain a deeper understanding of them, and experience how they change and fade.

TASK 22
Embracing your emotions through mindful observation

Whatever the emotion is, just observe it with curiosity and an accepting attitude, examining its presence, its form and its movement. Use these points as a guide to delve deeper into your emotions, and spend a sufficient amount of time reflecting on them, between 10 and 20 minutes.

Start by taking a few slow deep breaths.

Recognize your emotional distress and accept that you're feeling this way. Say out loud what's happening, and how you're feeling.

Try to immerse yourself in the emotion, allowing yourself to experience how it feels. Where in your body does it feel like the emotion is? In your head, maybe your chest or your stomach? Or are your emotions outside your body: above you, below you, behind you or in front of you? Are they to your left or to your right?

What colours would represent the emotions?

Does it feel like these emotions are solid and still, or do they seem to have movement? If they move, what is their speed, and in which direction do they move?

Notice how your emotions change in intensity. What is their intensity to begin with? As you observe and accept them, do they feel more or less intense?

Notice how some of your emotions might be inviting you to react in certain ways. Where are they trying to pull you?

Recognize your feelings as just feelings; they're not threats, nor are they literal truths. Separate yourself from your emotions by using phrases like:

'I'm having the feeling that . . .'

'I'm noticing that I'm having the feeling that . . .'

Notice how it feels when you say these words, and how there's a shift between you and the feeling, as you detach yourself from it, seeing it as something that happens to you, instead of it 'being you'.

Try to visualize your emotions as a cloud in the sky, even imagining writing the emotion onto the cloud. Then watch the wind move the cloud away from your vision, just as it does with all the clouds we see in the sky.

Take a few slow deep breaths, in through your nose, and out through your mouth and bring yourself back to the present moment.

Think of your ability to tolerate heated emotions as a bubble. The more you allow yourself to experience your emotions without trying to control or resist them, the more your emotional resilience bubble expands. This bubble can either grow or shrink depending on how you react to these heated emotions. When you encounter intense emotions such as anxiety or fear, it's common to want to pop the bubble and escape from the discomfort. However, this approach only makes you more emotionally fragile. Instead, try to observe and accept your emotions without judgement, and allow the bubble to grow in size. By intentionally expanding your emotional bubble, you're building up your ability to handle challenging emotions. With continued practice, your bubble becomes even more flexible and capable of withstanding difficult emotional experiences. Remember, your emotional tolerance level is not fixed, and with dedication, you can continue to grow your bubble and improve your emotional well-being.

Skill Two – Labelling Your Emotions

Labelling your emotions as they arise can provide valuable insight into your internal world. When you put a name to what you're feeling, it helps you understand yourself better and gives you clarity and insight into your emotional state. It's like shining a light on what you're experiencing. This awareness and understanding validates your emotions, which can make you feel less distressed. When you label your emotions, it also creates some distance between you and the emotions themselves. It's like watching them from the sidelines instead of being caught up in them. This distance allows you to deal with your emotions with more balance, rather than feeling overwhelmed by them. Importantly, labelling your emotions activates the prefrontal cortex of your brain, which is involved in emotional regulation and decision-making. This activation helps to regulate the intensity of your emotions and allows you to consider alternative perspectives or coping strategies, which can reduce your distress further.

It's important to not only recognize negative emotions

but also to acknowledge positive emotions. This allows you to appreciate the positive experiences in your life, even if they may seem insignificant due to anxiety. A positive outlook can boost your mood, balance your thinking, alleviate feelings of hopelessness and foster a sense of gratitude. Additionally, recognizing positive emotions can help balance out the negative emotions that may dominate your emotional experience. No matter how fleeting or minor positive emotions may seem to you, take a brief moment to acknowledge, label and reflect on them.

The Plutchik emotion wheel here is a really helpful tool to use to identify and understand your emotions. It gives a visual representation of different emotions and how they relate to each other. The wheel is based on the idea that there are eight primary emotions: joy, trust, fear, surprise, sadness, disgust,

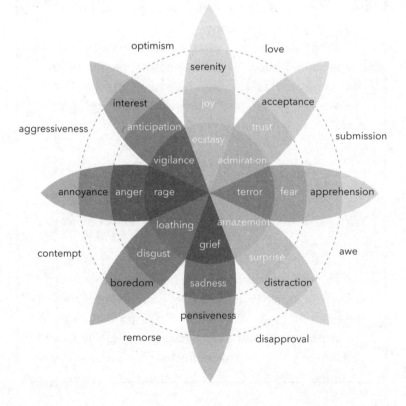

anger and anticipation. To use the wheel, start by identifying the emotion you're feeling and find it on the wheel. Take a look at the emotions adjacent or opposite to it and consider how these feelings relate to each other. Then consider the intensity of the emotion, and how it may be impacting how you're thinking, and the behaviours that you might respond with. The outer rings of the wheel show the intensity of each emotion, with the centre being the most intense and the outer area being the least intense.

TASK 23
Labelling your emotions positive and negative

Use the wheel above to help you recognize your emotions.

Verbalizing your emotions by saying 'I feel . . . [name the emotion], *which is a normal feeling given the circumstances*' can be a helpful way to label your emotions, or ask yourself '*How do I feel?*', referring back to the emotions in the wheel above if you need to.

You can also write about what you felt at a particular moment, and if there's any trigger to go with that emotion, note that down as well. For example: '*Today I felt so disheartened and frustrated when I couldn't get my words out at work.*'

As you practise labelling your feelings it will help you to note positive and even neutral emotional states too; again refer to the emotional wheel for the different types of feelings. Covering the whole range will give you the opportunity to really hone this skill.

The purpose of this exercise is straightforward: to recognize and label your emotions as they arise. It's a simple act of naming them and perhaps understanding the context behind them. Remember, this exercise is not about judging yourself as weak or inadequate for experiencing emotions that are hard to handle. Instead, it's an opportunity to show yourself compassion and understanding. In the next section you'll learn more about the concept of self-compassion.

Skill Three – Self-compassion

Self-compassion is about treating yourself with kindness, understanding and acceptance, particularly when things get tough or when you're not at your best. Think of self-compassion as giving yourself the same love and care you would offer to a close friend or family member who is struggling. Self-compassion is important because it helps you develop a positive and supportive connection with yourself. Instead of being overly hard on yourself or judgemental, self-compassion encourages self-acceptance and self-nurturing. It reminds you that it's normal to face difficulties and have flaws, because we're all human. It also helps cultivate emotional resilience, promotes a healthier perspective on success and failure, and it plays a vital role in managing anxiety and improving overall well-being. If you want to overcome anxiety, you'll need to develop a motivation to be compassionate towards yourself. Recognize that your experience is worthwhile and you are worth this compassion.

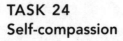

TASK 24
Self-compassion

The aim of this skill is to encourage you to be gentle with yourself and avoid being self-critical about your emotions. Remember, feelings just are, you can't help what you feel. By showing yourself compassion, you can improve your ability to confront and manage your difficult feelings. To develop more self-compassion towards your emotional distress, try asking yourself the following questions:

- How can I be more open to what I'm going through and the emotions I have?
- How can I be more sensitive to the feelings I experience?
- What can I say or do that would show more sensitivity?
- What do I tend to say or think about myself that could be considered insensitive?
- What do I need when I'm feeling this way?

Be compassionate in your tone of voice. A compassionate voice sounds different to an everyday voice; think about the words you use when your mind chats away and change them as you need to, for example:

Change this: *'I'm so sensitive for feeling so panicked and unsafe all the time.'*

To this: *'It's no wonder I'm having this emotion. I'm vulnerable to feeling unsafe because of everything that's happened to me.'*

Imagine if a friend or loved one came to you and said, 'I feel so pathetic and helpless, constantly overwhelmed by fear.' Would you respond with criticism and judgment, saying, 'Yes, you should just pull yourself together!'? Of course not. Yet that might be how you've been talking to yourself. Instead, practise speaking to yourself with empathy and understanding. Recognize that you're in pain and that your suffering deserves kindness and warmth, not self-criticism. Connect with the innocent and vulnerable child within you if that helps, and visualize that child or find an old photograph of yourself to evoke that connection. Visualizing ourselves as children can be a powerful way to cultivate self-compassion, especially when it may be challenging to show it otherwise. Take a moment to evoke an image of yourself as a child and use this image as a means to speak to yourself with gentleness, compassion and understanding. Imagine offering comforting words and extending the same warmth and care you would provide to a child in distress. Embracing this practice can help foster a deeper sense of self-compassion and bring about greater emotional well-being.

Here are some examples:

'I'm so sorry you're going through this; I know this is really hard.'
'You can count on me, I'm here for you, I will look after you.'
'I understand what you're going through.'
'I love you, I'm going to support you and help you.'

'I know how difficult this is, and I also know you'll get
  through this.'
'You're not alone, I'm here with you.'
'It's okay that you feel this way, it makes perfect
  sense.'

Skill Four – Self-soothing

Self-soothing strategies are practical ways to provide comfort, support and relief to yourself when you're going through emotional distress. These strategies aim to help you navigate difficult emotions and restore a sense of balance. By engaging in self-soothing activities, you create a safe and nurturing space that brings calm and comfort to you, even during difficult times. Self-soothing is a particularly helpful strategy after you've experienced acute emotional distress (there is tons of evidence for this) and also helps to reset your body after you've suffered physiological stress.[9] Self-soothing is different from general self-care, which usually involves regular activities to improve your overall well-being, although certain self-care practices can also provide soothing effects when you're experiencing emotional stress. Self-soothing, on the other hand, refers to specific actions that are used with the intention of calming and comforting yourself during moments of emotional distress. It's a more focused approach aimed at finding relief and restoring inner peace in challenging emotional situations. You'll find some self-soothing strategies in the box below, and you can also refer back to the tools in Chapter 3 (see pages 91–100), as well as the 'Fun Activities' list on page 378 for lots more inspiration and ideas on self-soothing, plus you may also have some ideas of your own already too.

TASK 25
Self-soothing

Try out different self-soothing strategies to see what works best for you. These are some of my favourites:

Try simple breathing exercises, like counting your breath as you breathe in through your nose for a slow count of three, hold your breath for a slow count of four, and breathe out through your mouth for a slow count of five. Keep going for at least five to ten minutes, or as long as you need.

Self-soothing physical touch can have a protective effect on distress. Self-hugging and self-touch are simple but powerful ways to soothe yourself. Find what type of touch feels most comfortable for you and use it for at least a few minutes each time. When you practise self-soothing touch, start by taking a few slow deep breaths. Then turn your focus towards the warmth and the physical feeling of contact between your hand and the body part you're touching. Here are some ideas of self-soothing physical touch:

- Placing your hand on your heart.
- Placing your hand on your stomach.
- Placing your right hand on the left side of your chest, and your left hand on your stomach.
- Stroking your upper arms.
- Stroking your cheeks.
- Hugging yourself as you stroke your shoulders.

Soothe yourself using smells: place a drop or two of essential oil on a soft, warm face cloth, lie down comfortably on your back and place the cloth loosely on your face. Focus on the smells as you breathe slowly and deeply.

Set aside time to listen to your favourite music, or music that helps you feel calm, content and relaxed. You can hum or sing along to the music. Spend some time creating a special playlist that you can go to at times of distress.

Pay attention to experiences that bring or have brought positive emotions for you. They can be simple things like noticing that you feel good, you look good, something made you laugh or you saw something interesting or inspirational. We want to capitalize on the experience of positive emotions as much as we can. Spend time thinking about them in as much detail as you can, including what triggered them.

People react warmly to positive emotions, so share your experience with others, telling them how you felt, and why. You can do this verbally or by a message to a friend saying, 'Hi, how are you, I'm feeling so good today', or 'I watched this movie last night – I laughed so much, have you seen it?' This skill can help broaden your mind's ability to focus on the good stuff too, hindering anxiety dominance in your mind.

Other self-care activities to soothe and help you with the emotion you're experiencing include taking a relaxing bath, cooking a special meal for yourself, watching your favourite movie, and wrapping yourself in a blanket and reading a book you love.

Skill Five – Productive Distraction

Productive distraction is the intentional redirection of your attention away from what is distressing you and onto something meaningful. This prevents you over-attending to distress in ways that can make things worse. Unproductive distraction involves avoidant behaviours aimed at escaping thoughts and feelings, which perpetuates anxiety problems. In contrast, productive distraction is not about suppressing these experiences, but rather acknowledging them before redirecting your attention. Productive distraction starts with accepting your emotional distress, understanding it, processing it, then shifting your focus to the present, onto something meaningful, or onto a soothing activity. Productive distraction can also include cognitive distractions: these require greater mental effort, and can be particularly useful when it feels more challenging to shift your attention.

Productive distraction is not a single or complete solution for managing emotional distress, but can be viewed as a complementary strategy to be used alongside other strategies. Its aim is to help you improve your ability to regulate your emotions while you continue to develop and refine your skills with longer-term strategies that will lead to more lasting change.

General distractions can be anything that is meaningful to you, a task that you've been meaning to get done, or an activity you enjoy. This could be DIY, baking, painting, drawing, knitting and so on. Physical exercise is also a great way to distract yourself in a productive way. Going for a walk, run, or practising yoga can help you stay present in the moment. Listening to music, reading a book or watching a movie are also good distractions. It's important to find what works best for you, what brings you joy and a sense of calm.

Cognitive distractions are activities that demand a higher level of mental engagement or have a high cognitive load. These are tasks that require deeper thinking and occupy your mind fully. Reading a book or watching TV may not be enough because they don't always require enough mental effort to distract effectively. In this section you'll find some specific ideas for cognitive distractions.

TASK 26
Cognitive distractions
Try these ideas for cognitive distraction:

- Count backwards in fives from twenty-five, then fifty, then a hundred. You can make this task more challenging, for example counting down from a hundred in multiples of six, seven, eight or another number.
- Pick a random number higher than a hundred, then keep subtracting it by another number, like six, seven or eight, until you reach zero. If you get to zero too quickly then pick another number in the next hundred and repeat the procedure.
- Do a complex puzzle or crossword, or use a brain training or brain game app.
- Phone a friend or relative that you've been meaning to get in touch with and talk about specific topics with them. Even better is to walk and talk at the same time, to double the cognitive load.
- Sort photographs of a recent holiday into a digital or physical album.
- Plan some home or garden improvements you've been meaning to get round to in as much detail

as you can. Do drawings, make lists, choose colours and themes, etc.

- Review your calendar for the next month, or three months, planning your schedule and activities.
- Go out for a walk or run, while listening to music or a podcast that really captures your interest.
- Use the alphabet to think of an animal that starts with each letter. Do some research to help you find one for every letter. Or choose another category.
- Plan an upcoming trip itinerary in as much detail as you can.

Once you have tried out some of the distraction techniques, it's important to reflect on their effectiveness. If a technique isn't bringing you relief, it's okay to adjust it or try a different strategy. You'll know when a particular distraction is working, as you'll feel a reduction in distress and be less overwhelmed. Experimenting with different distraction techniques can help you identify the ones that work best for you.

Ten Key Takeaways for Managing Intense Emotions

1. Remember that it's completely normal to experience a range of intense emotions alongside anxiety. These emotions can cause a lot of distress and can feel difficult to tolerate.

2. It's important to remember that the intense emotions accompanying anxious thoughts or sensations can sometimes make you believe something is seriously wrong,

even when it isn't. Be mindful of the tendency your mind has to interpret the emotions arising from anxiety as factual proof of a threat.

3. Feelings just *are*. You can't argue with them. Instead, focus on using the strategies outlined in this chapter to learn effective ways of coping with them.

4. Relying solely on emotional distress to make assumptions about anxiety can lead to engaging in behaviours that reinforce your anxiety. It's important to be mindful of this and avoid getting caught up in anxiety-reinforcing behaviours.

5. Avoid suppressing or avoiding your emotional distress as this can be counterproductive. While it may provide short-term relief, in the long run it can exacerbate anxiety problems, as well as undermining your ability to manage difficult emotions effectively.

6. It's essential that you understand the relationship between your emotional distress and your anxiety. By gaining this understanding you'll be better equipped to manage and regulate yourself.

7. Emotions that accompany anxious thoughts or sensations can often be misleading and they don't necessarily reflect the objective truth. Learning to establish a stronger connection with your inner experiences, and separating your emotions from your thoughts and sensations, will enable you to deal with them more effectively.

8. Acknowledge and accept your emotional distress. This can help reduce its negative impact on you, and free up your psychological resources to focus on productive ways to move forward.

9. Label your emotions as they arise, both the positive and negative ones. Develop self-compassion, learn to

self-soothe, and use productive distraction to build skills for managing your emotional distress more effectively.

10. Make a commitment to consistently practising emotional regulation skills, so they are integrated into your daily life. This will help you build resilience so you can cope better with anxiety over time.

 Rinse and repeat!

Repetitive activities like knitting, colouring, solving puzzles, cleaning, organizing, or playing an instrument can be helpful ways to calm your mind and reduce anxiety. Repetitive tasks can really absorb your attention and focus, distracting you away from anxious thoughts and feelings. Engaging in repetitive tasks allows you to shift your focus onto things within your control, rather than worrying about future uncertainties. Repetitive tasks can also be soothing and relaxing, making you feel more at ease. As you engage in tasks like these, you can also become more mindful and attuned to your senses, paying attention to the sensations and movements involved in the activity you're doing. Do you have any other ideas for calming repetitive tasks that might interest you?

Chapter 7:
How Can I Learn to Navigate Uncertainty?

Can we be absolutely certain about everything in life? Is that even possible? Living life means learning to live with uncertainty without it consuming you, and without it destabilizing your day-to-day life. Uncertainty is inevitable regardless of what we do, and the best choice we have is to develop our ability to tolerate it, so we can minimize the anxiety and distress it causes us. Recent global events, such as the Coronavirus pandemic, conflicts, and climate catastrophes, have vividly demonstrated the pervasive nature of uncertainty in life. At times uncertainty may even seem like a constant characteristic of life. If you struggle in your ability to tolerate uncertainty, witnessing it on a mass scale may make you more anxious. Like many of my patients, you may have attempted to eradicate uncertainty from your life in response to anxiety's demands, but deep down, you know this approach is futile and only provides temporary relief. The truth is, you cannot eliminate uncertainty entirely, and every attempt to do so only fuels more anxiety, hindering your path to recovery. While certain aspects of life are beyond our control, one crucial aspect you can control is how you choose to react and cope with uncertainty, and that's where your greatest advantage lies.

Recognizing and addressing uncertainty is absolutely vital

in overcoming anxiety. Throughout my clinical experience, I've noticed that every single patient struggling with anxiety has also grappled with uncertainty. For some patients I've been the first person they've consulted for help. Others came to me having seen other practitioners, therapists or counsellors. My own standard treatment protocol in the clinic always includes addressing problems with uncertainty. So, initially it came as a surprise to me that uncertainty intolerance was never a target in treatment for any of my patients who'd sought previous help. My clinical work spanning two decades and numerous research studies strongly support the notion that uncertainty fuels anxiety. As early as 1998, I came across a significant paper highlighting the pivotal role of intolerance of uncertainty in anxiety disorders.[10] Subsequent research, including a study in 2001 with 347 subjects, further reinforced the strong connection between intolerance of uncertainty and anxiety.[11] Over the past two decades, research has consistently shown the disruptive impact of uncertainty intolerance in clinical anxiety disorders. Uncertainty fuels anxiety and vice versa.

When it comes to managing anxiety, the constant pursuit of solving every uncertainty can feel like stumbling through an endless series of dark rooms. Each time, you're feeling your way around, trying to make sense of things by finding the light switch. But no matter how many times you turn on the light, there's always another dark room to navigate, with another door leading to even more uncertainty. Your desire to illuminate every dark corner is understandable, but ultimately it won't help you beat anxiety. It's natural to want to solve every uncertainty, but the truth is that it's impossible.

The key to finding peace is learning to accept uncertainty and building the skills to handle it with increased confidence.

In this chapter, we'll take a close look at the role of uncertainty in shaping your anxiety and explore effective strategies to manage it. I'll show you how to increase your ability to tolerate uncertainty. When you're able to do this effectively your anxiety will diminish. It's true that things don't always go exactly how we plan them to go, or want them to be. But if you allow space for uncertainty in your life, your ability to deal with these situations will get better and better. Through learning to master and tolerate uncertainty you'll have the resources to cope, even if or when bad things happen.

Understanding Uncertainty

Uncertainty is the psychological state of not knowing something. Uncertainty means that you can't predict the outcome. Neither you nor I can see into the future, so we will always be uncertain about some things. Every human being has a different tolerance of uncertainty. Some people don't seem at all bothered by it and cope pretty well. They actually enjoy the thrill and excitement it brings! They're the spontaneous types, up for new experiences, and they might even get a kick out of roller coasters, bungee jumps or horror movies. While these activities are generally harmless, sometimes people can cross the line of healthy uncertainty. This can lead to engaging in risky behaviours, excessively pushing boundaries or finding themselves in dangerous situations that pose potential risks. It's important to strike a balance between embracing novelty and adventure while still ensuring personal wellbeing. Personally, as I've gotten older, I must admit, I'm not exactly a fan of roller coasters, and I'm definitely not here to push you in that direction either! For other people, their tolerance of uncertainty depends on the situation. Finally, there are many people who find it challenging to tolerate even the slightest bit of uncertainty. Their aversion to uncertainty is so strong that it triggers unhelpful reactions. This becomes a real problem, as it generates high levels of anxiety and leads to engaging in behaviours that actually fuel anxiety further. It's a vicious cycle because these behaviours only reinforce the aversion to uncertainty. You stay stuck in trying to fight it, to eliminate it by controlling it, because you believe that you can't cope with it. As your anxiety worsens, so does your sense of uncertainty, and as that increases so does your intolerance of it.

You might believe that not worrying is bad, that it's better to be preoccupied with uncertainty, as otherwise it will lead to a bad outcome. Imagine anxiety as a school bully who's constantly telling you what to do and how to feel, and if you don't do what they say there'll be severe consequences. This bully is always telling you to worry about something, even if it's not reasonable or logical to do so. You may feel so intimidated and scared of the bully that you do everything it says, even if it's not helpful or healthy for you. The problem is that when you do have brief moments of not listening to this bully, you start to worry about not worrying. The bully has convinced you that if you don't worry, something terrible will happen. This fear of not worrying can create a vicious cycle of anxiety that's hard to break away from. But you don't have to be a victim to this bully. You can stand up to it and challenge its lies. Just like a bully loses its power when you confront it, anxiety loses its grip when you challenge its irrational thoughts. By practising and using effective tools, you can overcome the fear of not worrying and break free from anxiety's grip.

Let's take a closer look at the loop created by anxiety and uncertainty, and how each loop sets the stage for the next one, creating an ongoing cycle. Remember, problematic anxiety typically begins with a trigger, whether internal, external or so subtle that you may not even be aware of it. This trigger then gives rise to an anxious thought and/or sensation, which in turn generates a sense of uncertainty within you. To dispel this feeling, you are compelled to take some sort of action. However, each time you strive for certainty in uncertain situations, your aversion to uncertainty grows stronger. Can you see how focusing on controlling or eliminating uncertainty becomes a significant factor in perpetuating your anxiety? Take a moment to reflect on this diagram and observe how the cycle keeps your anxiety problems alive.

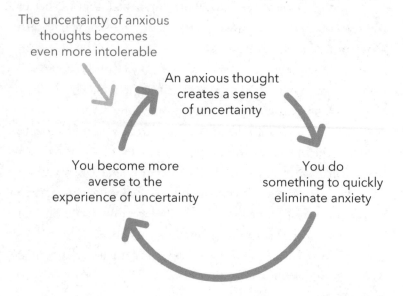

The uncertainty of anxious thoughts becomes even more intolerable

An anxious thought creates a sense of uncertainty

You do something to quickly eliminate anxiety

You become more averse to the experience of uncertainty

Each time you go round this anxiety loop it perpetuates your fear of uncertainty. Your reactions to trying to eliminate it undermine your confidence in managing it and tolerating it. As you go on like this, one loop feeds the next, and you continue down a spiral of worsening symptoms. People who suffer from health anxiety or panic attacks face distress stemming from the uncertainty surrounding their physiological sensations. Those with social anxiety struggle with the uncertainty of how they are perceived or how they come across to others.

Meanwhile, individuals with generalized anxiety constantly shift their worries from one possible uncertain scenario to the next. Regardless of the specific anxiety problem, individuals often experience heightened awareness, a continuous preoccupation with uncertainty, and a strong aversion to the unknown.

This heightened awareness itself serves as a trigger for experiencing increased anxiety and physiological sensations, as well as for misinterpreting them. Someone with social anxiety will often approach social situations with apprehension and a long list of uncertainties, influenced by a perception of social failure. For instance, one of my patients expressed concerns like, 'What if I say the wrong thing? What if I don't know how to sit or where to put my hands?' These uncertainties contribute to their ongoing cycle of social anxiety, making it even more challenging to take small risks, like initiating a conversation or introducing themselves in a group situation. Like my patient, you may find yourself investing significant time and effort into preparing for negative outcomes that never actually occur. If you've been caught in this pattern, it's important to recognize that even when you strive to make everything certain, things can still unfold in a way that you don't want them to, you'll be no further on, and your anxiety problems will still be there.

The Problems Caused by Uncertainty

Intolerance of uncertainty causes many problems, some of which you may already recognize in yourself. It keeps you trapped in a cycle of overthinking, constantly preoccupied with anxious thoughts. Additionally, it drives you to engage in behaviours that actually worsen your anxiety, perpetuating your problems further. Many of the things you do to manage uncertainty will be mentally and physically exhausting too. You undertake these actions with the intention of reducing the intensity of distress linked to uncertainty, to get rid of as much uncertainty as you can and to increase your perception of control over future outcomes. Here are some examples of behaviours that can arise from intolerance of uncertainty:

- You live with the assumption that uncertain events always have a bad consequence.

- You avoid situations that may feel uncertain or unsafe to you, even though objectively they are not. This tendency may arise from difficulty distinguishing between uncertainty and actual danger.

- Even in the face of a minute risk, you tend to hyper-focus on it, magnifying it into an imagined future catastrophe.

- You avoid going to new places because you feel anxious about the unfamiliarity and think of all the things that could go wrong.

- You reduce your exposure to situations where there are any unknowns; this is avoidance, which we will address in the next chapter.

- You try to prepare yourself for every uncertainty that you might face by imagining all the possible future scenarios.

- You do everything you can to remove uncertainty from everyday situations.

- In an effort to eliminate uncertainty and alleviate the discomfort it brings, you find yourself impulsively and hastily taking specific actions. These actions may include avoiding certain situations, cancelling plans, or sticking to familiar places.

- To manage your aversion to experiencing feelings of uncertainty, you avoid situations where there is a possibility of an uncertain outcome, such as a doctor's appointment or a social gathering.

- You fixate on bad news and worry endlessly about how it will or could affect you one day.

- You consume an excessive amount of information, often more than necessary. For example, you may feel compelled to gain encyclopaedic knowledge about specific health issues or obsessively track environmental risks.

- You ruminate on your anxious thoughts, continuously going round in circles, without ever reaching a conclusion.

- You frequently seek excessive validation about your health, or how you are perceived by others, or even decisions you need to make.

- Uncertainty drives you to engage in repetitive checking behaviours, both physical and mental. Physical checking may show up as health-monitoring behaviours such as repeatedly measuring your pulse, or constantly reviewing emails you've sent due to social anxiety. Mental checking involves obsessively reviewing past events and analysing your words and actions in excruciating detail.

- You resort to unhealthy coping mechanisms, such as excessive distraction, in order to avoid confronting uncertainty altogether. By keeping yourself constantly occupied and busy, you create a shield against any potential encounter with uncertainty, in the hope of escaping its discomfort.

- You procrastinate about making decisions.

Do you recognize any of these patterns in yourself? You may feel a sense of control over events by engaging in these behaviours. However, it's important to recognize that these actions do not actually reduce the risk of negative outcomes occurring. Despite the statistical likelihood of catastrophes being relatively low, my patients often attribute their non-occurrence to their own preventative actions. This belief further strengthens the inclination to continue these behaviours aimed at controlling uncertainty, and prevents acknowledgement and acceptance of how rarely such predicted and feared catastrophes actually occur. As a result, the opportunity to learn that controlling uncertainty does not lead to positive outcomes is missed, and the cycle continues.

Patient Example: Wasim's Heart

Take a look at this diagram based on the experience of my patient, Wasim. It illustrates how Wasim's uncertainty triggers an attempt to control it or eliminate it through checking and seeking reassurance. These behaviours, although aimed at managing uncertainty, are actually avoidant and controlling in nature. The relief gained from these actions is short-lived, and Wasim quickly finds himself back in a state of uncertainty, leading to the repetition of these behaviours. Over time, this cycle becomes more ingrained, with increased frequency and intensity, exerting a stronger grip on Wasim. Despite his repeated efforts, note that the actual likelihood of him having a heart problem remains unchanged. But, in the process, his tolerance for uncertainty weakens and his anxiety worsens.

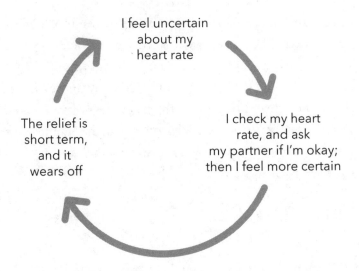

I feel uncertain about my heart rate

I check my heart rate, and ask my partner if I'm okay; then I feel more certain

The relief is short term, and it wears off

In addition to the behaviours mentioned earlier for managing uncertainty, you might also notice that you tend to avoid pleasurable aspects of life due to their potential unpredictability. This avoidance, which also commonly stems from uncertainty, causes you to miss out on activities and experiences that you would love to be a part of. One example is taking holidays or trips away from home. The change in environment and routine can trigger feelings of being out of control, leading to uncertainty and increased anxiety. Being in an unfamiliar place can expose you to new situations and environments that may further amplify your distress. Additionally, concerns about being far away from your usual support systems and infrastructure in case something goes wrong can contribute to anxiety. The uncertainty surrounding the possibility of getting sick or injured while on holiday can also be a source of anxiety. The constant pursuit of control over uncertainty can hugely diminish the joy in your life. It can create a persistent sense of impending threat, making it feel as though something ominous is always lurking nearby. For instance, my patient Jake was so drained by his intolerance of uncertainty that he sometimes wished the feared event, in his case, cancer, would just happen to put an end to the constant torment of living with uncertainty. Here are more insights into the thoughts of patients with anxiety who have grappled with uncertainty. These examples offer a further glimpse into the inner turmoil caused by uncertainty, and you may find them relatable:

'Even though the odds of something bad happening are really small, I think they will happen to me.'

'That tiny chance is me, and I can't get past it.'

'I can't cope with the fact that there's a possibility of it happening, it's like I need a guarantee.'

'I can't not know, I need to know, so I check and check and check.'

'I went to see two doctors because I wanted to be a hundred per cent certain, and after walking out I felt better. But later I still felt uncertain, and felt like I wanted to see another doctor.'

'I'm so uncertain about what the doctor will say, they will probably give me bad news, so I'm not going to go.'

'I feel like something is going to end badly, even if the outcome I'm imagining has a low probability.'

'Not knowing is threatening, unsafe and possibly dangerous, so I will stick to what I know.'

'I can't do things spontaneously, I just don't enjoy them.

*I need to know who, where, when, why, what, plus
everything else on top of that.'*

*'Not knowing is so scary for me, it's like when I don't know
it means there's something definitely wrong.'*

Understanding Your Experience of Uncertainty

You now have an understanding of the concept of uncertainty,
its intolerance and the problems this causes in worsening anxiety and hindering recovery if left unaddressed. You've also
gained insights into the motivations, behaviours and thoughts
experienced by those affected by it. We'll now move on to
looking at your experience of uncertainty and then proceed to
exploring strategies to address it. You'll have noticed throughout the book, there is a significant emphasis on gaining a
good understanding of things before attempting to make any
changes. This process enhances your awareness, enabling you
to recognize when you're engaging in behaviours influenced
by uncertainty and It empowers you to effectively apply the
strategies you need at the right moments. So let's get started
with your first task to help you deepen your understanding of
your experience with uncertainty.

> **TASK 27**
> **Understand your experience of
> uncertainty**
> Use the questions below to take a deeper
> look into the role uncertainty plays in your life. As
> you work through these, take notes in your journal or
> digital notes.

- How do you feel when you're uncertain about a possible future situation or event?
- How do you feel when you fixate on all the possible things that could go wrong?
- How much time do you spend immersed in thinking about these things?
- What kinds of things do you do to deal with your uncertainty?
- How has the need to control uncertainty affected your life, your relationships, your sense of enjoyment in things?
- How have the things you do to control for uncertainty impacted the duration and intensity of your anxiety? Has your anxiety improved, worsened or remained the same?

In this section, I will provide you with a range of strategies aimed at addressing your need for certainty, and enhancing your capacity to embrace uncertainty.

Pros and cons of requiring certainty

From my work in clinic, I have noticed a common pattern. Patients often find it challenging to let go of their need for certainty, even though they can see how it holds them back. If you're someone who struggles with accepting uncertainty, immerse yourself in Task 28. This particular task has been effective for many of my patients in overcoming their reluctance and becoming more comfortable with navigating uncertainty. It's possible that you hold positive beliefs about anxiety, particularly regarding uncertainty, and perceive your reactions as a helpful means of preventing negative outcomes from occurring.

At times, the experience of uncertainty can be so distressing that maybe you prefer to continue reacting and responding to it, rather than facing it head-on. However, it's important to remember that remaining in this position will hinder your progress in overcoming anxiety. You might perceive your reactions to uncertainty as a way of being prepared for the worst, believing that focusing on every uncertain possibility will prevent catastrophes. Additionally, you may think that reacting to uncertainty provides a sense of predictability and control in life. It's possible that you don't believe you have alternative strategies for managing the unknown, so you prefer to stick to what you know. These patterns might have become ingrained habits, and it can be challenging to see a way out of them. By completing this next task, which involves examining the pros and cons of requiring certainty, you will gain insights into the usefulness of your current patterns of behaviour influenced by uncertainty.

TASK 28
Pros and cons of requiring certainty

Work through the questions below, particularly when you encounter instances of increased uncertainty, and observe yourself responding in unhelpful ways. Working through this task will also help you in challenging your existing beliefs about uncertainty. Be sure to record your responses in either your notebook or digital notes.

- Has reacting to uncertainty made things more certain and more predictable for me?
- Has reacting to uncertainty changed the outcome of things that have happened in the past?
- How long have I been reacting to uncertainty?

- If controlling uncertainty is effective, I should be nearly recovered. During the time that I've been reacting to uncertainty, has my anxiety got better and better? Am I improving?
- Is it factually correct that (a) reacting with uncertainty fixes my problem, or (b) am I experiencing a short-term relief that gives me the perception that I have more control over negative events than I actually do?
- When I do things to deal with my uncertainty, how do I feel in the short term and in the long term?
- Does uncertainty keep my mind occupied with anxiety, fear, threat and all the worst possibilities? If so, how does this make me feel, and how does it affect my general emotional well-being?
- In what ways does reacting to uncertainty justify all the suffering it causes me mentally and emotionally?
- What are the pros and cons of continuing to require certainty in my life?

Acceptance and flexibility in the face of uncertainty

In Chapter 2, we learned about the crucial role that acceptance and flexibility play in dealing with anxiety. Embracing the distress of uncertainty is an integral part of this acceptance too. You owe it to yourself to embrace the full range of human emotions, with understanding, kindness and an open attitude. Acceptance is about recognizing that uncertainty is a natural part of life and allowing yourself to experience the associated discomfort it might bring without judgement. By accepting uncertainty, you open yourself to new possibilities, adapt to changing circumstances and cultivate a sense of inner peace and resilience in the face of the unknown. Acceptance involves acknowledging that you may experience discomfort for the time being while you're trying to work on changing your reactions and responses to uncertainty. By accepting this temporary discomfort, you shift from resisting it, trying to eliminate it, and engaging in unproductive responses. This allows you to make room for growth and progress.

If you resist experiencing uncertainty, you inadvertently invite more of it into your life. The struggle comes about when you attempt to respond and react to uncertainty, which stems from resistance. This resistance gives uncertainty more power, but when you simply allow it to exist without resistance, its influence begins to diminish. Remember, emotions are natural and inevitable; they simply *are*. The most effective way to navigate through them is to ride them out. Part of riding them out means not reacting to them in unhelpful ways. As you adopt this approach to dealing with uncertainty, you will notice that, over time, it gradually dissipates. By embracing uncertainty and consciously choosing not to be controlled by it, you reclaim your power and pave the way for more progress.

But how do you actually do this? To gain a more detailed understanding of how to employ acceptance strategies, I recommend that you refer back to the tasks outlined in previous chapters. The most relevant ones are:

- Task 6: My Acceptance Affirmation, page 73. A personalized reminder to acknowledge that anxiety is a natural part of your experience, that you can embrace it with kindness and understanding, allowing it to be present without judgement or resistance.

- Task 7: Thank Your Mind and Name the Story, page 77. This fosters gratitude towards your mind for trying to protect you, and consciously recognizes the narratives or stories that contribute to your anxiety so you can create distance from them.

- Task 22: Embracing Your Emotions Through Mindful Observation, page 210. This involves consciously and non-judgementally observing the flow of your inner experiences.

Acceptance and uncertainty

Remember that accepting means you're simply recognizing your fear of uncertainty as it arises, observing it, acknowledging its presence and allowing it to be there without reacting impulsively to it. To practise acceptance, take a moment to slow down and step back from immediately engaging in reactive behaviour. Instead, take note of what is emerging within you and how you are feeling. Pause and allow yourself to process the experience in a mindful and non-judgemental manner, talking yourself through your experience, for example:

'I'm feeling anxious because I fear the uncertainty of . . .'

'I realize that I always react to uncertainty by doing . . .'

I also realize that in the long term this just keeps my anxiety going. I want to move away from anxiety, not towards it. This is an opportunity to move towards overcoming anxiety. There are great benefits to me in not reacting to this uncertainty.'

After embracing acceptance, move towards cultivating flexibility in how you respond to uncertainty. Now that you've acknowledged the distress that uncertainty brings, it's time to approach your actions with adaptability. Explore the full spectrum of possibilities and refrain from repeating the same unproductive behaviours that have proven ineffective for you in the past. The inflexible approach involves resorting to the same reactive patterns. On the other hand, the flexible approach to dealing with uncertainty involves using your conscious awareness to make choices that move you closer to overcoming anxiety. By consciously considering your options and consciously choosing responses that align with what you want, you empower yourself to navigate uncertainty more effectively.

I'm faced with an anxious thought
again; it requires me to
make a choice

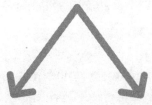

This choice moves me
AWAY from my goal of
overcoming anxiety,
and worsens my anxiety

This choice moves
me TOWARDS
my goal of
overcoming anxiety

Remember this diagram from earlier (see page 102)? Your power lies in choosing how you react. Every time you experience uncertainty it will result in you having to make a choice about what to do to deal with it. You can either make a choice that steers you further away from your goals, increasing distress and reinforcing anxiety, or one that acknowledges the presence of distress without worsening your anxiety problems, moving you closer to what you want.

You might argue that you don't want to tolerate the feeling

of uncertainty, that you can't, that it will be too hard. But it'll be harder the more you continue to resist it and avoid it. And yes, it may well be hard in the beginning, but I promise you it will get better and better when you continue doing this work on yourself. This is your opportunity to change how you do things and improve your quality of life in the long run.

So what can you do to be more flexible and make the choice that moves you towards your goal? There are various strategies you can employ to enhance your tolerance of the distress caused by uncertainty. Again, I recommend revisiting the relevant tasks presented in previous chapters. Some strategies in this book are interconnected and can be adapted and applied to different anxiety problems. Take a look back to Chapter 6, tasks 23–26 from page 214 which are all very relevant to flexibility.

Patients in my clinic have also found creating a personalized self-talk script to be immensely helpful in managing and soothing the distress of uncertainty. Here's an example that you can modify to reflect your own voice and words, keeping in mind to use a kind and reassuring tone, similar to how you would speak to a loved one or a child in a similar situation.

Self-talk sample script
Even though the feeling of uncertainty might linger in the background, I will move my attention onto something else, something absorbing and interesting. My mind deserves this break from all this difficult stuff. I really want certainty, but I accept it won't help me get better, so I'm going to accept its presence and observe its pull until it fades.

Managing your uncertain predictions

When living with anxiety, encountering the unknown can evoke a feeling of threat, which in turn triggers predictions and overestimations based on the presence of uncertainty, amplifying both the perceived likelihood and severity of the threat. Effective management of these predictions is crucial to overcoming anxiety. By consciously navigating these predictions, you can avoid reinforcing their validity through unhelpful actions, and stop yourself from becoming entangled in a distorted state where perception and reality are skewed by the presence of uncertainty. Let's consider the case of my patient Jake (who we met very briefly earlier).

Patient Example: Jake's Stomach Cancer Fears

Jake had an intense fear of stomach cancer, leading him to predict its presence on a daily basis. Whenever he was triggered by an unfamiliar or uncomfortable sensation in his stomach, he immediately associated it with a negative sign directly linked to cancer. This association stemmed from the uncertainty surrounding the origin of the discomfort. The belief that uncertainty equalled something negative became deeply ingrained in Jake's thinking. Through our work together, Jake gradually discovered that it is not rational to assume the worst simply because something is uncertain or lacks immediate clarity. The next diagram illustrates the struggle and anxiety trap Jake found himself in, how it was perpetuated, and the subsequent downward spiral he experienced.

Do you find yourself, like Jake, anticipating something negative simply because you're uncertain about it? Are you inclined to assume that uncertainty always leads to bad news or unfavourable outcomes? If so, you're not alone. Many anxious people tend to travel down this familiar path of anxious and uncertain thoughts, where feelings of uncertainty are often seen as a signal for impending disaster. When this happens you will feel very scared, and even more anxious, and this heightened emotional distress also causes a magnification of physical sensations, similar to what Jake experienced in his case.

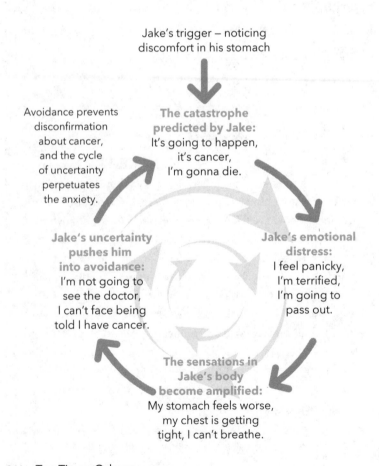

Jake's trigger – noticing discomfort in his stomach

The catastrophe predicted by Jake: It's going to happen, it's cancer, I'm gonna die.

Jake's emotional distress: I feel panicky, I'm terrified, I'm going to pass out.

The sensations in Jake's body become amplified: My stomach feels worse, my chest is getting tight, I can't breathe.

Jake's uncertainty pushes him into avoidance: I'm not going to see the doctor, I can't face being told I have cancer.

Avoidance prevents disconfirmation about cancer, and the cycle of uncertainty perpetuates the anxiety.

Developing the skill of consciously monitoring the predictions you make in response to uncertainty is crucial. It's important to recognize that not knowing does not automatically indicate a negative outcome. To help monitor your thoughts and behaviour in relation to this, you can keep a simple record, like the following table, where you note the date, the prediction arising from your uncertainty, and later follow up to confirm whether it actually happened or not. If it didn't happen, take note of what actually transpired instead. Regularly review this table to look at the probability of neutral or even positive outcomes that have occurred. The purpose of this monitoring exercise is to help you learn that uncertainty does not guarantee a negative outcome, and to cultivate a more balanced perspective on uncertain situations.

Date	What you assumed or predicted:	Did it happen?	Did something good or neutral come of it instead? What?
28th July	Because I'm unsure what this feeling in my stomach is, it must mean it is cancer.	No	Good – the doctor said I'm all clear. It put my mind at rest.

Building Resilience to Uncertainty

This section will help you build your resilience for coping with uncertainty. Through the use of these tasks, you will discover that the discomfort of uncertainty is transient; it will pass, and it is entirely possible for you to cope with it. These tasks, which are particularly impactful and among my favourites due to their effectiveness, are designed specifically to help you build resilience for uncertainty. The following tasks facilitate efficient learning through personal experience, enabling your mind to release any inaccurate ideas it may hold. By consistently practicing the skills outlined here, you can make faster progress in developing your resilience to uncertainty. The strategy employed in these tasks focuses on teaching your mind how to cope with uncertainty by modifying your responses and minimizing your efforts to eliminate or control it. This skill requires deliberately and intentionally embracing increasing levels of uncertainty to strengthen your resilience.

It's understandable if your uncertainty makes you hesitant to engage in any of the exercises in this chapter, especially when it has become the habitual norm from which your mind operates. It's expected that you may feel some apprehension about trying these strategies, but remember that the purpose is to provide you with tools to effectively deal with uncertainty, allowing you to accept the discomfort it brings and develop better tolerance for it. By gradually embracing this discomfort, you will discover that it can be endured, leading to improvement in your overall anxiety. This shift in approach will prevent you from fuelling your anxiety problems, bringing you closer to the goal of overcoming anxiety.

Patient Example: Oliver's Struggle with Uncertainty

My patient Oliver struggled with health anxiety, seeking absolute certainty not only in terms of his physical well-being but also across other areas of his life. To achieve certainty regarding his health, Oliver engaged in repeated doctor visits, multiple tests and extensive online research. Additionally, Oliver exhibited an aversion to uncertainty in his daily life, as evidenced by his avoidance of unfamiliar situations, strict adherence to routines, and strong preference for familiar places, including taking the same routes when driving. Sometimes people have particular needs that create a preference for routine and structure, some people naturally thrive on it, and there's usually no problem with this. It becomes problematic when it is driven by anxiety, resulting in habitual behaviours aimed at controlling or eliminating uncertainty.

To address his problems with uncertainty, Oliver implemented the task outlined below. He started with stage 1, which aimed to address his general uncertainty, followed by stage 2, targeting uncertainty specifically associated with his health anxiety. In Oliver's case, stage 1 involved building confidence by addressing his everyday tolerance for uncertainty. This initial stage focused on addressing lower-level uncertainties that were not as strong as the challenges and aversions he experienced regarding his health. By starting with smaller uncertainties, Oliver could develop confidence and practise the necessary skills to consolidate and improve them before tackling higher-level uncertainties.

Here's another way for you to understand how to build your tolerance for uncertainty and avoid giving in to anxiety's grip. Imagine the urge to check your phone, something many of us experience throughout the day. Instead of immediately reaching for your phone, try delaying the urge and simply observe the thoughts and feelings that arise without reacting to them. By practising this delay, you train your brain to understand that the urge will pass and you don't have to act on it immediately.

With consistent practice, you'll notice the urge gradually fades and loses its power. These exercises, along with others in this chapter, will enhance your ability to tolerate the discomfort of uncertainty. Over time, you'll become more comfortable with the idea that not everything requires an immediate reaction or resolution, and it's okay to sit with the discomfort of uncertainty.

I have set out some stages and provided a detailed description to help guide you through the process of dealing with uncertainty.

Stage 1 – Address General Uncertainty

Stage 1 focuses on situations that may not be directly linked to your main anxiety problem but still entail a certain level of uncertainty, at a lower anxiety intensity. By focusing on these specific targets, you will have the opportunity to practise and strengthen your ability to tolerate uncertainty. You will also gain confidence in accepting and embracing uncertainty, which sets a solid foundation for stage 2. For this first stage, you will actively expose yourself to uncertainty using simple every-day possibilities. You will find twenty suggestions to explore uncertainty. While these suggestions may appear simple, they are designed to evoke uncertainty. You don't have to do these exact things, feel free to adapt these suggestions or come up with your own ideas that elicit similar feelings of uncertainty.

TASK 29
Exploring general situations of uncertainty

Here is a list of twenty ideas for exploring and exposing yourself to general situations of uncertainty:

1. Read a book by an unknown author or in a new genre.
2. Make a deliberate change to your daily routine.
3. Try something completely random, such as changing the order of your activities, exploring a new genre of music, or playing an unfamiliar game.
4. Sample a spoonful of food you've never tried before or buy an unfamiliar fruit.
5. Eat an unlabelled food given by a loved one or try blindfolded tasting.
6. Take a different route when driving or try using alternative modes of transport.
7. Visit a new place or explore an unfamiliar location.
8. Attend an event that you normally wouldn't consider.
9. Let someone else plan and organize an outing or activity for you.
10. Shop at different a supermarket from your usual one.
11. Watch a movie without reading anything about it beforehand.
12. Dine at unfamiliar cafes or restaurants.
13. Experience eating out alone.
14. Engage in a new hobby that you've never tried before.
15. Experiment with a new hairstyle or with a different outfit.
16. Take a spontaneous day trip to a nearby town or city.
17. Explore a new form of exercise or try a taster fitness class.

18. Cook a meal using ingredients you've never used before.
19. Try a workshop or class on a subject that you have limited knowledge about.
20. Attend events that celebrate traditions or cultures different from your own.

Choose a range of activities from the provided list or your own ideas, moving from easy to more challenging. Begin by focusing on the easy and accessible everyday activities that you can repeat frequently. Reflect on your ability to tolerate discomfort after completing each activity and observe how your tolerance evolves over time. Use a table to track your progress, similar to the example shown below. Don't be discouraged if it takes several attempts to become comfortable with uncertainty, as this is normal. Stay committed to the task until you reach a point where the uncertainty no longer causes distress for you. The everyday activities will offer the most effective and consistent exposure to uncertainty, helping you build your tolerance over time. Some activities on the list require more resources and planning: they serve as inspiration for future opportunities when you have developed a greater capacity for uncertainty. This way, you can take advantage of the chance to engage in the experiences if and when they arise.

The purpose of the table is to track and record the changes in discomfort as you engage in your chosen tasks and observe how it gradually becomes easier over time. It serves as a visual representation of your progress, highlighting the positive impact of repeated exposure. As an example of progress tracking, let's consider someone who decides to rotate their visits among three different local supermarkets. Please remember that you have the freedom to choose activities that suit you best, and selecting the supermarket is not a mandatory task. This example simply serves as a demonstration of how to document and assess your progress. In another example, someone conducted a blindfolded taste test with various unidentified foods. Each attempt featured a different food, chosen based on what was readily available that day. Again, you are not required to undertake the food task, and if you choose to do so, there's no need to spend money on items specifically for this purpose. You can prioritize using what is already accessible to avoid unnecessary waste.

Chosen task to practise tolerating uncertainty	Discomfort level on a scale of 0 to 10, with 10 representing the highest level.
Alternating visits among three different supermarkets.	Attempt 1 (Supermarket A) – 6/10 Attempt 2 (Supermarket B) – 6/10 Attempt 3 (Supermarket C) – 5/10 Attempt 4 (Supermarket A) – 3/10 Attempt 5 (Supermarket B) – 2/10 Attempt 6 (Supermarket C) – 2/10 Attempt 7 (Supermarket A) – 0/10
Having a blindfolded taste test of an unidentified food, taking only a spoonful each time, without any prior knowledge of what it is.	Attempt 1 – 7/10 Attempt 2 – 6/10 Attempt 3 – 4/10 Attempt 4 – 2/10 Attempt 5 – 0/10

Stage 2 – Addressing Uncertainty Specific to Your Anxiety

After you've completed the activities in the initial stage, it's important you move directly to address uncertainty specific to your anxiety problems. Avoid delaying or hesitating, so you can maintain the momentum for progress. Before planning your tasks in this stage, I recommend you read through this entire section.

People who suffer with anxiety often employ methods to cope with their inability to tolerate uncertainty. You may have used these coping mechanisms, switching between them or employing multiple methods at different times. Relying on these actions to manage distress not only reinforces anxiety problems but can also lead to uncertainty paralysis, a state characterized by intense anxiety and discomfort that hinders you from taking constructive action. In the long term, depending on these methods to handle uncertainty is ineffective in overcoming anxiety. Below are several examples of common behaviours that people engage in to control, eliminate or minimize their experience of uncertainty. As you review these examples, take note of any behaviours that resonate with you. Please remember that this list is not exhaustive, so if there are additional actions that apply to you, make sure to acknowledge them as well.

Common uncertainty control behaviours
- Engaging in excessive over-planning and over-preparation.
- Persistently getting caught up in predicting a range of possible outcomes.

- Avoiding uncertain situations and information, or engaging in unhealthy distractions.
- Reacting quickly and impulsively to the discomfort of uncertainty.
- Asking repeated questions.
- Excessive reassurance seeking.
- Spending prolonged periods searching the internet.
- Consuming an excessive amount of information.
- Repeatedly checking things.
- Imagining all possible future scenarios.
- Procrastinating when it comes to making decisions.
- Maintaining rigidity and doing things the same way.
- Doing things that you don't really need to.

There are six specific steps to address uncertainty related to your anxiety problems. We'll now go through each of these steps, using a consistent example throughout to guide you through the process.

1. Identify the behaviours you use to manage feelings of uncertainty

What do you do to feel more certain? Refer to the list of common uncertainty controlling behaviours provided above for examples. Here is an example based on health anxiety about the heart:

Seeking constant reassurance from my partner.

Repeatedly checking my heart rate, often multiple times, or checking it hourly.

Spending hours researching online for information related to heart health.

2. Rank the behaviours based on the intensity of distress

To ensure a successful approach, it's best to start with smaller challenges and gradually build confidence before moving on to the next task. We want to strike a balance where the tasks are not too overwhelming or discouraging, yet still keep the momentum of progress going. Take a look at the list you created in the previous step and rearrange it in order, with the easiest task at the top and the most challenging task at the bottom. Assign a score from 1 to 10 to each behaviour on the list, where 1 represents the lowest level of uncertainty-based distress and 10 the highest. This indicates the level of distress or anxiety you anticipate if you were to resist engaging in that behaviour, and will help you rank the behaviours from lowest to highest. For example:

Spending hours researching online for information related to heart health, 6/10

Seeking constant reassurance from my partner, 8/10

Repeatedly checking my heart rate, often multiple times, or checking it hourly, 10/10

3. Make a prediction for each behaviour starting with the lowest score

The purpose of this task is to assess your ability to tolerate uncertainty and to demonstrate that resisting your typical reactions does not result in catastrophic consequences. You will perform this task for each behaviour you have ranked, starting from the lowest ranked one and progressing to the highest ranked one. This means that with each round, you will make a new prediction based on the specific behaviour at hand. In our example the lowest ranked behaviour is:

If I don't spend hours researching online for information related to heart health I might not be aware of symptoms and could miss something. If I do, I could have a heart attack and die.

Now, assign a percentage rating to indicate the strength of your belief in the uncertainty-based prediction you have made, *90 per cent*

4. Embrace uncertainty with new responses

This stage focuses on refraining from using the behaviours you typically employ to cope with feelings of uncertainty. In the example we're discussing, where the usual response to uncertainty is spending hours researching online, embracing uncertainty with a new approach could mean gradually reducing the designated time duration for this action (e.g. starting with twice a day) and restricting the duration to, let's say, 10 minutes each time. From there, the frequency can be decreased to once a day for 5 minutes, then progressing to alternating days, every three days, once a week and ultimately towards completely refraining from engaging in the behaviour altogether. You're basically repeating the task until your discomfort with uncertainty significantly diminishes and the percentage rating for how true you think your prediction is objectively decreases to at least 10 per cent or even zero! This process allows you to build resilience and gradually increase your tolerance for uncertainty.

Engaging in this practice of recording and evaluating the accuracy of your predictions can be helpful for several reasons. Firstly, it allows you to objectively assess the outcomes and challenge any distorted beliefs or exaggerated fears related to uncertainty. Secondly, it provides tangible evidence of your ability to tolerate uncertainty and demonstrates that refraining from your usual responses does not lead to catastrophic consequences. Lastly, it helps you track your progress over time, providing motivation and reinforcement as you witness your discomfort diminish and your confidence in managing uncertainty grow. Using the same example, I have shown you how you can document your experience, for instance you can choose to use a table, like the one below, or make notes in a way that works best for you.

Prediction: If I don't spend hours researching online for information related to heart health I might not be aware of symptoms and could miss something. If I do, I could have a heart attack and die. **Initial belief level before embracing uncertainty with new responses:** 90 per cent.

Final belief level in the prediction after embracing uncertainty with all these new responses: 5 per cent.

5. Review how your practice went

This is our review stage. After completing the practice of each targeted behaviour, it's important to review your progress to acknowledge the shift in your perception and reinforce the learning process. This review is instrumental in reducing the intensity of your attachment to the behaviours you use to control uncertainty. Consider the following questions to guide this review:

- What was the outcome? Was your prediction correct or incorrect?
- Despite feeling uncertain, was the outcome acceptable?

New responses to uncertainty	Did a heart attack occur by resisting uncertainty and using new responses to it?	Belief level in the prediction after embracing uncertainty with new responses
Reduce online research to twice a day for 10 minutes only	No	70%
Reduce online research to twice a day for 5 minutes only	No	60%
Reduce online research to once a day for 5 minutes only	No	50%
Reduce online research to alternating days	No	20%
Reduce online research to once every three days	No	10%
Reduce to once a week	No	5%
Completely refrain from online research	No	5%

- Was there any serious threat involved? Yes/No
- How did you feel during the practice? Was it as challenging as anticipated, or easier than expected?
- What did you notice as you continued to practise?
- What did you discover about the behaviour you typically rely on to cope with uncertainty? Is it truly necessary?

- What insights did you gain about your ability to handle uncertainty?

6. Repeat, persist and keep moving forward!

Once you've become comfortable with practising the skill of tolerating uncertainty and observing the outcomes, proceed to the next behaviour on your list and continue this progression until you have addressed all the behaviours you identified in stage 1. By consistently engaging in this practice, you will observe a noticeable improvement in your capacity to tolerate uncertainty, leading to a significant strengthening of this skill over time.

I have provided a complete example for you, focusing on the behaviour of online research to alleviate health anxiety related to the heart. However, it's important to note that individuals with different types of anxiety problems, varying temperaments and diverse coping strategies may use different behaviours to manage uncertainty. The following box offers insights into some common methods people use to cope with the distress of uncertainty, and ideas to address these. While you may find behaviours on the list that resonate with you, it's also possible that you employ other methods. Regardless of the specific behaviour, the six-stage approach above remains the same.

> **Addressing commonly used methods for coping with uncertainty**
> 1. **Over-planning**: Set limits, reduce the time spent on planning and limit how much information you will seek to satisfy your need for certainty. These limits can be time limits, or based on where you source information from.

2. **Repeated questioning**: Keep count of how often you ask questions over a two-day period, for example, then gradually reduce and eliminate this.
3. **Seeking reassurance excessively**: Set limits on how often you'll do this, perhaps at set intervals in the day or try alternate days. When the urge arrives, delay reacting to it for 10 minutes, then 20, 30, until you get up to an hour. Then keep progressing from there.
4. **Searching the internet for prolonged periods**: Set time intervals and duration limits. There are specific apps that can also help with monitoring this behaviour.
5. **Checking things repeatedly**: Set limits and keep reducing them.
6. **Asking for opinions/validation**: Set limits on how many opinions you're going to ask for. If you usually ask five people, ask four instead, reducing down to only one or two, as well as reducing the frequency with which you ask.

Gradually expose yourself to situations you avoid because of uncertainty. Start with milder instances and gradually work your way up to more challenging ones.

The more you struggle with uncertainty, the more important it becomes to practise the strategies in this chapter. If you need to, you can make it a daily habit to engage in tasks that promote uncertainty tolerance. Although it may be challenging at first, you'll soon realize that it requires less time and energy compared to striving for certainty. As you gradually build your tolerance, you'll find that you can let go of the problems uncertainty brings and cope more and more with not knowing. You'll discover that you don't need absolutes to feel satisfied, as they aren't attainable anyway. This process will free you from the suffering caused by uncertainty and help release anxiety's grip on you.

Enhancing your uncertainty-management toolkit

In addition to the strategies discussed in this chapter, I encourage you to revisit earlier exercises to enhance your uncertainty-management toolkit. By engaging in these prior exercises, you not only expand your toolkit for addressing uncertainty and anxiety, you also strengthen your skills in specific areas. Through practise, you can become proficient and more confident in using the skills I'm providing you with. There are several earlier tasks that are relevant, and your choice of these will depend on the specific scenario you are facing. Refer back to the tasks in Chapter 3 to calm your nervous system when you are triggered by uncertainty. Revisiting the tasks in Chapter 4 will help you address anxious thoughts related to uncertainty. Chapter 5 has valuable techniques to redirect your attention away from triggers associated with uncertainty so you can develop a more balanced and objective perspective. Expanding the scope of your attention beyond uncertainty can also reduce hyper-vigilance, allowing you to feel a sense of calm.

> **Ten Key Takeaways for Navigating Uncertainty**
>
> 1. Recognize the impact of uncertainty-related distress on your overall well-being and the anxiety problem you face.
>
> 2. Embrace the reality that uncertainty is an inevitable part of life and shift your focus towards enhancing your tolerance of it.

3. Understand how an intolerance for uncertainty leads to behaviours that worsen both your ability to tolerate uncertainty and your anxiety.

4. Acknowledge that engaging in unhelpful behaviours to control uncertainty provides temporary relief but perpetuates anxiety in the long run. Commit to breaking free from these patterns.

5. Examine your motivation for responding to uncertainty in ways that do not alleviate anxiety and explore healthier alternatives to overcome this struggle.

6. Embrace the fact that absolute certainty is unattainable in life, and work on developing the ability to live with uncertainty without allowing it to significantly impact your mental health.

7. Empower yourself by recognizing that you have control over how you choose to respond and deal with uncertainty.

8. Make a dedicated effort to increase your willingness to tolerate uncertainty by employing the strategies described in this chapter. Seek to understand, accept and respond flexibly to your experiences of uncertainty.

9. Embrace experiential learning as an effective approach to address difficulties with uncertainty. Engage in more general day-to-day activities that help you develop a better tolerance and reduce triggers associated with uncertainty.

10. Consistently practise and challenge yourself to tolerate increasing levels of uncertainty related to your anxiety problem. As your tolerance improves, you will also notice a reduction in anxiety symptoms.

Countdown for calmness!

Counting backwards from a high number, for example between 500 and 5000, can be a helpful tool for diverting your mind away from feeding into anxious thoughts. By focusing on counting, you're giving your mind a break from engaging with imagined future catastrophes. When you're counting backwards, your mind has to put in mental effort, meaning there's less mental effort available to focus on racing thoughts that feed anxiety. Counting backwards can also be helpful in regulating your breathing. By timing your breath with each number, you can slow down the rate of your breathing, which will also help you feel more relaxed.

Chapter 8:
How Can I Face My Fears?

Avoidance and safety behaviours play a significant role in perpetuating anxiety and are a primary focus for overcoming it. Avoidance involves steering clear of situations, thoughts, images or triggers associated with the negative outcomes you fear. For instance, you may avoid visiting the doctor because you fear receiving a devastating diagnosis, or you might avoid social gatherings due to the fear of rejection. Safety behaviours are subtle forms of avoidance where you engage in actions with the belief that they will protect you from potential harm. Both avoidance and safety behaviours have the aim of reducing the distress associated with your worst fears. Safety behaviours and avoidance worsen anxiety by providing temporary relief while preventing you from confronting your fears and learning to tolerate anxiety-provoking situations. This perpetuates the belief that the situations are genuinely dangerous, that you can't cope with them; it reinforces anxiety and restricts your life experiences.

In this chapter, we will take a close look at the concepts of avoidance and safety behaviours to provide you with a comprehensive understanding of their impact on your anxiety. After this we will explore practical strategies to reduce and ultimately eliminate avoidance and safety behaviours by facing your fears. Let me share an example of my patient

Izzy's experience, illustrating the detrimental effects of safety behaviours and avoidance in worsening anxiety.

> ### Patient Example: Izzy's Avoidance
>
> Many patients I've worked with have seen their world shrink, with some becoming housebound due to safety behaviours and avoidance. Izzy, for instance, developed severe anxiety centred on the fear of panic attacks in public. It all began one year prior when she had a panic attack while shopping in a crowded place, leaving her feeling trapped and convinced she was having a heart attack. She described being engulfed in a whirlwind of terror, suffocated by the impending doom that cast a dark shadow over her thoughts. In an attempt to prevent future attacks, Izzy relied on safety behaviours such as avoiding triggering situations, seeking reassurance, distracting herself with gaming apps, carrying lucky objects and planning escape routes. However, these behaviours only reinforced her fear and gradually isolated her from the outside world, leaving her unable to comfortably leave her home. Izzy was able to regain control of her life and find a sense of normality by breaking free from the reliance on safety behaviours and avoidance as coping mechanisms for her anxiety. Her journey towards this progress stemmed from her determination to release the grip of safety behaviours, diminish avoidance, and confront her fears head-on.

What Is Avoidance?

Avoidance is a coping strategy aimed at avoiding situations in which you anticipate negative outcomes or unpleasant feelings. Avoidance causes you to remove yourself from being in situations where you believe bad things could happen to you. The other goal of avoidance is to prevent facing up to unpleasant feelings or thoughts related to the outcomes you fear. Avoiding situations can create a temporary reduction in anxiety, leading to the belief that you are successfully eliminating risk to yourself. For instance, a person who is anxious about public speaking may experience temporary relief when calling in sick on the day of a presentation. By avoiding the situation, their self-confidence erodes further, perpetuating a cycle of avoidance and reinforcing the idea that they are unable to engage in public speaking. The more avoidant they become, the more their anxiety grows. Anxiety problems promote avoidance. Your anxiety seeks to shield you from distressing mental images and urges you to escape or avoid situations that could trigger your worst thoughts and feelings. This avoidance of situations where your worst thoughts could come true and your worst feelings could surface gives your anxiety centre stage. People who rely on avoidance tend to accept their beliefs without questioning them, as they find solace in the conclusion that there was no bad outcome, because of their avoidance. This relief strengthens their attachment to avoidance, seeing it as the only way to eliminate or control risk.

Avoidance not only reinforces your anxious beliefs about worst-case scenarios but also exacerbates rumination. By engaging in avoidance behaviours and reducing your activities, you create more time and opportunity for rumination to take hold. As rumination intensifies, so does your anxiety. Consequently, your world begins to shrink. When the mind becomes habitually avoidant, it tends to extend avoidance to various aspects of life, gradually transforming the person into a mere shadow of their former self. While the extent of this impact may vary for each person, it is commonly seen in the lives of almost all those with anxiety.

Avoidance is like sweeping dust under a rug: it gives you the impression that you've cleared your mind and body of any difficulties and struggles. But anxiety still lingers beneath the surface, and each time you engage in avoidance behaviours, the dust of anxiety accumulates and grows bigger, ultimately becoming a huge obstacle that hinders your ability to move past it. It's crucial to recognize this illusion, and understand that facing your fears is your path out of anxiety. To illustrate this further, let's look at another clinical example.

The diagram illustrates how Zara's increasing avoidance behaviour contributed to a worsening of her anxiety. She experienced more frequent and intense spikes of distress,

---

Patient Example: Zara's Avoidance

Zara was gripped by an intense fear of discovering a lump on her body, strongly convinced that it would be a clear indication of cancer. This fear took hold of her after she became aware of someone else's cancer diagnosis, leading her to believe that the same would happen to her too, despite the absence of any symptoms or supporting evidence. Consequently, Zara actively avoided situations where she might confront the possibility of finding a lump, such as skipping regular check-ups, avoiding mirrors and self-examinations and refraining from consulting doctors or attending health checks. The mere thought of encountering a lump filled Zara with overwhelming terror, as she firmly believed it would undoubtedly be cancerous and lead to her death. This paralysing fear drove her to avoid any activities that might bring her face-to-face with the potential discovery of a lump. Despite providing temporary relief, her avoidance behaviour perpetuated her deep-seated conviction that a lump existed. Consequently, her anxiety continued to worsen.

---

further reinforcing her belief that avoidance was the only way to cope with her fear. As time went on, this pattern of avoidance led to even more pronounced episodes of anxiety, intensifying the perceived severity of her fear.

When Zara avoids the triggering situation she experiences immediate relief. But next time, the intensity of her anxiety is heightened again.

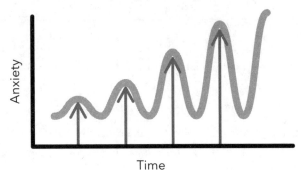

Before we move on to looking at safety behaviours, take a moment to reflect on your own avoidance patterns. Use the following questions to help with this. As you go through them, make notes in your journal or digital notes, and keep these handy, as they'll form the basis of what we do later in this chapter, when we work on facing your fears.

TASK 30
Identify your avoidance behaviours
1. What situations do you tend to avoid?
2. What specific thoughts do you try to avoid?
3. Which emotions or physical sensations do you try to avoid?

4. Why do you find these avoidance behaviours helpful? What benefits or relief do they provide?
5. What do you fear will happen if you were to stop your avoidance behaviours?
6. Have you noticed any patterns in how you feel both in the short term and the long term following your avoidance behaviours?

What Are Safety Behaviours?

Safety behaviours are actions or thoughts that a person engages in to reduce distress in situations that they perceive as threatening or dangerous. Safety behaviours are used as a coping mechanism; like avoidance, they may provide temporary relief from anxiety, but they ultimately reinforce and maintain the underlying anxiety problem. This is because the sufferer never has the opportunity to learn that the perceived danger is not actually as threatening as they originally thought, because they never fully experience the situation without the safety behaviours. Safety behaviours can show up in various forms depending on the specific anxiety problem. Here are some examples:

Social Anxiety:
- Avoiding eye contact during social interactions.
- Preparing and rehearsing conversations in advance to feel more confident.
- Consuming alcohol or substances before social situations as a means of reducing anxiety.

Generalized Anxiety:

- Carrying a specific object, such as a lucky charm or comfort item, to alleviate anxiety.
- Wearing specific clothing or accessories that provide a sense of security or reassurance.

Health Anxiety:

- Seeking constant reassurance from others, such as repeatedly asking for medical opinions or checking symptoms online.
- Avoiding situations or activities that trigger health-related fears, such as avoiding hospitals or medical appointments.
- Engaging in excessive checking behaviours, such as frequently monitoring bodily sensations or conducting repetitive self-examinations.

Panic:

- Restricting body movement to avoid triggering physical sensations like increased heart rate, shortness of breath or sweating.
- Engaging in controlled or shallow breathing patterns to regulate respiration and minimize sensations linked to panic.

People use the above, and other actions, to prevent their worst fears from coming true. They also use them to reduce the intensity of the distress they feel in triggering situations. Often people's preference is to completely avoid situations that cause them anxiety. But when they can't avoid a situation altogether, they will use safety behaviours as a more subtle way to avoid fully experiencing the situation. Safety behaviours can seem like a logical response to the perception of threat, but they are a tremendous obstacle in overcoming anxiety. Engaging in these behaviours is like sitting in a rocking chair constantly moving back and forth, which can make you feel like you're doing something helpful. But really you're not getting anywhere. The actions and movement might give you a sense of control and comfort, but ultimately, it isn't productive in overcoming your anxiety. To make meaningful progress, it's essential that you get off the rocking chair and start moving in a more constructive direction. In this chapter, I will share strategies to help you do just that.

The examples of safety behaviours mentioned earlier are just a glimpse into the wide range of behaviours that people may engage in to cope with their anxiety. Safety behaviours are highly individual, and each person will have their own unique ones. The nature of the behaviour is less significant than the underlying reason behind its use. This distinction is crucial because at times people may engage in the same behaviours without experiencing anxiety. For example, someone leaning on a wall might do so out of tiredness, rather than to prevent a fear of fainting from coming true. Similarly, sitting near an exit in a cinema might be motivated by the need to leave promptly for the next commitment, rather than a fear of being trapped. It is not the behaviour itself that poses a problem, but rather the purpose for which it is being used. I often ask my patients, 'Would you feel anxious if you were unable or not allowed to engage in that behaviour?' If their answer is 'Yes', it is likely a safety behaviour; whereas if they can easily change or discontinue the behaviour without experiencing any anxiety, it is probably not a safety behaviour. This question can assist in identifying personal safety behaviours, although exceptions may exist. Here are some examples to show the purpose behind common safety behaviours:

Safety behaviour	Why it's used
Going into a social situation but choosing not to speak.	If I talk I could embarrass myself by saying something stupid; I'll be rejected.
Arriving too early for a class/meeting.	If I'm late everyone will be watching me walk in, and I could trip over, blush or embarrass myself.
Trying to breathe in a particular way.	If I don't breathe like this, I won't get enough oxygen, and it could be dangerous.
Checking yourself, checking objects and things. Using medical devices and testing. Monitoring your vitals using a smartwatch.	If I don't check I might miss something serious; I could end up unwell, or dead.
Seeking reassurance by asking others, or looking up information.	If I don't keep asking others if they think I'm okay, I could die.
Sitting down or lying down more than needed. Trying not to move excessively. Avoiding physical exertion.	If I move around too much, I will raise my heart rate and could have a panic attack, or even bring on a heart attack.
Scanning for exits and sitting near exits.	If I don't sit near the exit I won't be able to leave quickly in case of an emergency. Medical services won't be able to reach me if I fall ill.
Relying on persistent distractions, such as keeping the TV or radio on, to evade thoughts, emotions or physical sensations.	If I pay too much attention to what I'm going through, something bad will happen.

Being accompanied by someone every time you go out.	If I go alone something bad could happen to me, and there'll be nobody there to help me.
Carrying a good luck charm or other item.	If I don't take my good luck/special item with me something bad will happen.
Sticking to the same familiar places and familiar people.	Going to a new place is unpredictable, unsafe, and something bad could happen to me; I won't be able to handle it.

As you can see from these examples, safety behaviours are preventative, aimed at averting negative outcomes. These negative outcomes usually relate to the prevention of death, illness, humiliation, rejection, embarrassment, unpredictability, or harm in varying degrees, ranging from minor to major.

Jinxing as a safety behaviour

Jinxing is another concept that falls under the realm of safety behaviours, and many of my patients struggle with this. It involves you engaging in superstitious actions or rituals to prevent a negative outcome from occurring.

You engage in superstitious practices like touching wood or adhering to the belief that acknowledging positive or neutral situations might 'jinx' them into turning negative. As a result, you intentionally resist acknowledging things as positive, neutral or as they truly are, opting instead to remain entrenched in a pessimistic mindset. It's almost as if you believe that by doing so, you are safeguarding against unfavourable outcomes. But these actions are not based on rational evidence or actual control over the outcome, rather on a subjective sense of control and the desire to reduce anxiety or uncertainty.

Your thoughts and reactions hold no power to influence or control events or outcomes. There is no logical connection between feeling less anxious, accepting positivity and tempting fate. The fear of jinxing oneself is a direct result of anxiety. Reflect on whether you would entertain these thoughts if you were not anxious. The fear of jinxing serves as another reactive strategy to manage anxiety, providing a false sense of control in situations where you feel powerless. Consider it an attempt to control anxiety. It's important to recognize that there is no unseen force waiting to punish you for not remaining anxious or for enjoying life. If you struggle with jinxing fears, you can address them using the strategies provided in this chapter, and you may also find it helpful to refer back to the section in Chapter 4 on jinxing and the strategies in Chapter 7 for improving your ability to deal with uncertainty.

Regardless of the specific safety behaviour, when you employ it and come out of a situation unharmed, you attribute the positive outcome to the safety behaviour itself, reinforcing its continued use. The major issue with this is that it prevents any acknowledgement and acceptance of how rarely such predicted and feared catastrophes actually occur. Over time, your confidence in your ability to cope diminishes, the range of safety behaviours expands, the desire to rely on them also increases, and with it your anxiety worsens. Here is a diagram illustrating another patient, Katie, who would only go out if accompanied by a friend.

As you can see from the diagram, Katie experiences temporary relief through her safety behaviour, which leads her to rely on it repeatedly. This creates a cycle of increasing anxiety and heightened avoidance, reinforcing her anxious thoughts and eroding her confidence. Can you relate to a similar

Katie thinks:
I can't go out on my own, I could pass out.

Having a friend there gives her temporary relief, but it reinforces and strengthens her belief that she is unsafe when alone.

Katie then feels:
I fear fainting in public, it's embarrassing and I'm concerned that nobody will help me.

Katie's safety behaviour:
I'll take my friend with me.

pattern in your own experience? This cycle continues to loop, causing a downward spiral where thoughts become more convincing and anxiety worsens. The thoughts gain a stronger grip on you, intensifying your desire for safety and leading you to engage in the safety behaviour again. This repetition further solidifies the cycle, perpetuating the pattern over and over again.

Before we move on to the strategies to deal with avoidance and safety behaviours, it is crucial to develop a thorough understanding of your own situation. This will pave the way for the practical section of our work. To facilitate this process, here are some questions for you to consider and reflect upon to gather more information about your safety behaviours.

TASK 31

Identify your safety behaviours

1. What safety behaviours do you rely on?
2. How many safety behaviours are you using?
3. For each safety behaviour, take note of what you think it appears to prevent or protect you from.
4. What are your fears regarding the potential consequences if you were to stop using these safety behaviours?
5. How long have you been using these safety behaviours?
6. Has your anxiety improved or worsened over the time period that you've been employing these safety behaviours?
7. What have you noticed about how you feel in the short term and the longer term when you use safety behaviours to cope with your anxiety?

Your short-term relief prevents your anxiety from ever reducing in the longer term. One of the best ways to deal with this is to face your fears.

Facing Your Fears

Facing your fears is about dropping safety behaviours and eliminating avoidance, enabling you to reclaim the freedom you once enjoyed, so you can pursue what truly matters to you. Healing comes from confronting the things you try to avoid, they hold the power to bring you forward on your journey to recovery.

I'm sure you must have come across the idea that confronting your fears is the key to overcoming them. While this holds true, it's important to acknowledge that facing your fears requires a thoughtful approach. It needs to be a gradual, well-planned, carefully executed and properly reviewed process, carried out with momentum. When you adopt this approach, you'll notice a natural reduction in your anxiety levels, and sometimes this can even happen at a rapid pace.

Facing your fears is a challenge, but one that you are now prepared for, thanks to the range of strategies you've acquired in the previous chapters. As you expose yourself to face your fears, it's normal to experience a temporary increase in anxiety. With the foundation of the strategies you've established and practised, including managing your nervous system stress, addressing anxious thoughts, directing your attention, managing uncertainty and coping with emotional distress, you are well prepared to navigate the initial challenging moments of facing your fears. These strategies have equipped you with the necessary tools to approach anxiety-provoking situations with confidence and resilience. By using these techniques, you'll be able to confront your fears and gradually diminish anxiety while fostering a sense of control and empowerment. By following the appropriate steps for facing your fears, you'll witness a decrease in anxiety, reduced feelings of uncertainty, and a transformation in your anxious thoughts. This natural decline in anxiety occurs as you persist in confronting your fears and letting go of avoidance and safety behaviours. Confronting your fears allows your mind to naturally re-evaluate and challenge the beliefs that contribute to your anxiety. By facing your fears, you gradually learn that the anticipated negative outcomes or threats are not as severe or likely as you once believed. This process helps to rewire your brain's response to anxiety, leading to a reduction in overall anxiety levels over time. In addition to that you gain a greater sense of control and mastery over the situations that once triggered anxiety. This newfound sense of control instils confidence and reduces the need for safety behaviours, as you realize that you are capable of managing and coping with challenges.

Confronting your fears goes beyond simply engaging in the feared activity. It also involves confronting the thoughts, images, emotions and physical sensations associated with that situation. Getting straight into exposing yourself to the fear without a structured approach can be overwhelming and ineffective. That's why I am here to provide you with a comprehensive self-help plan that will equip you with the necessary strategies to effectively face your fears, and navigate this process with confidence.

It is crucial that you understand the therapeutic value of confronting your fears without relying on avoidance and safety behaviours. The next diagram illustrates that while triggers may activate your anxiety, your reaction to these triggers is within your control. When you choose avoidance and safety behaviours, it perpetuates your suffering and maintains the cycle of anxiety. The path to freedom lies in moving forward and breaking free from this cycle. By consciously facing your fears and refraining from engaging in avoidance and safety behaviours, you empower yourself to overcome anxiety and make significant progress towards your goal.

Looking at this cycle, you can see that when anxiety emerges, it sets off a cascade of painful thoughts, emotions, mental images and physical sensations. These experiences can feel overwhelming, prompting the use of avoidance and safety behaviours as a way to cope. But relying on these strategies hinders your progress and perpetuates a cycle of distress. In contrast, when you actively confront your fears and bravely

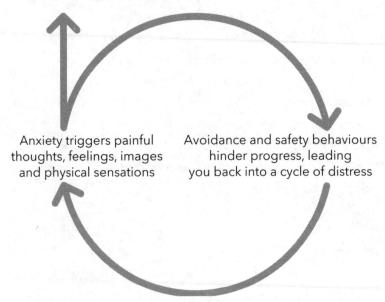

Facing your fears and
breaking free from the cycle of anxiety

Anxiety triggers painful
thoughts, feelings, images
and physical sensations

Avoidance and safety behaviours
hinder progress, leading
you back into a cycle of distress

face the situations or triggers that evoke anxiety, you disrupt
this cycle, and exit from it.

Now, let's move on to the process of how to face your
fears. Maintain a positive mindset, continue moving forward,
and have faith in your own inner strength and resilience. You
are fully capable of overcoming these challenges. You've got
this!

A Four-Step Approach to Facing your Fears

Having identified your avoidance and safety behaviours in
Tasks 30 and 31 (see pages 269 and 277), you can now follow
these four steps:

1. RANKING distress levels

2. FACING your fears

3. REVIEWING your progress

4. REPEATING the process with the next ranked behaviour

Now, you can follow the same approach as Nick by identifying and ranking your own avoidance and safety behaviours, selecting the easiest one to start with. Similar to Nick, you can then create a precise plan that breaks down the tasks into manageable steps. The table on page 284 illustrates

---

Patient Example: Nick's Journey with Facing Fears

Nick exhibited several behaviours related to his health anxiety, including avoiding doctor visits due to the fear of receiving a negative diagnosis (10/10), engaging in repetitive bodily checking (8/10), conducting excessive online research about diseases and illnesses (6/10), and seeking repeated and unnecessary reassurance from his girlfriend and parents about his well-being (4/10). We ranked both the avoidance and safety behaviours based on the distress they would cause if discontinued, assigning each behaviour a score out of ten (numbers added in brackets). We then approached these behaviours in order, from the least distressing to the most distressing.

To help Nick overcome his fears, we focused on addressing each behaviour individually, beginning with the easiest one. In this case, it was to stop seeking repeated unnecessary reassurance from others. We created a detailed plan to guide Nick in achieving this goal because simply stopping the behaviour outright was too challenging and ambiguous, lacking clear starting and ending points. Like Nick, when you follow the correct step-by-step plan you will witness your anxiety scale down repeatedly, and this experience helps the mind to automatically readjust its thinking patterns.

Nick's precise plan, where tasks were structured in a way that facilitated his progression. Throughout the process, Nick recorded his anxiety ratings, which helped him gauge the impact of his efforts. This step is crucial, as you should only proceed to the next task once your anxiety rating reaches a minimal level. If your anxiety does not decrease, it may be necessary to break down the task further or repeat it until your anxiety subsides.

1. Ranking distress levels

To assess your distress levels accurately, you will need to refer again to the insights gained from analysing your avoidance and safety behaviours in Tasks 30 and 31 (pages 269 and 277). This information plays a crucial role in determining your objectives, identifying the avoidance and safety behaviours that need addressing, and establishing their order of priority. If you are dealing with multiple avoidance or safety behaviours, which is a common experience for many individuals with anxiety, then address them individually, starting with the behaviour that is easiest to confront. Once you've identified the behaviour you are starting with, it's important to rate the level of belief you have in the necessity of carrying out that particular safety behaviour. This rating helps to assess the strength of your conviction and provides a baseline for measuring changes in belief as you progress through this process.

Let's take a closer look at Nick's example to highlight this process. Nick exhibited several avoidance and safety behaviours, which we ranked by assigning a distress score out of ten to each behaviour, with a score of 0 representing no distress and 10 indicating the highest level of distress. Next, we organized the behaviours in order of their distress level, from the most distressing to the least distressing. Nick needed to overcome each behaviour in a sequential manner, beginning with the easiest and gradually progressing to the most challenging. Here are the behaviours Nick displayed:

- Avoiding going to the doctor due to fear of receiving a physical health diagnosis (10/10).
- Engaging in repeated bodily checking (8/10).
- Conducting excessive internet research about diseases/illnesses (6/10).
- Seeking reassurance from girlfriend and parents regarding his well-being (4/10).

Nick's first target was the behaviour ranked lowest in terms of distress: *Stop seeking repeated unnecessary reassurance from others.* Nick's belief that he must engage in this behaviour for his safety was extremely high: he gave it a distress rating of 10/10.

2. Facing your fears

In this step I'd like you to create and follow a personalized plan for facing your fears. Like Nick, who had never faced his fears before and initially felt anxious, you can experience success by taking a gradual approach. Nick's plan demonstrates how tasks were carefully divided into manageable steps. By diligently confronting each task, Nick faced his fears head-on and achieved significant progress. Throughout the process, Nick rated his anxiety levels to assess the impact of his efforts. This rating system also ensured that he only proceeded to the next task once his anxiety reached a minimal level. If anxiety reduction wasn't evident, tasks were further broken down or repeated until anxiety subsided.

My plan to face my fear of letting go of unnecessary reassurance seeking	Anxiety rating before task (0–10, 0 being no anxiety)	Anxiety rating after task completion (0–10, 0 being no anxiety)
1: Limit reassurance seeking to only my girlfriend. Eliminating my parents from this. Do this for 3 days.	Day 1 – 10/10 Day 2 – 7/10 Day 3 – 4/10	Day 1 – 6/10 Day 2 – 3/10 Day 3 – 1/10
2: Limit reassurance seeking to twice daily with my girlfriend: morning and after work. Ask only one question each time. Do this for 3 days.	Day 1 – 7/10 Day 2 – 5/10 Day 3 – 3/10	Day 1 – 5/10 Day 2 – 2/10 Day 3 – 1/10
3: Ask my girlfriend one reassurance question per day, exclusively in the morning, for 3 days.	Day 1 – 6/10 Day 2 – 2/10 Day 3 – 1/10	Day 1 – 4/10 Day 2 – 3/10 Day 3 – 0/10
4: Ask my girlfriend one reassurance question every other morning before work if I need to. Stick to one question per session. Do this for 7 days.	Day 1 – 7/10 Day 2 – 6/10 Day 3 – 5/10 Day 4 – 5/10 Day 5 – 4/10 Day 6 – 2/10 Day 7 – 0/10	Day 1 – 5/10 Day 2 – 4/10 Day 3 – 4/10 Day 4 – 3/10 Day 5 – 2/10 Day 6 – 1/10 Day 7 – 0/10
5: Only seek reassurance from my girlfriend once a week, limiting it to one question per instance. Continue this practice for 14 days.	1/10	0/10
6: Stop seeking reassurance from my girlfriend about illness and diseases. Consult my doctor for any new concerns.	0/10	0/10

In creating your plan be sure to challenge yourself without overwhelming difficulty so you can achieve steady progress. Break down tasks into manageable steps, referring to Nick's plan for inspiration. Confront your fears by working through the tasks and continue until you see a significant reduction in anxiety. Rate your anxiety levels throughout the process to evaluate your progress. Adjust the plan if needed by breaking tasks down further or extending repetitions. Remember, this plan is tailored to your journey of overcoming safety behaviours and avoidance, so it is flexible to accommodate your needs and your rate of progress.

3. Review your progress

Take a moment to reflect on the process of facing your fears and evaluate your progress. This is an essential step in consolidating your experience and learning. It's important not to underestimate the value of this step as it allows your mind to embrace new perspectives and approaches to thinking and behaving. It's important to do this while the experience is still fresh in your mind, as this makes it much easier to get an accurate picture. Pay attention to what transpired during the process and how you felt throughout. Carefully consider your observations, emotions, and the changes you noticed. In this stage you should also re-rate the degree of belief in the necessity of carrying out the safety behaviour. Additionally, assess what aspects went well, what didn't go as planned, and the lessons you've learned. Identify any areas that require modification, repetition or further exploration. Here are some questions to help you review your progress:

Reviewing progress

1. What happened?
2. Were you able to complete the tasks you set out to?
3. Were you able to progress at a quicker rate than anticipated in your plan?
4. What has happened to the urge to engage in avoidance/safety behaviours as you've continued?
5. How have your beliefs about your ability to manage without depending on avoidance or safety behaviours changed?
6. What has happened to your overall anxiety?
7. Have you uncovered any threats or dangers?
8. Has your belief in any previously perceived threats reduced?
9. What have you learned about your ability to cope with these challenges, and how can you apply this knowledge to progress further?
10. How strongly do you now believe that you must engage in this behaviour for your safety?

Patient Example: Nick's Review of His Progress

1. **What happened?**
   As I went through the process, I noticed that the urge to seek reassurance became easier to resist. In the beginning, it was hard, but as I continued, the intensity of the urge reduced.

2. **Were you able to complete the tasks you set out to?**
   Yes, I was able to complete the tasks I set out to.

3. **Were you able to progress at a quicker rate than anticipated in your plan?**

Yes, it got easier as I repeated the tasks, I realized that my mind had fixated on excess reassurance as a helpful behaviour when, in reality, it wasn't necessary.

4. **What has happened to the urge to engage in avoidance/safety behaviours as you've continued?**
The urge to keep asking for reassurance was hard to resist in the beginning but the intensity really went down as I carried on. It got so much easier to not do it.

5. **How have your beliefs about your ability to manage without depending on avoidance or safety behaviours changed?**
I realized that my anxiety had led me to believe that I needed to engage in these behaviours for safety when, in reality, I can cope much better than I initially thought. I learned that seeking reassurance doesn't change the facts of my situation.

6. **What has happened to your overall anxiety?**
It's still there but it has definitely gone down. I don't have any anxiety about reassurance seeking, but I still need to work on the other things I avoid.

7. **Have you uncovered any threats or dangers?**
No I haven't. I can see that things really weren't as my anxiety led me to believe. I realized that my anxiety magnified my fears.

8. **Has your belief in any previously perceived threats reduced?**
Yes, I recognized that my anxiety magnified the significance of these threats, and through facing them without engaging in reassurance seeking, I realized they were not as relevant as I originally thought.

9. **What have you learned about your ability to cope with these challenges, and how can you apply this knowledge to progress further?**

I've discovered that I am much more capable of coping than I previously believed, despite what my anxiety led me to think. I can now see that not seeking reassurance didn't result in any negative outcomes. My mind became fixated on the idea that seeking reassurance was helpful when, in reality, it wasn't. I've also realized that I can handle situations without constantly seeking reassurance, as it doesn't change the facts of the situation. I need to remember that falling into the pattern of seeking reassurance, thinking it helps, can easily happen even though it doesn't provide lasting relief. Using this knowledge, I will try my best to be more mindful of my actions and their impact on my anxiety.

10. **How strongly do you now believe that you must engage in this behaviour for your safety?**

My belief that I must engage in reassurance seeking for my safety has significantly weakened; now I'd rate it as 0%.

Modifications in Nick's Approach

As Nick worked through his tasks, he gained momentum, resulting in some tasks being completed faster than initially planned. There were instances where Nick managed to accomplish two tasks in one go, because he felt able to do so without it being stressful for him. Adjustments to the plan were made based on Nick's reactions as he worked through it.

Just like Nick, it's important for you to maintain flexibility as you work through your own tasks. You may find that you can make modifications to your tasks as well. If you feel the urge to push yourself further, embrace that confidence and give it your all. Flexibility plays a crucial role in your journey, allowing you to make necessary adjustments and seize opportunities for growth. So, when you notice moments of confidence, harness their power and take full advantage of them.

If you were unable to complete the tasks you planned, it's important to take a moment to reflect on and review this too, so you can create a new, more effective plan. Start by considering why you were unable to complete the tasks and identify any obstacles you encountered along the way. Reflect on the reasons behind these challenges and consider what modifications, repetitions or further planning may be necessary. This could involve breaking the tasks down into smaller steps, increasing repetition, or adjusting the pace of your progress.

4. Repeat the process with the next ranked behaviours

Once you have successfully faced one fear from the list you created in Step 1, it's time to move on to the next ranked

---

Patient Example: Nick's Progress with His Other Ranked Behaviours

Once Nick successfully addressed reassurance seeking, he continued with a step-by-step plan to tackle his remaining three issues, prioritized based on their ranking. He first addressed his behaviour of conducting excessive internet research about diseases/illnesses. Then, he moved on to tackling his repeated bodily checking. Surprisingly, just three days after tackling his body checking, Nick took a bold step and made a doctor's appointment to confront his fear of avoiding medical visits. This accelerated progress of completing the doctor's visit sooner than planned demonstrated Nick's increased confidence as a result of the previous work he'd completed.

---

behaviour. Pace yourself and progress through the full list at a manageable speed to keep building your confidence.

As you progress with facing your fears, you'll notice a significant shift in how you perceive and approach the final, most frightening one. The completion of earlier tasks can naturally reduce overall anxiety, creating a cascading effect on the intensity of distress associated with the remaining fears. What once seemed daunting and overwhelming during the initial planning stage will now appear more achievable and manageable. Your perception of the most intense fear will have evolved through completing this full step-by-step process, allowing you to view it from a new perspective. While the idea of facing the final fear may still evoke some discomfort, it will no longer carry the same magnitude of distress as before you faced any of your other fears.

Facing fears for different anxiety problems

Recognizing the individuality of anxiety problems and avoidance and safety behaviours, it's crucial to personalize the 'facing your fears' approach. There is no one-size-fits-all plan that can be universally applied, even for people with the same anxiety problem. Each person's experience with health anxiety or social anxiety will involve unique avoidance and safety behaviours. Personalization is key, and tailoring the approach to your specific needs and challenges will give you the most effective results. To give you further insight into common safety behaviours associated with different anxiety problems, I have provided clinical examples. When developing a plan to address avoidance or safety behaviours for any of these anxiety problems, refer back to the four-step plan.

1. RANKING distress levels. Create a ranked list of fears and identify the least challenging behaviour to start with.
2. FACING your fears. Gradually face the feared situation or behaviour, step by step.
3. REVIEWING your progress. Reflect on your progress and the valuable lessons you have learned, while considering any adjustments that may be needed for you to continue.
4. REPEATING the process with the next ranked behaviour. Progress through your list of ranked fears, gradually confronting increasingly challenging ones as you repeat the process.

Health anxiety

We've already looked at the example of my patient Nick who suffered from health anxiety. Here are some other common avoidance and safety behaviours that I've targeted in my patients with health anxiety:

- Excessively googling or researching health, illness and disease.
- Excessive repeated self-monitoring using medical devices.
- Excessive body checking.
- Excessively asking for reassurance.
- Over-focusing on bodily sensations.
- Using a smartwatch to constantly self-monitor.
- Avoiding medical professionals, clinical environments, medical tests and test results.
- Having too many medical tests.

- Seeking too many medical opinions.
- Having someone with you all the time, in case of an emergency.

Ways to face these fears:
- Gradually reduce and eliminate excessive researching, self-monitoring, body checking and excessive reassurance seeking.
- Gradually expose yourself to clinical environments, for instance first driving past then walking past, waiting in the car park, entering the building then leaving, staying for longer time intervals, and finally building on these actions.
- Communicate honestly and openly with your doctor about the concerns you have about medical tests/ opinions, and also take guidance on the circumstances in which you should continue to use these.
- Gradually build up the periods of time you can be alone, from a few minutes up to a whole day, and so on.

Panic attacks

Panic attacks are characterized by sudden and intense waves of anxiety, accompanied by significant physical discomfort. The fear that a situation, sensation or thought may trigger another attack often perpetuates the cycle, causing people to become fearful of bodily sensations. This heightened state of physiological and emotional activation often leads to the development of avoidance and safety behaviours, which keep people trapped in an anxiety-maintaining cycle. Overcoming panic-related fears often involves directly experiencing the feared sensations and gradually exposing yourself to avoided situations. It requires staying in contact with deliberately induced sensations until the distress subsides. Below are some common avoidance and safety behaviours associated with panic attacks:

- Avoiding activities to prevent a racing heart and/or engaging in behaviours to maintain a normal heart rate and rhythm.
- Trying to stay in cool or cold environments to avoid discomfort.
- Avoiding certain movements due to fear of triggering sensations.
- Shying away from exercise out of fear of experiencing physical sensations.
- Avoiding situations that cause breathlessness.
- Avoiding specific places such as shopping centres, unfamiliar locations, public transport, cinemas, and busy or crowded areas.
- Restricting yourself to familiar places without venturing further.
- Avoiding small or enclosed spaces like lifts.

Ways to face these fears:
- Perform short bursts of running in place, gradually increasing the duration starting from 10 seconds.
- Allow yourself to be in a hot environment, such as sitting in a hot room, car, or bath, gradually increasing the duration.
- Practise gradual movements to learn to tolerate associated sensations, gradually increasing the duration of the movements.

- Engage in exercise for a short period and gradually extend the duration over time.

- Hold your breath for 15 seconds.

- Challenge yourself to breathe rapidly for 5 or 10 seconds, gradually increasing the duration up to 1 minute.

- Pinch your nostrils closed and breathe through your mouth, gradually increasing the duration.

- Gradually spend more time in places you typically avoid, starting with short durations and gradually increasing.

- Expose yourself to places or situations similar to where previous panic attacks have occurred, starting with brief periods and gradually extending the duration.

Social anxiety

Social anxiety revolves around the fear of negative judgement from others during interpersonal interactions and social situations. The common avoidance and safety behaviours I've noted in social anxiety include:

- Remaining quiet in front of others due to a fear of embarrassing yourself.

- Rehearsing every word before speaking.

- Avoiding engaging in small talk.

- Wearing headphones to discourage others from initiating conversation.

- Avoiding eye contact to evade imagined negative reactions.

- Being excessively self-focused, worrying about how you come across.
- Taking excessive time to respond to phone calls, messages or emails.

Ways to face these fears:
- Gradually start by saying something, beginning with simple sentences or asking basic questions, and progressively building up from there.
- Challenge yourself to spontaneously say something neutral in conversations.
- Practise brief greetings with people such as staff in shops or cafes. Ask them how they are, wish them a nice day, or inquire about the location of a specific product, and gradually expand on these interactions as appropriate.
- Gradually increase the duration of time without relying on safety behaviours like wearing headphones or avoiding eye contact.
- Gradually shift your focus outward, paying attention to external factors rather than constantly self-monitoring.
- Set limits for yourself, gradually reducing the time it takes to respond to messages or emails.

Death anxiety

Death anxiety is an extensive topic that warrants its own dedicated book! While I'm not able to do full justice to the topic of death anxiety here, I couldn't overlook its potential importance either. Death anxiety is deeply intertwined with existential concerns, which are often magnified in people with anxiety problems. People with health anxiety, in particular, can be significantly impacted by death anxiety. Their excessive worry about personal health or the well-being of their loved ones can be rooted in an underlying fear of death. Panic disorder also frequently involves a fear of dying, through say a heart attack. In Chapter 9 we will explore the connection between trauma and anxiety, including how experiences of loss, violence or life-threatening events can give rise to deep-seated fears about death, which can play a significant role in the broader landscape of anxiety problems.

For now, let's shift our focus back to the topic of avoidance and safety behaviours. As humans, whether consciously or unconsciously, we are inherently aware of the inevitability of our mortality, despite our tendency to avoid contemplating it. People who experience death anxiety often engage in avoidance and safety behaviours to shield themselves from thoughts of death, reminders of mortality and the possibility of dying. They may also avoid confronting triggers associated with death. Below are some common avoidance and safety behaviours associated with death anxiety:

- Avoiding contemplation of death.
- Steering clear of death-related themes in movies, TV shows, music and other forms of media.
- Shying away from thoughts, conversations or plans related to death.
- Avoiding attending funerals, visiting cemeteries, or encountering life insurance advertisements.
- Excessively fixating on imagined catastrophic scenarios tied to the impact of death on loved ones.

Ways to face these fears:

- Listen to songs that address the topic of death.
- Engage with fiction that explores themes of death and loss.
- Watch movies or TV shows that tackle the subject of death.
- Consider preparing a will, discuss the matter with acquaintances, and ultimately create a will.
- Gradually expose yourself to funeral homes and cemeteries during your travels.
- Reflect, discuss or write about your funeral preferences.
- Contemplate how loved ones or others you know have coped with bereavement.

The objective in these situations is to gradually reduce avoidance. Some of the suggestions I've listed may trigger discomfort, including the mere mention of death. Confronting death anxiety and its associated avoidance can be challenging. Some individuals I have worked with have experienced traumatic losses or events linked to death. The complex trauma resulting from such tragic experiences can give rise to a more intricate manifestation of death anxiety, wherein those death-related traumas and fears hold significant influence over the present. In these cases, the anxiety can be more effectively solved by treating the original trauma. If this resonates with you, I encourage you to seek the help of a qualified and experienced professional who can help you work through your death anxiety. Please refer to page 364, where I provide details on how to find the appropriate support. If you have experienced trauma that significantly contributes to your anxiety, Chapter 9 will provide valuable self-help strategies for coping with this impact.

Obstacles and Solutions

If you're experiencing difficulties and feel stuck in the process of facing your fears, it's important to recognize that there's usually a valid reason behind this. Understanding and addressing these stumbling blocks can help you overcome them, so you can go on to make progress. Here are some common challenges that you might encounter along the way, along with practical tips to help you navigate through each of them.

'I'm too anxious to get started'

Facing the things that trigger your anxiety, especially the ones that deeply terrify you, can be challenging. It's important to remember that you are not required to do it all at once. Working gradually is not only acceptable but recommended. If you find yourself overwhelmed and unable to start, it's perfectly okay to make your starting point more manageable and gradually build up from there. For instance, let's say you're struggling with social anxiety and find it challenging to speak in front of others or engage in small talk. A great way to start is by practising saying one or two short phrases or asking simple questions. If you're more at ease interacting with people you don't know as well, it can be a good idea to practise making small talk with an assistant in a shop, or the person who takes your coffee order. You can then gradually build from there. Once you start feeling more at ease, you can progress to speaking in front of a small and supportive group of friends or colleagues. As your confidence grows, you can then expand to larger audiences and ask more questions, working up to sharing more of your thoughts and ideas. You can also use your imagination to boost your confidence: take some time to imagine yourself speaking confidently and think about what you want to say in the comfort of your own home, or in front of a mirror. It's normal to feel some anxiety when you're just starting out, but it shouldn't be so overwhelming that it holds you back from getting started; if it does then break things down further. If you're still unsure about getting started, I recommend going back to Chapter 6 and practising the strategies shared there to better manage your distress before moving forward. Once you feel more prepared to deal with your fears, you can gradually face them and expand your comfort zone.

'I can't handle the anxious thoughts that arise when I confront my fears.'

It's completely normal to experience troubling thoughts and images when you're facing your worst fears. This is to be expected: you're facing your worst fears, so why would you not? After all, why wouldn't they surface? During these tasks, it's important to understand that a state of calm and ease may not be realistic and nor is it expected. It's natural for these situations to evoke feelings of discomfort and anxiety. Accept your distress and ride it out; what's the worst that will happen? If you find yourself experiencing these kinds of thoughts during the process of facing your fears, you can revisit the worst-case scenario exercise we discussed in Chapter 4 (see Task 15, page 149). Additionally, recall the work you've done on acceptance and consider reviewing those concepts too if needed. Remind yourself why you picked up this book in the first place: to become ten times calmer. You want to overcome your anxiety problems so that you can reclaim a meaningful life. Temporary distress is a small price to pay as you work through these challenges. Embrace the discomfort, knowing that it is a necessary part of your journey towards greater calm and a fulfilling life. You can also refer back to Chapter 6 How Can I Manage My Intense Emotions? (page 195). There you will find strategies to help you regulate your emotions as you go through this journey of facing your fears.

'I don't know if it's working, and if I should carry on'

This reservation is why it is very important that you review your progress as you work through your tasks by rating your level of anxiety. Your mind needs to be able to see this progress. Take a step back and re-evaluate your progress. If you haven't recorded any ratings, reviewed and reflected on your progress as shown in stage 3 (see page 285), then try a new or alternative task, ensuring that you measure as you go, noting your anxiety ratings before and after each task, and be sure to work through the stage properly.

It is also vital that you make your tasks long enough and frequent enough. Once in a while is not enough: you really need to be as frequent as you can and stick with the same task until the level of anxiety it causes has dropped significantly. If you face your fears in a more cursory way, it won't have the desired effect, and additionally brief periods of facing your fear are actually a form of avoidance, reinforcing your mind's belief that it's too scary and should be avoided.

A last important note: facing your fears only works if you do it *without using any safety behaviours*. If you use safety behaviours while trying to face your fears, you're not actually facing your fears, you're just reinforcing your anxiety. Again, if you feel that you simply can't face your fears unless you have safety behaviour, then you need to look at breaking your task down even further.

> ### Ten Key Takeaways for Facing Your Fears
>
> 1. Recognize that avoidance involves consciously avoiding situations, activities or thoughts that trigger anxiety, and that this behaviour perpetuates the underlying anxiety problem.
>
> 2. Recognize that safety behaviours are actions taken to feel safer from feared consequences, and that these are subtle forms of avoidance.
>
> 3. Keep in mind that avoiding or escaping situations, thoughts, images or triggers associated with your fears worsens your anxiety problems.
>
> 4. Understand that avoidance and safety behaviours are used to prevent or minimize worst-case scenarios from occurring, and to gain a sense of control over the distress level being experienced.
>
> 5. Work on addressing avoidance and safety behaviours to overcome anxiety problems, by consistently embracing the process of facing your fears.
>
> 6. When you avoid facing your fears, they become stronger. Embrace acceptance of the situation rather than persistently avoiding it, as fighting the situation through avoidance worsens anxiety problems.
>
> 7. Fully face your fears to experience a natural reduction in anxiety and to train your mind to accurately appraise danger.
>
> 8. Implement the structured four-step plan for facing your fears. Develop a clear and predictable strategy that details each step to gradually confront your fears. Repeat the

process regularly to build resilience and progress towards overcoming anxiety.

9. Approach facing your fears with flexibility, adapting and adjusting the required actions to maintain a balance between challenge and achievability.

10. Apply the structured four-step plan to address various anxiety problems such as general anxiety, health anxiety, social anxiety and panic.

 Stimulate your senses!

Engaging your sensory system can help reduce anxiety by grounding you in the present moment, shifting your attention away from anxiety. Your senses connect you to your external world, placing you firmly in the here and now, away from anxious thoughts that might be pulling you into future uncertainty. For double the benefit you can find sensory activities that are also pleasurable to you: these can release feel-good neurotransmitters like dopamine, reducing anxiety and boosting mood. Here are some ideas to stimulate your senses: use a kaleidoscope, appreciate art or nature, listen to the sound of rain falling or birds chirping, play with play dough or clay for touch, use fidget gadgets, enjoy a massage, try popping candy for taste, smell herbs or scented candles, the list goes on! Can you think of any others that you might find appealing?

Chapter 9:
How Can I Manage Anxiety Related to Trauma?

We already know that the causes of anxiety problems are wide-ranging. In this chapter we'll take a look at trauma and post-traumatic stress disorder (PTSD), so we can understand more about the nature of both of these. Importantly, we'll look at the relationship between trauma and anxiety, with a focus on the different types of anxiety problems. Your commitment to reading this book and taking steps to heal yourself is a tremendous display of strength. Be proud of your resilience in surviving what you have experienced and seeking ways to heal. Your dedication is truly admirable. In this chapter, I will guide you through various self-help strategies that can help you in soothing and calming a traumatized nervous system.

Imagine your brain as a sturdy boat and trauma as a tumultuous storm at sea. Just as a fierce storm can toss and jostle a boat off course, trauma can disrupt the delicate equilibrium in your brain. After weathering the storm, the boat needs time to regain stability and find its bearings again. It may require attention, care, improvements to its sails and any holes or leaks must be fixed to restore its sturdiness, solidity and strength. Similarly, after experiencing trauma, your brain needs time and support to restore balance. Like guiding a boat back to calm waters, you can offer yourself patience, kindness, compassion and self-care to navigate through the turbulence of trauma and rediscover inner peace. By doing so, you can help your mind and body realign and get back on course. Taking the time to soothe and care for yourself, as well as reaching out to loved ones or professionals if necessary, can all help your brain find its way back to a place of stability and calm. With time and care, your brain can regain its strength, and just like the boat, set sail again.

Please note: The information provided in this chapter is not intended for diagnostic purposes. If you suspect you may have PTSD, it is recommended that you consult a doctor to explore this further. Only a licensed professional can officially diagnose PTSD and guide you towards effective treatment. For additional support and resources related to trauma and PTSD, please refer to the information provided on page 392.

Trauma or PTSD?

Trauma and post-traumatic stress disorder (PTSD) are not the same. Trauma is an emotional response to a painful event or experience. Trauma is not an official diagnostic label, whereas PTSD is. PTSD is a mental health disorder resulting from the direct experience of major trauma or witnessing a major trauma. PTSD develops after a traumatic event, but not all traumatic events result in PTSD. Following a traumatic event, some people will develop symptoms that meet the criteria for a diagnosis of PTSD. Other individuals will have symptoms of trauma, while others may have symptoms that subside and fade away. PTSD typically creates significant and persistent distress, significantly affecting various aspects of a person's life and functioning. In contrast, the impact of trauma can be less pervasive and may not cause the same level of ongoing impairment.

Trauma

Trauma is an emotional response to a painful event or experience. Trauma is not an official clinical diagnosis, but a way to describe this emotional response. Traumatic experiences are a common part of human existence, and it is rare to find someone who has not encountered some form of trauma in their life. We all fall on a spectrum of suffering, with varying degrees of frequency and intensity. For some people, their families may have unintentionally or intentionally contributed to their challenges. Others may have had families who were unable or unwilling to offer support during difficult times. Even those with supportive and loving families may have experienced things going wrong sometimes. In adult life some people are estranged from their families due to the experiences they've had. Throughout life, most of us encounter universal experiences such as disappointment, hurt, rejection, humiliation, failure, conflict, fear, and even terror.

There is a prevailing hypothesis that attributes all trauma to childhood experiences, and some therapists may place blame solely on parents for such trauma. I advise caution regarding this viewpoint as it is not only flawed but can also be potentially harmful. It is important to recognize that not all trauma is linked to childhood or parental factors. While it is true that childhood experiences can contribute to trauma, we must also acknowledge the experiences of individuals who had positive childhoods but still go on to face trauma or anxiety in adulthood. It is crucial to adopt a comprehensive perspective that considers the diverse origins and complexities of traumatic experiences beyond childhood and parental influence.

One person may experience something as traumatic, but another person may not experience that same thing as traumatic.

This difference can be related to many factors such as temperament, personality, resilience, social support, nervous system function, among many others. Traumatic experiences can leave people with a significant sense of uncertainty and feelings of powerlessness. It doesn't matter whether it's a major event or a small event, what matters is the impact it's had on you.

Trauma really comes down to your personal experience of distress relating to what has happened to you. It doesn't make the impact on you any less if the next person seems unaffected by the same type of event. This is not how trauma works: you have different bodies and different minds, so you will react differently. Please don't be hard on yourself if you feel as if you should be able to cope and can't, or haven't been able to. As you read through this chapter you'll learn more about how you can cope, and there are lots of things you can do to soothe your nervous system's experience of trauma.

> *It doesn't matter whether it's a major event or a small event, what matters is the impact it's had on you.*

PTSD

As stated, PTSD is a mental health disorder resulting from the direct experience of major trauma or witnessing a major trauma. Major traumas characterized by PTSD can include exposure to death, serious injury/harm or another extreme threat to your physical integrity. Situations that are considered to have a serious threat to existence and integrity can include sexual abuse, being the victim of serious crime, violence, accidents or health-related incidents, being in war zones, experiencing natural disasters, and exposure to any of these situations through emergency crisis work. There are of course others; this is just to give you a broad idea. Symptoms of PTSD include the following:

- Recurrent, involuntary, intrusive thoughts and memories of the event.
- Re-experiencing the event through flashbacks or recurrent nightmares.
- Sleep disturbance.
- Hyper-vigilance and hyper-arousal.
- Feelings of detachment and numbing.
- Avoidance.
- Changes in perception.
- Dissociative reactions.
- Intense or prolonged psychological distress at exposure to internal or external cues that relate to aspects of the traumatic event.
- Marked physiological reactions to internal or external cues that relate to aspects of the traumatic event.
- Persistent and exaggerated negative beliefs or expectations about oneself, others or the world.
- Irritability and/or anger without provocation.
- Recklessness.
- An exaggerated startle response.
- Problems with concentration
- Persistent inability to experience positive emotions.

The Relationship between Trauma and Anxiety

The impact of exposure to traumatic events on all aspects of mental health are well known, with studies confirming the existence of anxiety symptoms in those exposed to traumatic experiences.[12] Childhood adversity is one cause of trauma, but it isn't the only source of trauma that can lead to the development of anxiety problems. Trauma can occur at any age, and even though much of the research focuses on adverse experiences of childhood, there are many experiences in adult life that can influence the onset of anxiety problems. I've seen countless patients with anxiety problems whose anxiety developed after experiencing childhood trauma. I've also seen countless patients with anxiety problems whose anxiety developed after undergoing trauma in adulthood.

Childhood adversity is strongly linked to the development of various mental health issues, including anxiety disorders. The term 'childhood adversity' encompasses a wide range of negative experiences during childhood, including poverty, low socioeconomic status, family conflict, domestic violence, parental instability, neglect, maltreatment, and tragic loss, among others. Research indicates that adverse childhood environments are associated with heightened physiological reactivity, commonly referred to as stress reactivity.[13] Stress reactivity refers to a person's physiological and psychological response to stressors or challenging situations. It involves the body's adaptive mechanisms, such as changes in heart rate, blood pressure, hormone levels and emotional responses, in order to cope with and manage the perceived stress. High stress reactivity implies a more intense and sensitive response to stressors, while low stress reactivity suggests a less pronounced response. Note that not all individuals who have experienced trauma develop problems with stress reactivity, or indeed anxiety problems.

Many of the studies on contributors to stress reactivity in childhood have focused on the relatively severe experiences of adversity. The extent to which only severe adverse events, such as abuse, contribute to changes in stress reactivity remains uncertain. Making premature assumptions in this regard is unwarranted due to the current limited understanding and lack of comprehensive knowledge in this field. Similarly, the specific aspects of childhood environments that contribute to maladaptive stress reactivity are also not well understood, and further research is needed.

Maladaptive stress reactivity is characterized by an exaggerated, prolonged or unhelpful reaction to stress that is not adaptive or beneficial in managing the stressful situation. This can manifest as excessive anxiety, heightened physiological activation, impaired coping skills, difficulty in regulating emotions, and an inability to effectively adapt to and recover from stressful events. Maladaptive stress reactivity can increase the risk of mental health problems including anxiety. While further research is needed to fully understand this view, one possible explanation cited for this increase is the impact on the developing stress response system.[14] As discussed in Chapter 3, the stress response system is your body's innate 'fear alarm'. Traumatic experiences can disrupt child development, potentially affecting the proper development of the stress response system. If this is the case, then the stress response may not function as optimally as it should.

Let's move on to explore clinical examples of anxiety problems and their connections to trauma.

Patient Example: Katie's Generalized Anxiety

Katie struggled with both generalized anxiety and health anxiety. Her parents had demanding schedules, often working long hours, which left Katie to manage on her own for extended periods, though not overnight. Even when her parents were present at home, Katie was left to handle things on her own, with her parents giving her too much responsibility at a young age. This overwhelming sense of responsibility made Katie believe that she had to cope with her problems alone and that everything rested on her shoulders. It was undoubtedly a difficult experience for her as a child. Katie rarely shared her problems or worries with her parents, and nor did she confide in others. She internalized her concerns, becoming a chronic worrier. Katie's worries would shift from one thing to the next: comments people made, her work, being on time, her family, her partner, money, world events, her health, other people's health, the list went on. Whenever one worry seemed to subside, another quickly emerged. Katie's core beliefs, influenced by her childhood experiences, revolved around vulnerability, the constant possibility of things going wrong, and the fear of being at fault if something bad were to happen.

Katie's example demonstrates the impact of childhood neglect on the development of generalized anxiety. On the other hand, Laura's case demonstrates how generalized anxiety can emerge from experiencing trauma in adulthood. As well as childhood causes there are a wide range of traumatic experiences in adulthood can trigger generalized anxiety. These can include experiencing an assault, natural disasters, accidents or witnessing violence. Turbulent relationships, difficult breakups or divorces and the loss of a loved one can also cause profound emotional distress and contribute to generalized anxiety. Job loss, financial instability and ongoing work-related stress can generate chronic worry and anxiety. Additionally, significant life events that introduce uncertainties and pressures can contribute to heightened anxiety levels.

Patient Example: Laura's Generalized Anxiety

Laura developed generalized anxiety as a result of multiple stressful life events. Firstly, she experienced a sudden job loss due to the company downsizing, leaving her uncertain about her financial stability and future career prospects. Shortly after, her long-term relationship ended, adding emotional distress and a sense of loss. Laura then had to relocate to a new city, leaving behind her established social support network and familiar surroundings. Understandably, these events were a lot for Laura to handle all at once, overwhelming her usual ways of coping. They disrupted her sense of stability, security and familiarity, significantly impacting her daily functioning, mental health and overall quality of life. Laura's generalized anxiety manifested as constant worrying about life, finances, job prospects and finding happiness in a new relationship. This worry extended to everyday tasks as well, including work responsibilities, time management, getting enough sleep and so on.

Patient Example: Jack's Health Anxiety

I met Jack when he was in his early thirties. Growing up, Jack was surrounded by numerous health problems within his family. His father battled with serious and chronic health issues, and Jack had experienced the loss of his grandparents due to illness. Of course, it is important to note that these circumstances were beyond anyone's control, including Jack's.

The trauma of witnessing a parent in a vulnerable and uncertain state shaped Jack's perception of his own body's integrity and safety. Over time, this developed into a fear of acquiring specific illnesses and diseases. Jack's sensitivity to bodily sensations was heightened, leading him to extensively monitor and match up any experiences with online disease criteria. Jack's health anxiety was influenced by his traumatic experiences, leading to the development of specific beliefs related to safety, security and stability. As a result, Jack held firm convictions that he was in constant danger, that threats lurked everywhere, and that he was destined for harm.

Patient Example: Polly's Health Anxiety

Polly's health anxiety was influenced by her mother's own struggles with the condition. Her mother's health anxiety extended to Polly and her siblings, leading to repeated checks on their well-being. Polly's mother had two overwhelming fears: the fear of dying and leaving her children to struggle, and the fear of any one of her children experiencing illness or death. Polly shared that her mother would often become emotionally erratic and 'freak out' at even minor signs of illness. Although I had never personally met Polly's mother, learning about the depth of her concern for her children evoked a profound sense of compassion within me. The intensity of her love and worry for her family resonated deeply, highlighting the universal instinct of parents to protect and nurture their children. As a result of her experiences, Polly internalized a belief that she was fragile, viewing her own body as delicate and susceptible to illness or harm. Polly saw the world as a dangerous place, harbouring a general sense of apprehension and hyper-vigilance towards potential risks and dangers. This led to a constant need for monitoring her own health and the health of her partner and pets.

Perhaps you find yourself in a similar situation to Polly's mother. If that's the case, please know that you're not alone. It's quite common for parents and caregivers of any gender to experience health anxiety in relation to their children. Now, you might be concerned about whether your own worries and behaviours could potentially traumatize your family, just like Polly's experiences with her mother. It's completely understandable to have this anxiety, and I want to address this directly. In fact, I chose to discuss Polly's situation as an example because I recognize how many people share these worries. It's true that our behaviour as caregivers can have an impact on our children. They absorb so much from what they observe in us. However, the fact that you're here, reading this book and seeking ways to address and work on yourself, speaks volumes. By taking steps to feel calmer and improve your own well-being, you are creating a positive ripple effect that can benefit your family as well.

You might be wondering what happened to Polly and whether her story proves that parents can irreparably damage their children, causing lifelong anxiety. I want to assure you that it's not true. I have witnessed countless instances of change and transformation. Following appropriate treatment, Polly experienced a significant improvement in her anxiety problems. She gained insight into the root causes of her anxiety, particularly the influence of her mother's behaviour. Learning coping strategies to manage her worries and developing a healthier perspective on safety and risk played a crucial role in her progress. Over time, Polly's anxiety decreased, and she developed a sense of confidence in her ability to handle life's challenges. Polly's case serves as a powerful example of how we can process and heal from past traumas and embrace a more balanced and fulfilling life.

As you make progress in your own journey, if that includes being a parent, you can encourage your children to take healthy age-appropriate risks, and you can talk to them about anxiety. If they ask questions you can answer them and provide them with understanding. You can introduce them to some of your own self-help skills, be that breathing or mindfulness Explaining to them how it works and why it helps can be incredibly valuable. Within the strategies you're learning in this book, there are countless ways for you to support yourself with your anxieties, and you're equipping yourself with the tools and resources necessary to be a more present and balanced caregiver. What's more, each of these strategies can also be expanded upon in support of that role. By nurturing your own growth, you're not only benefiting yourself, you're creating a positive ripple effect that extends to the well-being of your family too.

Patient Example: Amy's Health Anxiety

Amy's encounter with trauma occurred in adulthood, disrupting her previously anxiety-free existence. It all began when she received a misdiagnosis of thyroid cancer, sending her on an emotional roller-coaster ride. The confirmation of the diagnosis initially forced Amy to confront the frightening nature of her own mortality. She embarked on treatment for thyroid cancer, a condition that is typically curable. But then, the unimaginable happened – Amy was informed that a grave error had been made with her diagnosis. While encounters with misdiagnosis like Amy's are thankfully very rare in my clinical experience, they do occur on occasion. In the aftermath of this traumatizing experience, Amy became consumed by health-related preoccupations. She engaged in repetitive body checks and expended considerable financial resources on private medical consultations in a relentless pursuit to eliminate any possibility of illness. Amy's anxiety symptoms persisted for several years until the trauma stemming from the misdiagnosis was addressed and treated. It is a testament to the resilience of people like Amy that they can navigate through such challenges and find a path towards healing and recovery.

The patient case examples I've provided here show how the traumatic events Jack and Polly experienced in their childhood led to the development of health anxiety. In contrast, Amy developed health anxiety as a result of a traumatic event in her adult life. Aside from the examples given, it's important to note that there is a wide range of traumatic experiences in adulthood that can contribute to the development of health anxiety. Based on my clinical experience, these experiences have included going through a health crisis personally or witnessing someone close dealing with one. Additionally, the sudden loss of a loved one, whether due to illness or other causes, can generate anxiety surrounding health and mortality, leading to heightened health concerns. Being involved in a traumatic accident or experiencing an injury can intensify awareness of physical vulnerability and potential health risks. Exposure to a major public health scare, such as a pandemic, either directly experiencing it or closely following a significant health scare in another part of the world, can be traumatic and instill fear and anxiety about personal health and safety. Managing chronic or ongoing health conditions that require frequent medical attention or treatment can be traumatic too, contributing to health anxiety. The constant focus on health and medical care can amplify concerns about potential additional health problems. Lastly, being a victim of or witnessing medical errors or malpractice can diminish trust in healthcare systems and professionals, leading to heightened health anxiety.

Patient Example: Josh's Social Anxiety

To illustrate how trauma can contribute to social anxiety, let me share the story of my patient, Josh. During his school years, Josh endured horrible and relentless bullying. A so-called 'friend' would oscillate between treating Josh well and treating him terribly. This bully also encouraged others in their group to join in the torment, engaging in name-calling, hitting, spitting, tripping, and making him eat things he didn't want to. They even mocked Josh's voice and actions. Naturally, this constant abuse made Josh excessively self-conscious, never wanting to do or say the wrong thing in case it led to more bullying. Josh did his best to blend in, desperately trying to avoid drawing attention to himself. These traumatic experiences led Josh to develop a deep-seated belief that he was inherently flawed, unworthy, and incapable of being accepted by others, no matter what he did. As the years went by, Josh became increasingly socially anxious. In his adult life he'd become accustomed to not speaking around others to avoid saying anything wrong. This affected not only his social life, but also his relationships, and hampered the career he wanted.

Patient Example: Emily's Social Anxiety

Emily, who described herself as a careful person, had never experienced social anxiety until a specific incident at work. She was tasked with delivering an important and high-stakes presentation to a large audience, but encountered several technical difficulties. The slides became disorganized, the microphone malfunctioned and her anxiety heightened in that moment. She stumbled over her words, eventually breaking down in tears and hastily leaving the stage in front of everyone. The profound sense of embarrassment and humiliation she felt had a significant impact on her. Emily became consumed by the fear of being judged by others, replaying the incident in her mind and constantly worrying that she would be seen as incompetent. Her confidence was shattered and self-consciousness overwhelmed her, causing her to doubt her abilities and anticipate similar future failures or embarrassments. As a result, Emily began actively avoiding public speaking engagements and declining invitations to all professional events. She withdrew from social gatherings, isolating herself due to the fear of judgement and the possibility of experiencing further humiliation.

Persistent bullying, emotional abuse and humiliation can have a significant impact on self-esteem, heightening the risk of developing social anxiety, as demonstrated in Josh's example. Similarly, traumatic experiences in adulthood, such as Emily's, can serve as triggers for social anxiety. From my clinical practice, I have observed additional causes of social anxiety resulting from traumatic events in adulthood, including embarrassing public incidents, social mishaps, perceived failures in performance, high conflict interactions, workplace harassment, discrimination or enduring hostile environments. Regardless of the specific trigger, such experiences can lead individuals to develop beliefs about their own inadequacy, incapability, and lack of worthiness. They live in constant fear of negative judgement from others, perpetuating their social anxiety and hindering their ability to fully engage in social situations.

Patient Example: Zane's Panic Attacks

I have encountered numerous patients who have found their first panic attack to be a deeply traumatic experience. Zane is one of these patients. Prior to his first panic attack, he had never experienced anxiety or panic. Zane's first panic attack occurred during a boat trip while on holiday with his friends. They rented a small boat to sail around an island, but at one point, the boat stopped at some distance from the shore, which made it difficult to return quickly. As Zane, who was not a strong swimmer, contemplated being stranded on the boat, a sudden rush of fear overcame him. Compounding this, it was a scorching hot day, and Zane had consumed energy drinks to stay alert due to a late night. This overload of caffeine led to a jittery sensation in his body. Since Zane had never experienced a panic attack before, he had no idea what was happening to him when he began to feel 'weird'. His heart raced, he became irritable, struggled to breathe, and was convinced that he was on the verge of dying on the boat. He believed that if he were to pass out, there would be no way for an ambulance to reach him. Zane's friends quickly brought him back to the hotel to see a doctor, and by the time they arrived the panic attack had subsided. Zane eventually learned that what he had experienced that day was a panic attack. He shared with me that his life changed on that very day, and he hadn't felt the same since. In an effort to avoid triggering similar sensations and experiences, Zane made significant changes to his lifestyle. He completely eliminated all caffeine-based products from his diet and actively avoided specific situations and places that triggered anxiety or reminded him of the panic attack. Additionally, he became cautious about engaging in physical activities that could evoke sensations similar to those experienced during the panic attack, as they would provoke anxiety and fear of another episode occurring. The physical distress during the panic attack was truly overwhelming, but what made the experience even more traumatic for Zane was the profound and helpless belief, in that moment, that he was on the verge of dying with no hope of rescue.

Patient Example: Emma's Panic Attacks

Another example illustrating how panic attacks can be traumatizing is the case of my patient, Emma. Emma had attended a special work event in an unfamiliar city and was returning home by train. The train was packed with people, and although Emma had a seat, the aisles and doorways were crowded. Unexpectedly, the train came to a halt in the middle of nowhere. Initially, Emma didn't think much of it, but as the minutes passed without any movement, she started to worry. An announcement explained that there was a signal problem causing the delay, but the duration of the delay was unknown. The train remained stationary for nearly an hour. During this time, Emma began to feel hot, then noticed her heart racing. A sense of dread washed over her, intensifying her already rapid heartbeat. She felt a strong conviction that she was unwell, and on the brink of collapsing. She felt trapped and helpless, unable to get help due to the train's overcrowding, its remote location in the middle of nowhere and her inability to exit from it. Emma's breathing became rapid, her body trembled and tears welled up in her eyes, all while she desperately tried to hide these reactions from her fellow passengers, fearing the embarrassment it would bring. After what felt like an eternity, the train finally resumed its journey. Emma described the remainder of the trip as nothing short of 'torture,' but she felt a great sense of relief and comfort wash over her as she stepped off the train and made her way home. Emma consulted her GP, who recognized her symptoms as a panic attack and prescribed medication for future use in case of a recurrence. Although apprehensive about the possibility of another attack, Emma remained fine until one evening when she was lying in bed and her heart started to pound again in exactly the same way. It felt as if she were reliving the initial attack, which triggered yet another panic episode. Emma developed a strong aversion to sensations in her body, particularly those that were reminiscent of the panic. Emma would avoid all situations and places where there could be any possibility of sensations being re-experienced.

Zane and Emma's case examples illustrate how panic attacks in adulthood can serve as traumatic triggers. Now, let's look at a different patient case where panic attacks arose as a consequence of traumatic childhood experiences.

Patient Example: David's Panic Attacks

David developed panic disorder due to traumatic experiences in his childhood. These significantly influenced his perception of physical sensations. Growing up in a conflict-ridden household kept David constantly on edge, never knowing what to expect. This constant state of hyper-vigilance extended from his surroundings to his own body and the physical sensations he experienced. He would meticulously monitor sounds and behaviours in his environment and certain sounds would evoke familiar bodily sensations that reminded him of the intense conflicts. It was as if these sensations acted as a distress signal, triggering a sense of 'It's happening again.' Consequently, David became hyper-aware of any changes in his body, often panicking in anticipation of conflict, whether it occurred or not. Sometimes, these episodes resulted in panic attacks. As an adult, David remained hyper-aware of the slightest bodily sensations. He perceived these sensations as potential threats, triggering recurrent panic attacks. The traumatic events from his past had rewired his brain to interpret physical sensations as dangerous and catastrophic. Any alteration in heart rate, breathing pattern, or bodily sensation would throw him into a state of panic.

Trauma and death anxiety

The concept of death is universally unsettling, and it can be argued that anxiety about death is a shared experience that affects all of us to varying degrees at different points in our lives. For some people, death anxiety becomes a severe and intrusive problem that significantly impacts their daily life, and in some cases it can be traced back to a traumatic event. Traumatic experiences related to death or dying can occur during early life, childhood, or even in adulthood. Many people have faced tragic circumstances that have deeply traumatized them, leading to a constant preoccupation with the fragility of life, their own existence, and the well-being of their loved ones.

Clinical examples of death anxiety induced by trauma or post-traumatic stress disorder (PTSD) encompass a wide range of experiences. These examples serve as a glimpse into the multitude of connections between death anxiety and trauma. They can include the sudden and unexpected loss of a parent or loved one, witnessing someone's death, experiencing a serious illness, being affected by a violent act, and numerous other distressing events. Losing a loved one under ordinary circumstances already highlights the vulnerability of our own existence, but when coupled with a traumatic event, the impact intensifies. Not only does it heighten our awareness of the preciousness of life, but the trauma itself can create intense experiences of uncertainty.

In my clinical practice, many people developed death anxiety following the sudden loss of a family member. In some cases, the cause of death was an unexpected diagnosis or health problem, often accompanied by a rapid deterioration in health. Other patients I have worked with had pre-existing health conditions that traumatized them, leading to a visceral realization of mortality. Even when these conditions were not life-threatening, they were enough to shake the foundation of their existence and raise questions about the certainty of life as they once knew it. Even after recovering fully from their health issues, the death anxiety persisted because the trauma of the experience had left an indelible mark on them. Life took on a different meaning for them.

Trauma-related cognitions

Cognitions are thoughts that encompass experience, knowledge, perception, judgement and memory. Through the examples I've provided, we can see how traumatic experiences contribute to the development of anxiety problems. One common factor among these experiences is the presence of underlying cognitions. Those who have experienced trauma often develop specific beliefs, coming away from the traumatic situation thinking in a very particular way, and often these beliefs are self-directed. These beliefs are shaped by the experience itself, the knowledge acquired (whether accurate or not), the judgements made, the impact on perception, and the consolidation of all this into memory. When working with patients to resolve trauma-induced anxiety problems it's important to recognize the beliefs they've come to hold because of what's happened to them. The next image shows some common examples of cognitions that can arise from traumatic experiences.

We now have a good understanding of how traumatic experiences can impact anxiety, and how trauma disrupts the functioning of our nervous system, leading to fear and anxiety. There are various practices you can incorporate into your life to help your body and mind feel safe, thereby soothing your nervous system. Let's delve into those strategies next and explore how they can bring about positive change for you.

The experience I've had has left me believing . . .

I can't trust others

I don't have choices

I am weak

I can't trust myself

I can't handle it

I am a failure

I can't succeed

I am damaged

I am helpless

I am powerless

I am a disappointment

I am not in control

I am odd

I am not safe

I am worthless

I am in danger

I am not good enough

Soothing a Traumatized Nervous System

When individuals have experienced trauma, they can often become triggered by intrusive images, unwanted memories, flashbacks and overwhelming emotions. A crucial aspect of trauma treatment involves learning strategies to manage this heightened activation and soothe a traumatized nervous system. These self-calming techniques have the ability to reduce heightened physiological activation, subsequently lowering the likelihood of catastrophically misinterpreting situations. Distancing and detaching yourself helps to reduce heightened activation, enabling you to separate the past from the present, providing a sense of safety and security instead of experiencing escalating distress triggered by traumatic memories. While acknowledging the reality of past experiences, we don't need to remain trapped in them; we can keep those memories intact while calming ourselves in the present moment.

Sometimes, even after the trauma has ended, your nervous system can struggle to settle down, or it can become easily activated by triggers that remind you of the trauma. Trauma can induce changes in different parts of the brain, resulting in an over-activation of the brain's danger monitoring system. Even the slightest hint of threat, whether realistic or not, can trigger anxiety, stress and overwhelm. Using strategies that help soothe these nervous system reactions can support your mind's natural ability to heal and process aspects of the trauma that currently disturb you. These strategies aid in regaining balance when you are triggered, as they help your mind learn, integrate and differentiate between the present and past. They assist your mind in recognizing that you are not in any current danger.

A significant part of healing involves understanding that the marks left by trauma are understandable and normal. It's not surprising that when something feels reminiscent of a trauma, your mind transports you back there in an attempt to help and protect you. While we cannot erase everything, we can reduce the intensity by consistently helping our stressed nervous system feel safe and protected, reminding it that the danger has passed and you are safe now.

Trauma is stored in both the body and the mind, so when we're working to help a traumatized nervous system we need to support both of these. I will describe several strategies that can both help manage the heightened physiological activation in your body and support your mind through these times. These strategies serve as soothing techniques that aim to calm your nervous system, but it's important to note that they are not a substitute for professional trauma treatment. While these strategies can provide relief and support, addressing and healing underlying trauma requires specialized professional help (see page 392). In the meantime, I hope that these techniques can offer you some comfort and aid in managing your symptoms. When traumatic experiences are retriggered, it can be challenging to practise more complex skills, so the strategies presented here are simple and easy to use. As you'll see, it's best to make them personal to you, which will make them more powerful, and they'll also feel more natural to who you are. If these strategies are new to you, allow yourself time to learn and practise them when you are in a calm state, so they become second nature. This way, you will be able to access them more easily when you need them the most.

Soothing objects

A soothing object is something that you can hold in your hand; the most important thing about this object is the comfort it brings you, the special meaning it carries and the soothing quality it has; it may also have warm memories attached to it. When you're feeling distressed or anxious, this object can be a source of solace and help redirect your attention. This object can be used to soothe you and help you turn your attention towards something else when you experience distress and anxiety. You can use your soothing object and your attention skills discussed in Chapter 5 (see page 184) to really get into focusing your attention on all the soothing qualities it offers. It's helpful if your soothing object is portable, allowing you to take it with you wherever you go, so you can hold, touch, feel, wear or squeeze it whenever you need to soothe yourself. Here are some examples of soothing objects:

- A favourite book.
- A soft toy, teddy or plushie.

- A meaningful scarf or piece of fabric, maybe with a special scent.
- Scented items, such as citrus fruit or a lavender pouch.
- A keyring with personal significance.
- A stone or pebble.
- A wooden ornament or item.
- A seashell.

Soothing images

The purpose of a soothing image is similar to that of a soothing object. It represents a special visualization of a place or situation that brings you comfort and a sense of safety. It's a place where you love to be, a place that brings you joy, where you can feel calm and content. You can use soothing images whenever you need to calm yourself. Can you picture an image of a place or situation that signifies this calming effect for you? In my clinical practice, I often ask my patients, 'What is your favourite place in the entire world, where you feel the most content, calm and relaxed?' Take a moment to reflect on that place for yourself. It can be indoors or outdoors, quiet or bustling with people, filled with sounds and colours. It could even be a room in your current or past home, a garden, or a place where you engage in activities you enjoy, such as a sport, spending time with a pet, or indulging in a spa experience. Here are some examples of soothing images:

- A cherished holiday.
- Majestic mountains.
- A serene, snowy landscape.
- Being immersed in a tranquil library.

- A museum or gallery.
- Relaxing on a picturesque beach.
- Walking or running through the beauty of nature.
- Swimming in an expanse of open water.
- Being engaged in creative activities, like painting, cooking or sewing.
- Lounging in an open meadow.
- Sharing a picnic with loved ones.

These examples serve as inspiration, but remember that your own soothing image is unique to you. It's a personal representation of a place or situation that brings you a profound sense of calm and relaxation.

Regardless of the type of place you choose in your soothing image, infuse it with as many soothing and calming elements as possible. Once you have envisioned a place, bring it to life using your imagination and engage your senses, picture it as vividly and as detailed as you can. Stand as if you are physically present there and slowly rotate 360 degrees, taking in every visual aspect. Walk around the space, moving from one end to the other, absorbing all the details. Immerse yourself in the sounds of this special place – how many different sounds can you hear, and how do they change? Imagine the scents that permeate the air – nature, food, flowers, or any other aromas that bring comfort. Delve into the sensations on your skin – whether you are sitting, standing or lying down – and pay attention to how the surfaces feel against your skin. Consider how the weather feels on your skin – is it warm or windy? Take the time to focus and be fully present in your soothing image.

Practical tasks can help enhance the richness and vibrancy of your image. For instance, you can create an album of photographs, either your own or ones you find online or in magazines, that relate to your image. These can be placed in your journal or compiled into a digital album to represent your soothing place. If you enjoy arts and crafts, you could draw, paint, or create a collage depicting your soothing place. I've observed that the more effort my patients invest in creating a powerful soothing image, the more impactful it becomes when they need to use it, and they can easily immerse themselves in the image when they require its soothing qualities. Take some time to walk through your image, try to bring it to mind throughout the day. The more you practise using your soothing image, the more proficient you'll become at accessing it, and the more readily available it will be to you during moments of distress.

Some of my patients also find it helpful to contemplate how they will transition to their soothing place from their current location. They imagine an image that connects them to the place they want to be in. Some imagine drifting away on a cloud, a glowing portal appearing for them to walk through, a comforting hand reaching out to guide them, or the presence of a loved and trusted person to walk them there. If you find it beneficial to include a connecting image, go ahead – it serves the purpose of providing you with a quick and simple route to your soothing place.

Soothing phrases

Soothing phrases consist of affirmative words that are comforting, and help you feel calm. They serve as reminders that you are safe, resilient and you are surviving. Here are some examples of soothing phrases:

- I am safe.
- I am strong.

- I am okay.
- I am capable.
- I have overcome challenges before.
- I have survived.
- I will continue surviving.
- I believe in myself.
- I believe in my strength.
- I am living, I am breathing.
- I am growing.
- I am healing.
- I've made it through tough times.
- I will keep making it through.
- I have incredible power within me.
- I am courageous and determined.
- I possess strengths that helped me survive.
- I can navigate difficult moments.
- I am embracing my inner strength.
- I am learning and growing from my experiences.
- I am creating a brighter future for myself.

Your soothing phrases should be personal to you, hold meaning for you and help you feel grounded. A collection of one to three phrases tends to work best for my patients. Once you have your phrases, make a habit of saying them every day. Repeat them at various intervals throughout the day, write them down, create artwork with them, or place them on sticky notes around your house. You can also set reminder alerts on your phone or computer to display your soothing phrases at different times. Use these phrases to affirm your strength, safety and well-being as frequently as possible. All these things will help you consolidate your soothing phrases, making them easily accessible in times when you need to calm yourself.

You can also support your mind when you experience anxiety by being aware of whether it has wandered back to the past, and back to a place associated with trauma. When you notice this, acknowledge that it is normal, and it's how you will feel when your mind goes back there. Recognize the anxiety that arises when your mind revisits traumatic experiences. Then, remind yourself that the past is behind you, and focus your attention on the present moment. Verbally state the time and date, describe what you are currently doing or about to do, and affirm, 'My mind went back to the past, but I am here now, not there, and I am safe.' Repeat this affirmation as needed while redirecting your focus to your breath, which serves as an unbreakable tether to the present. If you still feel unsafe, consider taking journal notes that provide factual evidence of your current safety. Even if you may not fully believe it at first, engaging in this practice can help your mind in gradually restoring a sense of safety.

You can also incorporate phrases that directly address your nervous system. Assure it that despite feeling unsafe, scared and terrified, it has also known how to feel safe. Acknowledge that difficult experiences have occurred and that it will take time for your nervous system to regain confidence in its safety. Express your commitment to helping it reach that state by being kind, compassionate and patient as it learns to regulate itself again.

Soothing positions

When we are triggered, afraid, upset or distressed, our bodily changes and posture often reflect what we are going through in our minds, and the way we carry ourselves changes. These physical positions can be linked to past traumatic experiences or serve as an expression of our anxious state. Our body position can come to be a reflection of what we are experiencing in our mind, it might link to a past traumatic experience, or be a reflection of how we feel emotionally. Thoughts, intrusive images, unwanted memories and flashbacks can all influence how we position ourselves physically, and these positions can mirror the distress and hurt of what we experienced.

When you find yourself in a state of distress, you can also manage your heightened activation by adopting powerful and soothing poses – physical positions (most of which are from yoga practices) that make you feel strong and grounded. The choice of these positions will be personal to you, and I have provided some examples that I use with my own patients. You may also discover other positions that work for you or already know of a pose that makes you feel better. Some people find standing positions more helpful, while others prefer sitting or lying down. Experiment with different poses to determine what feels best for you, what helps you feel safe, strong, comfortable, or brings about the feeling that you desire. Again, be sure to practise the poses regularly so that they become well established for when you need them at times of distress. If you have any concerns regarding physical health or mobility in relation to using these positions, it is advised that you consult with your doctor before using them.

Some of my patients have found it helpful to dim the lights while practising these poses. You may choose to use them in silence too, or alongside your favourite calming or empowering music. Whichever pose you choose, aim to hold each position for a few minutes. If it feels challenging at first, start with just one minute and gradually increase the duration as you become more comfortable. Find a timeframe that works best for you and allows you to experience the full benefits of these poses.

Warrior poses

These first two poses are designed to open up your chest, promoting a sense of expansiveness and allowing your inner

strength to develop. These powerful stances can help you connect with the courage within you, enabling you to find a grounded place of stability.

Powerful poses

The expansive and solid postures of these powerful poses can cultivate a sense of strength and confidence. In the first pose, you have the option to hold your hands wide open or as fists, whichever gives you the greatest benefit.

I'm sure you're familiar with this well-known and empowering pose. It can provide you with a sense of strength and can feel very soothing.

Child's pose

I love the child's pose, it provides a great deal of comfort as it opens up your hips and relaxes the pelvic floor, which can in turn activate the rest and digest branch of your nervous system. This branch is responsible for mitigating the fight-or-flight response triggered by anxiety. Additionally, it elongates your back, alleviating tension held within the body and soothing the nervous system. It has the double benefit of allowing you to breathe deeply. There are two variations – one where

you can place cushions or blankets beneath yourself to provide some extra support to your body and one without.

Waterfall pose

This is a deeply relaxing posture that has the potential to calm the nervous system and induce a deep sense of relaxation. By engaging the parasympathetic nervous system, it promotes a state of calm and aids in stress relief. There are two variations: one supported by a wall and the other without any support. While I personally cannot hold my legs in this pose without the support of a wall, some individuals find strength and empowerment in being able to settle into the pose independently. Please choose the variation that suits you best. This pose is believed to counteract the effects of gravity, providing your heart with a respite from the arduous task of pumping blood throughout your body. It is said to help lower the heart rate and regulate blood pressure, consequently alleviating heightened activation of the nervous system.

Resting your legs

In this pose, you can place your legs on either a chair or a sofa. If you choose to use a chair, it may be helpful to put a cushion on it to enhance the comfort of your legs. Similar to the waterfall pose, this position is known for its ability to calm the nervous system and reduce stress reactions by regulating blood flow.

Goddess pose

Our final pose opens up the chest and shoulders, creating a sense of stability. It also promotes a feeling of openness and can have a soothing effect on both the mind and body. Once again, there are two variations of the pose: one that induces relaxation and another that inspires a sense of power and strength. You can choose the one that resonates with you the most. Although the pose is commonly referred to by a feminine name in the yoga world, it can of course help people of any gender.

Soothing self-touch

Over the years of my experience working with people who have experienced trauma, I've learned about lots of different ways to soothe a dysregulated nervous system. Soothing self-touch is another one of these: it offers quick and easy relief in moments of overwhelm and helps calm the nervous system. Here are two examples from my clinical work. However, it's important to note that you may discover additional ones or already have your own form of soothing self-touch, which is wonderful. Regardless of the type of self-soothing touch you choose, remember that consistency is key. When you keep using it, it continually reinforces the message to your nervous system and brain that you are safe, enabling you to return to a state of calm.

One form of self-soothing touch is to give yourself a hug. Embrace yourself firmly and comfortably, allowing for a sense of security and relief, especially when you feel anxious, triggered or unsafe. You can even visualize hugging the part of yourself that feels scared or hurt or in need of comfort. Start by placing each hand on the opposite shoulder, or if possible reach around to your back. Then, gently stroke both hands downwards and upwards, providing a soothing motion.

Another comforting form of self-soothing touch is to hold your own hand. This simple act can provide a profound sense of reassurance and support to the frightened part of yourself. As you hold your hand, take a moment to gently remind yourself that you are present for that part of yourself that feels frightened. Despite the overwhelming emotions you may be experiencing, affirm to yourself that you are safe, even if it doesn't always feel that way.

This gesture of self-compassion and connection can help soothe anxiety, calm the nervous system and cultivate a greater sense of inner security. Take the time to acknowledge and validate your emotions, offering yourself the comfort and care you both need and deserve.

Getting Further Help for Trauma

It is entirely possible for you to recover from anxiety symptoms, even when they are triggered by trauma. As mentioned earlier, traumatic symptoms can sometimes subside on their own. Our brains need time to process and make sense of the experiences we have been through. However, in cases where symptoms persist and do not resolve over time, I advise you to seek further in-person help. Current guidelines recommend two specific trauma-focused psychological treatments: trauma-focused cognitive behavioural therapy (TF-CBT) and eye-movement desensitization and reprocessing (EMDR). I love EMDR! It is a go-to treatment for me, the gold standard, and has been proven to be the most effective and scientifically supported treatment for trauma. EMDR has been shown to bring rapid reductions in negative emotions and the intensity of disturbing images and memories. In my own clinical practice, I have witnessed incredible progress that was simply not achievable with other therapies. Witnessing people who have been suffering make contact with their painful experiences and heal from them right before my eyes has been truly extraordinary. For more information on accessing EMDR for trauma, please refer to page 365.

Ten Key Takeaways for Managing Anxiety Related to Trauma

1. Remember that anxiety problems have diverse causes, stemming from environmental, societal, biological, temperamental and other factors. Trauma is also recognized as a contributing factor to anxiety-related problems.

2. It's important to differentiate between trauma and post-traumatic stress disorder (PTSD). Trauma refers to the emotional response triggered by a painful event or experience, while PTSD is a specific mental health disorder that arises from directly experiencing or witnessing a major trauma.

3. Note that trauma is not an official clinical diagnosis but rather a term used to describe the emotional response to an overwhelming experience. Many people have encountered some form of trauma at some point in their lives.

4. Traumatic experiences can leave people with a profound sense of uncertainty and powerlessness. Keep in mind that the impact of an event on you personally, regardless of its scale, is what truly matters.

5. Note that trauma leads to changes in thinking, emotional responses, perception and therefore reactions. These alterations can often affect your nervous system, causing it to become distressed.

6. Understand that traumatic experiences can contribute to the development of generalized anxiety, health anxiety, social anxiety and panic attacks.

7. You can use self-help strategies to gain relief from anxiety symptoms associated with trauma, although some people may also need to seek in-person professional help.

8. Use soothing strategies to help yourself. Since trauma is stored in both the body and mind, intentionally soothing both can be incredibly powerful in bringing relief to your nervous system.

9. There are numerous self-soothing strategies that can help calm your nervous system, including using soothing objects, visualizing calming images or phrases, and adopting soothing positions for your body. Practise these with consistency to help consolidate the effects.

10. Help yourself heal by engaging in regular compassionate self-soothing strategies that soothe your nervous system. You have the ability to survive because you have already done so.

 Dance it out!

Did you know that dancing is not only great for your physical health but also for your mental well-being? Scientific studies show that dancing can be an effective way to reduce anxiety. When you dance, your brain releases endorphins, which are natural chemicals that make you feel happy and positive. The physical movement of dance helps reduce the level of cortisol in your body too, a hormone that is linked to stress and anxiety. So why not put on some music and dance in your kitchen, like nobody's watching?! It's a great way to relieve stress and have fun. If you're feeling up for it, dancing with friends can help reduce social isolation too, whether it's a class or a social event.

Chapter 10:
How Can I Move Forward from Here?

This chapter focuses on the maintenance of both your mind and body, empowering you to create a roadmap towards a calmer future, enabling you to move forward from your current state and effectively manage future anxiety. Imagine your mind and body as a garden that requires continuous care and attention. How can you ensure the ongoing maintenance of this garden? Just like tending to a garden, it involves regularly weeding it, keeping a watchful eye and remaining committed to practising the strategies that help it flourish. It also entails preparing for unpredictable or stormy conditions by making plans and being proactive. Taking a forward-looking approach will contribute to a sense of calm, help you plan for continued success in consolidating your new ways of thinking and being, and keep you psychologically healthy.

Overcoming anxiety is not a one-time task where you simply implement strategies and consider it done. It requires ongoing practice and maintenance to strengthen the necessary aspects. The garden metaphor helps illustrate this concept. Imagine your mind as a vibrant and diverse garden, abundant with green grass, colourful flower beds, majestic trees, graceful climbers and well-kept hedges. It serves as a sanctuary for you. Just as you tend to a garden by nurturing its plants, your mind requires attention and care to allow healthy thoughts to flourish and grow stronger. Additionally, troublesome thoughts must be pruned away, like removing weeds from a garden, addressing them promptly when noticed. Patience is key as you await growth and witness the changing seasons. A cluttered and chaotic garden loses its inviting nature, so maintaining your mind's state through regular visits, keen observation and patience is crucial. Stay focused on what you can change, utilizing the strategies you have, and accepting the occasional setbacks that are inevitable. Embrace these moments as opportunities for reflection and learning, restoring calm and equilibrium. Identify areas that require attention to achieve your desired state and commit to maintaining them, while acknowledging life's unpredictable circumstances. Dedicate yourself to cultivating a calm sanctuary within your mind, bringing joy and fulfilment. Your mind's garden relies on your ongoing efforts to provide the nourishment necessary for its growth and overall well-being. The more you invest in nurturing your mind, the more it will thrive and bloom.

Continue Practising

With the range of strategies outlined in this book, you now have numerous ways to respond to and manage your anxiety issues. In my clinic and on social media, people frequently ask me, 'What should I do? Please tell me what to do?' That is precisely why this book is packed with actionable advice. *Ten Times Calmer* provides you with a comprehensive programme to overcome your anxiety. You now possess many strategies that you can use to help you achieve and maintain a sense of calm. To make these skills your automatic response, it is essential to practise them extensively. This practice is vital for successfully overcoming your anxiety problems. The more you practise, the greater your progress will be. When there are still areas that require improvement, you become more susceptible to setbacks. Triggers and symptoms can resurface when you are confronted with future stressors. Strive to minimize your anxiety as much as possible. Focus on investing time in the strategies that have proven most effective for you and keep enhancing your ability to apply them. Remain mindful of the ten key concepts presented in this book; these are listed below in chapter order. Take a moment to review them and identify any areas that require further attention. If you identify aspects that need additional work, revisit the respective chapters and continue your efforts in those specific areas. By doing so, you can continue making progress in your journey towards overcoming anxiety.

1. Maintain a good understanding of your anxiety, retaining an awareness of why its presence makes sense.
2. Approach your anxiety differently by adopting an accepting and flexible mindset as a new way of being.
3. To calm your stressed nervous system, continue using exercises that trigger the relaxation response in your body.
4. Work consistently on managing your anxious thoughts, addressing the tendency to catastrophize, as this lies at the core of all anxiety problems.
5. Continue to practise skills that strengthen your ability to shift your attention away from anxiety-provoking stimuli.
6. Continue using emotional regulation strategies to soothe the intense emotions that often accompany anxiety.
7. Strengthen your ability to navigate uncertainty by actively engaging in activities that boost your tolerance for uncertainty.

8. Keep facing your fears by addressing safety behaviours and avoidance.
9. Recognize that anxiety related to trauma can be managed by consistently calming your nervous system using soothing strategies.
10. Stay proactive in continuously managing your anxiety, avoiding the temptation to revert to old coping mechanisms that can trigger it to resurface.

Create a Mini-toolkit

Out of all the strategies presented in *Ten Times Calmer*, which three have become your favourites and helped you the most in managing your anxiety? Make a note of these in a 'mini-toolkit' either in your journal or digital notes, and ensure that you continue using these effective strategies. You can use this mini-toolkit as a quick and accessible reference guide for moments when you need immediate support. Let me illustrate this with some more patient examples. Once you have reviewed these, I encourage you to create a mini-toolkit of your own, highlighting the strategies that have been most effective, frequently utilized, or essential for your needs. This will serve as a quick valuable reference for your ongoing journey towards overcoming anxiety.

Patient Example: Lucy's Thoughts-based Mini-toolkit

Let's start with my patient Lucy, who primarily struggled with her thoughts. Instead of immediately assuming the worst outcome, Lucy consistently referred back to her mini-toolkit, which included the strategy for dealing with worst-case scenario thoughts (Task 15, page 149). This enabled her to take an alternative approach to her thinking instead of automatically jumping to negative conclusions. In addition, Lucy committed herself to accepting that her mind had developed a habit of thinking in worst-case scenarios as a result of past fearfulness. She recognized that her mind generated these thoughts with the intention of assisting her, but she realized that to overcome this habit, she needed to change her response and not react to them in the same way. Her preferred acceptance tool to help consolidate this involved reciting her acceptance affirmation, which she could do from memory (see Task 6 on page 73 for a reminder of how to do this). Furthermore, Lucy worked on replacing her 'what ifs' with 'even ifs', as detailed in Task 17, page 156, Dealing with 'What Ifs' and Question-Based Thoughts.

Patient Example: Bella's Bodily Sensations-based Mini-toolkit

Bella grappled with excessive focus on bodily sensations, which often led her to search for symptoms online. As part of her mini-toolkit, Bella committed more time to her most effective strategy, which involved expanding the scope of her attention, using Eight Skills to Improve the Scope of Your Attention in Chapter 5 (see page 184). Bella complemented this with a regular relaxation routine, utilizing the breathing exercise (see page 92) and relaxation (see page 95). Bella's third favourite strategy involved continuing to practise and increase her ability to confront feelings of uncertainty, as described in Chapter 7.

> ### Patient Example: Mohammed's Avoidance-based Mini-toolkit
>
> Mohammed struggled with high levels of avoidance, and incorporated effective strategies into his mini-toolkit. Mohammed embraced the tools for facing his fears using the Four-Step Approach to Facing Your Fears (see page 280), tackling them one by one until he achieved his outcome. This included confronting situations, places and fears related to bodily sensations. Additionally, Mohammed utilized strategies to help him accept and observe his emotions using Task 22 Embracing Your Emotions through Mindful Observation (see page 210), which allowed for a different approach in place of resorting to avoidance.

Dealing with Setbacks

Setbacks are a completely normal part of overcoming anxiety. Setbacks are simply points in time where particular things happen that appear to worsen anxiety. While setbacks can make it feel like the progress you've made was for nothing, in actual fact something has created a vulnerability, which has triggered anxiety symptoms, and this recurrence makes you think you're back to square one. You are not. Things go wrong sometimes, or things don't go as planned or how we want them to go. If this happens, don't see it as a failure, or that you're back where you started. This is an opportunity for you to consolidate your skills. View setbacks as an unpleasant but temporary state that will be overcome even more quickly and efficiently than when you first started out on this journey. This time you know exactly what to do, and that's your greatest advantage.

While setbacks may feel unpleasant, they can be helpful in certain ways. They provide valuable information about areas that require further work and the source of your distress. Reflecting on setbacks enables you to learn more about yourself and your anxiety, empowering you to make informed choices about what you want to do. Here are some things to consider when reflecting on and learning from setbacks:

- Reflect on why you experienced this setback. Is it a recurring pattern or something you have encountered before in a similar way. What makes sense about its reoccurrence?

- Reflect on why it is understandable that you experienced this setback. Has it happened before in a similar way? Is it a pattern you are familiar with?

- Identify the trigger that caused the setback.

- Determine which skills you can employ to effectively manage this setback based on what you've found most effective.

- Consider other factors that may have contributed to your vulnerability to this setback, such as fatigue, sleep deprivation, neglecting self-care activities or experiencing isolation.

Considering these factors will help identify areas where changes may be necessary and help foster both self-understanding and self-compassion. Avoid beating yourself up after a setback, as it will only worsen how you feel and this could hinder your progress. Instead, recognize setbacks as understandable responses with underlying reasons. Even if you don't encounter a major setback, be attentive to any signs of things slipping. If you notice small issues starting to arise, proactively utilize your strategies to address them promptly and prevent them from worsening.

Planning Ahead

Just as we might prepare in advance with a detailed route map, proper equipment and training for a physical challenge like climbing a mountain, we can apply the same approach to managing anxiety setbacks. Instead of relying on last-minute improvisation, it's beneficial to have a well-prepared plan in place. Think of this plan as your personal toolkit for navigating anxiety challenges. By having a plan ready, you empower yourself to respond effectively and minimise the impact of future setbacks. It's like having your own customised strategy to tackle anxiety head-on when you might need it most. So, take the time to create your plan and ensure it includes the coping mechanisms and techniques that have proven most effective for you. Just as thorough preparation enhances your chances of success in physical challenges, your tailored plan can strengthen your resilience against anxiety setbacks.

Patient Example: Mohammed's Plan

Mohammed, who was introduced earlier, understood that if he noticed himself engaging in new avoidance behaviours, it was a signal to implement his prevention plan and prevent the avoidance from worsening. His plan involved confronting and being present in the situations or places he wanted to avoid. If necessary, he used related techniques like widening the scope of his attention, relaxation or distraction to facilitate this process, so he was less fixated on physical sensations. Additionally, Mohammed incorporated assessing the thoughts that triggered his avoidance. For instance, if he declined an invitation to a movie due to the thought 'I might get trapped, I'll be unable to seek help, and could suffer a heart attack', he would evaluate the likelihood of that scenario occurring. Mohammed's prevention plan encompassed three key elements. Firstly, he remained vigilant for the emergence of new avoidance patterns, recognizing that these could be indicators of escalating anxiety. Additionally, he paid attention to any tendencies to excessively focus on bodily sensations, knowing that this could contribute to heightened anxiety. Lastly, Mohammed recognized the importance of evaluating his catastrophic thoughts accurately, challenging their validity and assessing whether they aligned with reality. By incorporating these three strategies, Mohammed equipped himself with an effective prevention plan.

Think ahead and set up your plan

In this section, we will delve deeper into the process of preparing a plan that you can readily deploy when needed. Having a prepared plan will minimize the impact of recurring anxiety and reduce the likelihood of reacting in ways that exacerbate your anxiety. It will also prevent you from falling back into old coping behaviours that your mind may have been accustomed to. To establish your prevention plan, it's essential to examine four key areas: identifying potential triggers, observing changes in thinking patterns, noting any alterations in your behaviour and considering any upcoming events. Let's look at each of these areas in more detail, and as you progress through them, be sure to take notes that you can use later to develop your plan.

Identify possible triggers

Take a moment to reflect on your usual triggers, referring back to the notes you made during the exercise in Chapter 1 (Task 2: Identify Your Anxiety Triggers, page 29). Drawing from your past experiences, identify potential triggers that could cause anxiety to resurface in the future, and note these down. Additionally, consider moments when you have felt particularly vulnerable too. Here are some common triggers:

- Experiencing a physical sensation of anxiety.
- Having a minor illness.
- Going through a life stressor.
- Having a period of poor sleep.
- Not eating well.
- Having to attend events.
- Having to travel.
- Having to be around others.
- Having to attend health appointments.

Identify changes in thinking

As anxiety resurfaces, it's important to be mindful of the changes that may occur in your thinking patterns. Notice if there is an increase in negative or catastrophic thoughts, where you find yourself expecting the worst outcomes and dwelling on potential dangers. Be aware of getting caught up in repeated patterns of overthinking and rumination. Pay attention to whether you're engaging in 'what if' scenarios, constantly imagining and worrying about negative outcomes. These thinking patterns often lean towards a fearful outlook and can intensify anxiety and stress. Take note if you find yourself leaning towards these tendencies again. Remember that the importance of recognizing these changes in your thinking is so you can return to practising strategies to address your anxious thoughts. Here are some examples of the types of thoughts that can commonly arise when anxiety is resurfacing:

- 'I know something terrible is going to happen.'
- 'This situation is going to end in disaster.'
- 'I won't be able to handle it if things go wrong.'
- 'Nobody likes me or wants to be around me.'
- 'What if something bad happens and I can't handle it?'
- 'What if I embarrass myself in front of everyone?'
- 'What if people judge me or think negatively of me?'
- 'I won't speak up in meetings because I fear being judged.'
- 'My heart is racing; I must be having a heart attack.'
- 'I feel light-headed; I'm going to pass out.'
- 'I have a headache; it must be a sign of a serious medical condition.'
- 'I can't go to that social event; it will be too overwhelming.'
- 'I'll avoid driving on motorways because I might have a panic attack.'

Identify changes in behaviour

Take a moment to consider any behaviour-based indicators that might suggest you are reverting to unhelpful anxiety patterns. Reflect on the actions you might start engaging in or the activities you may stop doing. Similar to Mohammed, perhaps you might notice a tendency towards increased avoidance of certain things. Identify specific instances of avoidance that come to mind. What about any superstitious behaviours or actions like touching wood that may have re-emerged during anxious moments? Here are some examples of common anxiety-related behaviours to help you further in this identification:

- Engaging in self-monitoring and excessive self-analysis.
- Increased checking behaviours, such as constantly checking yourself or searching the internet for reassurance.
- Avoiding specific places or situations because they trigger anxiety.
- Doing things that your anxious thoughts tell you to do, when you don't actually need to, and you know you're only doing so because you feel anxious.
- Seeking excessive reassurance from others.
- Ceasing the use of relaxation techniques or coping strategies.
- Withdrawing from activities and social interactions.
- Resorting to comfort eating or using alcohol/drugs as coping mechanisms.
- Skipping meals as a result of increasing anxiety.

It might also help you to take a look back at the behaviours you exhibit when struggling with anxiety, as discussed in Chapter 1, so if necessary, refer back to Task 4: My Reactions to Anxiety, page 54. Create a list of your anxiety behaviours and keep it easily accessible to catch any creeping back of these behaviours. Additionally, consider seeking the opinion of a loved one. Those closest to us often notice changes in our behaviour before we do. Ask them to politely and sensitively alert you if they observe you engaging in certain behaviours from your list. You can also inquire about any general changes they notice in you when you become more anxious, and add those behaviours to your list as well.

Consider upcoming events

I recommend using your calendar to identify upcoming events that could make you more vulnerable to anxiety. These events may include holidays, being away from home, weddings, work events or social gatherings. Look ahead to the next month, three months, six months or even the next year to identify potential anxiety-inducing situations. How can you ensure that you catch any emerging symptoms quickly as these events approach? Also consider whether there are specific strategies that you could benefit from working on more as these events approach.

Patient Example: Bella's Prevention Plan

Thinking ahead	Examples	Plan
What things might retrigger my anxiety?	Experiencing a new physical sensation. Or an old sensation coming back. Getting a minor illness, like a cold or a sore throat.	I can re-read the relevant sections in the book and firm up my understanding of how anxiety can produce sensations. I can use acceptance skills, to allow discomfort to be there during a brief and minor illness.

How might my thinking change?	I'll start having more anxious thoughts. I will spend more time thinking about my anxious thoughts, and this will make me quieter and more withdrawn.	I can review the strategies in the anxious thoughts chapter. My most effective ones were dealing with worst-case scenario thoughts, and 'what ifs'.
What things will I start to do, or even avoid when my anxiety is retriggered?	I will start keeping a close eye on my body, looking at it, checking it too. I will start googling again. I will ask my husband for more and more reassurance. I'll stop doing fun things and become quieter.	I can use the tools on tolerating distress and uncertainty to help resist giving in to checking urges and reassurance seeking. I will need to increase how much I use the attention skills to make sure I'm not over-focusing on my body. I will look at my fun activities list and see what I can schedule to keep me busy with nourishing activities.
What upcoming events or situations might cause an increase in anxiety?	Having to travel is a big one for me; I hate being away from home. I always assume something bad will happen.	I can use the tools in the anxious thoughts chapter, especially the 'evaluating' ones.

Now that you have covered the four key areas: identifying triggers, observing thinking patterns, noting behavioural changes and considering upcoming events, it's time to create your own plan based on the notes you have taken. Use Bella's example plan as a reference, and keep your plan flexible, as circumstances may change and you may need to make amendments. Having a plan like this will enable you to proactively handle challenges before they arise. It's especially helpful because as anxiety intensifies, it becomes more difficult to think clearly and problem solve effectively. By having a plan that you can refer to as soon as you notice signs of increasing anxiety, you can navigate through those moments with more ease.

Lifestyle Tips

Success is not solely about relieving stress and suffering; it also involves focusing on overall well-being to strengthen your inner resources. Anxiety problems can be all-consuming, occupying significant mental space and dominating your thoughts. The efforts you put into managing or controlling anxiety consume time and energy. As you start feeling better and your anxiety becomes less burdensome, you'll find yourself with more time and more mental capacity. It's crucial to consider how you can make use of this newfound space and establish lifestyle factors that enhance your progress while reducing your vulnerability to future anxiety problems. This means creating a fulfilling and engaging life that brings you joy. Here are some ideas to help you explore this further:

- Reflect on the activities you were unable to pursue due to anxiety. What are some things you'd like to be able to do?

- Are there any hobbies or sports activities you used to enjoy that you'd like to revisit? Take some time to research how you can re-engage with them.

- What captures your interest, brings you pleasure and holds importance for you? Make an effort to engage in activities related to these interests.

- If you didn't have any previous interests, refer to the Fun Activities list at the back of the book (see page 378) for inspiration. Consider if there's anything on the list you'd like to try?

- Are there any home projects you've been meaning to tackle, such as organizing, decorating, gardening, DIY or learning new cooking skills?

- Are you interested in making changes to your work life, such as returning to work or exploring different career paths? Perhaps anxiety has hindered your pursuit of these goals. Consider actions you can take to further explore these ideas, such as enrolling in a course to enhance your knowledge, or speaking to a mentor or a careers advisor.

- What would you like to do regarding your social connections? Are there any changes you'd like to make in terms of who you spend time with? Adequate social contact is crucial for maintaining good mental health. Can you reconnect with a friend you've lost touch with?

- Look at your friendships and identify the people who make you feel valued and comfortable. Can you dedicate more time to nurturing those relationships? If you're interested in making new social connections, are there leisure activities that align with your interests and provide opportunities to meet like-minded people?

- You're already aware of the benefits of physical movement for both your mental and physical health. Regular exercise brings pleasure, improves strength, enhances cardiovascular health and reduces the risk of injury. What types of physical activities would you like to try and commit to on a regular basis?

- Remember to maintain balance by incorporating 'me' time, rest, sufficient sleep and a nourishing diet into your routine wherever possible.

Mark Your Progress

Acknowledge your achievements and give yourself the credit you deserve by rewarding yourself. Celebrating your progress will help maintain a positive outlook. Remember that success is not immediate, and it is not achieved overnight. Stay mindful of the small yet significant steps you take towards overcoming anxiety and reaching your ultimate goal. It's easy to overlook these small victories, especially if you have been critical of your anxiety or have held a negative perception of yourself as weak or inadequate. Many people fall into the trap of thinking, 'If I'm not completely better, then it's not worth it.' If you feel like you've been trying for years and nothing seems to work, you may perceive it as a failure. Try to view this differently: it's not a failure, it's a learning experience. You have gained insights into what doesn't work, allowing you to let go of ineffective strategies and continue cultivating the ones that do work. It's common for people to be harsh and self-critical, focusing on their failures and shortcomings while downplaying their successes, especially the smaller ones.

It's natural to experience discomfort or to cringe when it comes to celebrating and embracing progress, whether significant or minor. You might feel more comfortable criticizing yourself for not making faster progress. But fixating on past challenges or the length of time you've dealt with anxiety will only dampen your motivation. You need that motivation to propel you towards your desired outcome. Part of this is about moving away from self-criticism and instead acknowledging and taking joy in your achievements. By doing so, you can sustain your motivation and momentum. Recognizing your progress enables your mind to acknowledge the strides you're making towards overcoming anxiety.

So, how can you mark your progress? You can use a notebook or a calendar to track your achievements. Set aside a specific time each week to reflect on your overall progress and record what you have accomplished. Writing down these achievements not only boosts your confidence but also reinforces the notion that your efforts are effective. Even if you don't initially think highly of the positive achievements you note down, continue recording them. They can still have a positive impact on your thinking and can reshape your perception when you stay consistent with them. Recognizing your achievements also keeps you energized. Your brain craves this positive feedback, along with the rewards for your accomplishments. Your brain has a reward circuit that regulates your ability to experience pleasure. When this circuit is activated, your brain releases a combination of electrical and chemical signals that generate feelings of accomplishment, pride and happiness. It's a wonderful feeling that motivates you to keep going and to achieve more.

Rewards don't have to be extravagant or expensive material possessions. In my opinion, immersing yourself in experiences that bring you joy can be more fulfilling than material items. Consider activities that genuinely make you happy. What do you enjoy doing? Make a list of a few things you can indulge in. It could be something as simple as taking a scenic drive, preparing a special meal or drink, watching a movie you love, or another way to pamper yourself. Embrace your progress and savour the rewards you give yourself along the way.

Visualizing Your Future Self

Visualization is a powerful tool used for various mental health issues, and there is substantial evidence supporting the use of visualization techniques for anxiety. Additionally, the application of visualization and imagery is known to improve well-being, decrease blood cortisol levels, alleviate pain and enhance sleep quality. Visualization incorporates vision-, hearing-, touch-, taste- and smell-based sensations, resulting in a rich multisensory experience. By focusing on these sensory aspects in conjunction with images, thoughts and emotions, you can access meaningful elements of your situation. The following exercise outlines how you can practise visualizing your progress and envisioning your future self. The purpose of this last visualization technique is to provide you with a calming practice that allows you to acknowledge and value the progress you've achieved. It also serves as a tool for envisioning a future free from anxiety with optimism and positivity. Before attempting it, I recommended you read through the entire exercise and even consider recording an audio version to help you relax and listen to the instructions while practising. Feel free to practise this exercise as frequently as you wish, but try to establish a regular routine, even if it's just for ten minutes once a week.

TASK 32
Visualization exercise

Find a comfortable position, either sitting or lying down.

Take a few deep breaths, inhaling slowly through your nose, holding your breath for a few seconds before slowly exhaling through your mouth.

Allow yourself to relax into your position, into how your body settles.

Embrace the sense of calm that washes over you.

Notice the contact, pressure and difference in temperature between your body and the surface you're resting on.

Begin to envision how you would like to be, how you wish to perceive yourself when you imagine a life free from anxiety. What does this image look like?

Notice what it feels like to visualize yourself in this anxiety-free state.

Now, think of a favourite colour, one that evokes feelings of serenity, contentment and relaxation. Imagine this colour radiating around and through you as you visualize your future self.

Notice how safe and how comfortable you feel in this visualization.

Look at yourself and connect with the calmness you're visualizing.

Observe your surroundings. Have you transported to a specific location? If so, where are you?

What do you see within this visualization?

Engage your sense of hearing. What sounds do you hear in this visualization? Is it the sound of nature, peaceful music or something else? Allow these sounds to enhance the experience.

Engage your sense of taste. What flavours and tastes do you imagine? Imagine enjoying something delicious that brings you a sense of calm and relaxation.

Pay attention to the sensations that arise as you picture yourself in this anxiety-free state.

Take note of the safety and comfort that envelops you during this visualization.

When anxiety is absent, visualize yourself engaging in various activities. Observe how it feels to witness yourself being capable of performing these actions now.

Gaze at yourself and establish a connection with the tranquillity you are seeing.

Ask this envisioned version of yourself if they can share a message or offer words of wisdom that could further assist you.

Acknowledge how your future self recognizes that vulnerabilities may exist but also embraces your strengths and courage.

The version of yourself you are visualizing represents the person you aspire to be, the person you are and the progress you have already achieved and will continue to make.

Remain in this visualization for as long as you like. When you feel ready, shift your focus back to your breath. Take a few slow, deep breaths, then gradually bring your attention back to your body. Notice how it feels as you gently move your fingers and toes. Then gently move the rest of your body and bring your awareness back to the room you're in.

Switch the scene!

When anxiety starts to creep in, a quick change of environment can be very helpful. Stepping away from a situation that triggers anxious thoughts can help disrupt the pathway that anxious behaviour would normally follow. It's not about avoiding things you don't like, or running away, but about moving yourself away from a situation that is fuelling anxiety. As an example, suppose you're sitting at your computer and anxious thoughts begin to arise, which then create an unhelpful urge to google. In this scenario, you can move to a different room, make a drink, step outside, or even complete a short task. This change of scene can give you a fresh perspective and free you from feeling trapped. Being in new surroundings can provide different stimulation, which can help shift the focus away from anxious thoughts and urges.

A final note from me . . .

I wish you well, and I wish you every success as you continue on this transformative journey to becoming ten times calmer. Thank you for trusting me to be your partner through this journey.

Ten Key Takeaways for Moving Forward

1. Embrace the principle of regular care and attention for both your mind and body. Just like a garden, they need continuous nurturing to flourish and thrive.

2. Review the ten key concepts presented to identify areas that need further attention and revisit the corresponding chapters to continue your progress in those specific areas.

3. Reflect on the strategies presented in *Ten Times Calmer* and identify your most helpful ones to create a mini-toolkit in your journal or digital notes for quick reference to these strategies.

4. Remember that setbacks are a normal part of the journey and may occur when specific events or circumstances trigger you. Setbacks do not erase the progress you have made. Instead, they indicate a temporary vulnerability.

5. Foster a forward-looking mindset, focusing on consolidating positive changes and planning for continued success.

6. Take a proactive approach by planning ahead to implement strategies that minimize the impact of potential future triggers. Recognize how your thoughts and behaviours may shift as anxiety worsens, and be mindful of upcoming situations that could heighten vulnerability to anxiety.

7. Utilize the newfound time and mental space, previously occupied by anxiety, to engage in activities that enrich and enhance your life.

8. Celebrate and acknowledge your accomplishments, both big and small, as a means of maintaining a positive perspective and staying motivated.

9. Regularly harness the power of visualization to facilitate anxiety recovery and enhance your overall well-being.

10. Never underestimate the value of your efforts, always remember and appreciate the milestones and progress you have achieved. Above all, continue moving forward with determination and resilience.

Finding the Right Professional Help

If you need further professional help, it is advisable to consult with your doctor who can provide guidance and support in exploring further avenues. The following information may also assist you in locating a suitable mental health professional. Although my expertise is primarily focused on the United Kingdom and its healthcare system, comparable public and private healthcare organizations, regulators and accrediting bodies exist worldwide.

A word of caution: In the UK, individuals are legally allowed to label themselves as psychotherapists, irrespective of their training or qualifications. While some practitioners undergo extensive training programmes lasting many years, others may have completed short six-week courses or have no formal training whatsoever. Therefore, I recommend seeking a regulated professional.

Regulated Professionals

Mental healthcare professionals who are regulated are mandated by law to register with a government body responsible for safeguarding the public. Various professions fall under this type of regulation, including:

- Clinical Psychologists – Registered with the Health and Care Professions Council (HCPC) and accredited by the British Psychological Society (BPS)

- Counselling Psychologists – Registered with HCPC and accredited by the BPS

- Health Psychologists – Qualification in Health Psychology, registered with HCPC and accredited by the BPS

- Psychiatrists – Trained in medicine, and registered with the Royal College of Psychiatrists

- Registered Mental Health Nurse – Registered with the Nursing and Midwifery Council (NMC)

EMDR Practitioners

EMDR is a complex treatment, one that should only be delivered by properly trained and qualified practitioners. If you would like to find an EMDR practitioner, here are some further details:

- The EMDR Academy therapist directory: emdracademy.co.uk/find-a-therapist

- EMDR Association lists accredited therapists in UK and Europe: emdrassociation.org.uk/find-a-therapist

- EMDRIA is the international association for EMDR, where you can find EMDR trained practitioners worldwide: emdria.org/find-an-emdr-therapist

- EMDRAA – The EMDR Association of Australia: emdraa.org/find-a-therapist

How to Find the Right Person

Even when you come across a regulated professional, it is advisable to conduct some due diligence to ensure they are the most suitable person to help you in addressing your difficulties. The quality of available help can vary greatly, so it is crucial to understand how to obtain the best possible support. Here are some points you may wish to consider:

- Always inquire about a practitioner's qualifications and training, including the duration of their training. A reputable practitioner will be more than willing to share this information. If they are unwilling or defensive, it is advisable to consider finding someone else.

- Discuss with the practitioner whether they plan to set goals for your treatment together.

- Ask the practitioner about the specific type of therapy they propose for you, including the underlying model and its evidence base for your particular problems.

- Request any relevant reading materials or resources that can provide further insight into their approach.

- Ask the practitioner if they will offer direct advice on resolving the problem you are facing or if they will not provide direct advice.

- Inquire about the practitioner's approach to reviewing your progress, and ask about the frequency of such reviews and what actions they usually take when there is a lack of progress.

- Discuss the practitioner's expertise and experience in dealing with the specific problems you are facing. You may even ask them about the number of patients they have treated with similar issues.

- Request an estimation of the recommended number of sessions. Clinical guidance for anxiety disorders typically suggests a range of approximately 12 to 15 sessions.

Common Symptoms and Sensations of Anxiety

Here I have listed the common symptoms and sensations of anxiety. I know that physical sensations can be a source of great stress for many sufferers, so having this information readily available may be helpful. This list is not meant to be exhaustive, and there may be other symptoms or changes that I haven't included. To make it easier for you to navigate, I've organized symptoms and sensations into different categories. My aim in providing this information is to help you feel more at ease by gaining a better understanding of the types of anxiety symptoms that exist.

Sensations Affecting the Whole Body/ Generalized Sensations

Aches and pains • Tension and stiffness • Muscle pain • Back and shoulder pain/tension • Pulsing feeling in muscles • Throbbing feeling in muscles • Weakness • Agitation • Restlessness • Restless legs • Jelly/wobbly legs • Heavy tired legs • Body jolts • Body zaps • Body shakes • Body tremors • Tingling in the body • Prickly feeling in the body • Pins and needles • Buzzing sensations • Shooting sensations • Pulsing sensations • Vibrations • Heavy body • Numbness • Fatigue • Exhaustion • Tiredness • Low energy • Tired but wired feeling • Excess energy • Inability to relax • Weight gain • Weight loss • Changes in body temperature • Feeling too hot/cold • Sudden hot/cold flashes • Excessive sweating • Night sweats • Feeling unsteady • Sensitive reflexes • Sensory sensitivity

Head-based Sensations

Dizziness • Light-headedness • Feeling faint • Swaying sensation • Headaches • Head zaps • Head pressure • Sore scalp • Tingly prickly scalp • Brain fog • Burning face/head • Hot face/head • Numb face • Lump in the throat • Tight throat • Difficulty swallowing • Choking sensation • Throat clearing • Psychosomatic cough • Mouth tingling/numbness • Tongue sensations • Aching jaw • Teeth grinding • Excess yawning • Neck pain • Feeling of a tight band around the head

Heart/Chest/Respiratory Sensations

Chest pain • Chest discomfort • Chest flutters • Chest tightness • Chest pressure • Chest vibrations • Chest tremors • Full feeling in chest • Hot feeling in chest • Shooting chest pains • Ribcage tightness/pressure • Tight band around the ribcage • Tight band around the chest • Heart palpitations • Racing heart • Skipped beats • Pounding heart • Irregular heart rhythm • Heart flutters • Left arm pain • Breathlessness • Increased demand for oxygen • Feeling of air hunger • Suffocated feeling • Out of breath • Shortness of breath

Stomach/Bladder/Bowel

Nausea • Vomiting • Butterflies • Upset stomach • Appetite changes • Fatty/salty/sugary cravings • Frequent urination • Urgent need to urinate • Overactive bowel • Urgent need to empty bowels • Constipation • Diarrhoea • Belching/burping

Skin-based Sensations

Flushed skin • Blushing • Loss of colour in skin • Tingling skin • Burning sensations • Crawling sensations • Skin sensitivity • Numbness on skin • Prickly feeling on skin

Sleep

Insomnia • Difficulty falling or staying asleep • Vivid dreams • Waking with a jolt • Night waking • Sleep paralysis • Nocturnal panic attacks

Ear-related Sensations

Tinnitus • Humming • Ringing • Buzzing • Hissing • Pulsing • Auditory sensitivity • Ear popping • Pressure and pain • Burning ears

Eye-related Sensations

Visual sensitivity • Eye strain • Dilated pupils • Contracted pupils • Blurred vision • Dry eyes • Watery eyes • Eye tics • Visual flashes • Light sensitivity • Tunnel vision

Mind-based Changes

Feeling of terror • Feeling of impending doom • Irrational fears • Constantly afraid • Anticipating the worst • Predicting the worst • Negative thoughts • Repetitive mental chatter • Mood changes • Irritability • Feeling trapped • Afraid of being trapped • Overwhelm • Fear of a heart attack • Fear of a serious illness • Fear of allergic reactions • Fear of embarrassment • Fear of dying • Fear of losing control • Fear of passing out • Fear of being in public • Fear of making a mistake • Fear of losing your mind • Fear of harm • Heightened self-awareness • Feeling self-consciousness • Fear of being alone • Obsessing about sensations • Obsessing about not getting better • Racing thoughts • Repetitive thoughts • Ruminating • Intrusive thoughts • Seeing scary images • Feeling 'crazy' • Feeling detached • Feeling out of touch with reality • Feeling unreal • Depersonalization • Derealization • Dissociation • Feeling spaced out • Feeling snappy • Feeling frustrated • Feeling emotionally unstable • Difficulty concentrating • Memory difficulties • Difficulty thinking • Reduced problem-solving ability

Behaviours

Avoidance of places • Avoidance of people • Avoidance of situations • Scanning exits • Sitting near exits • Not leaving the house • Giving up driving • Staying in 'safe' places only • Withdrawal • Comfort eating • Not eating • Restrictive/selective eating • Smoking • Using alcohol / drugs • Fidgeting • Skin picking • Hair pulling • Scratching skin • Habit behaviours • Excessive checking • Monitoring • Body checking using medical devices • Reassurance seeking • Excessive research

Types of Anxiety Problems

Here you will find descriptions of different types of anxiety problems based on the International Classification of Diseases, 10th Edition (ICD-10) and the Diagnostic and Statistical Manual of Mental Disorders, 5th Edition (DSM-5). The information is intended for general purposes only and should not be used to make a diagnosis. If you'd like to explore an official diagnosis of your anxiety problems, please consult with your doctor. Only a qualified healthcare professional with the appropriate licensure can accurately confirm a diagnosis.

The specific symptoms experienced vary from person to person. To read more about the types of physical symptoms associated with anxiety problems see page 368.

Generalized Anxiety Disorder (GAD)

Generalized Anxiety Disorder (GAD) is characterized by uncontrollable worry and anxiety. While normal levels of worry are typically short-lived and may involve problem-solving, people with GAD experience excessive and persistent worrying about various aspects of their lives. People with GAD may experience the following symptoms:

- Experiencing anxious thoughts most days, for at least six months

- Having a multitude of different anxious thoughts simultaneously
- Having anxious thoughts that appear disproportionate to the situation
- Experiencing anxious thoughts that interfere with the ability to accomplish day-to-day tasks in a reasonable manner
- Persistent 'what if' thoughts
- Difficulty controlling and/or dismissing anxious thoughts
- Frequent difficulty in problem-solving anxious thoughts
- Believing that worrying is beneficial for planning or preventing negative outcomes
- Avoiding specific situations or scenarios
- Struggling to tolerate uncertainty and having an aversion to taking risks
- Constantly contemplating all the potential things that could go wrong
- Experiencing anxiety about a variety of topics, including:
  o Concerns regarding loved ones
  o Worries about job-related matters
  o Academic work-related matters
  o Performance-related issues
  o Punctuality concerns
  o Fear of things not working out
  o Financial worries
  o Anxiety about natural disasters or world events
  o Concerns about environmental problems

Illness Anxiety Disorder

Health anxiety became officially known as Illness Anxiety Disorder (IAD) in the Diagnostic and Statistical Manual of Mental Disorders, 5th Edition (DSM-5). Beyond the specific diagnostic criteria, it is common for many clinicians to continue using the term 'health anxiety' as it is widely understood. People with health anxiety are persistently anxious and worried about their health and well-being, even when there is no medical reason to be so. This impacts their daily thoughts, emotions, and actions. People with health anxiety may experience the following symptoms:

- Consistently experiencing anxiety and worry regarding health and wellbeing
- Encountering catastrophic thoughts and mental images associated with illness, disease, chronic conditions and death
- Spending considerable time fixating on health, illness, disease and bodily symptoms
- Seeking frequent comfort or reassurance from others, including doctors, to alleviate concerns about health
- Undergoing repeated and unnecessary medical testing
- Worrying that doctors may have overlooked a serious condition
- Engaging in frequent body checks and self-monitoring for any signs or symptoms
- A hypervigilance of bodily sensations, feelings, marks or lumps
- Becoming overly preoccupied with specific body parts

- Avoiding certain activities due to the belief of having an undetected and undiagnosed condition
- Excessively seeking illness/disease-related information
- Avoiding things related to illness/disease, such as television programs, medical information, doctors, clinical environments and conversations
- Sensing signs and sensations attributed to a specific illness/disease after exposure to related information
- Visualizing distressing future scenarios, like being diagnosed with a severe condition and contemplating its impact on loved ones
- Believing that unless constant vigilance is maintained over the body, signs of a serious condition may be missed
- Having the persistent belief that something significant is wrong and attempting to suppress it, only to have it resurface in the form of recurrent distressing thoughts

Social Anxiety Disorder

People who experience social anxiety are highly anxious when in the presence of other people. They often fear coming across as foolish, clumsy, embarrassing themselves, or being negatively judged by others. People with social anxiety may experience the following symptoms:

- Avoiding social situations entirely or to the greatest extent possible
- Experiencing excessive worry about possible embarrassment

- Experiencing intense anxiety prior to, during, and after social situations, as well as engaging in post-event analysis
- Experiencing intense anxiety prior to entering social situations, as well as during the social situation and afterwards when analysing what happened
- Holding the belief that others will be judgemental and critical
- Being preoccupied with the idea that others are constantly observing and scrutinizing their actions
- Experiencing such heightened anxiety that they are unable to express themselves or engage in interaction
- Repeatedly ruminating on potential embarrassing scenarios that could transpire in social situations
- Analysing and worrying about their conduct and contemplating how they should have behaved differently following a social event
- Disliking both interactions with others and being introduced to new people
- Struggling to enter shops, cafes, restaurants or other public places
- Feeling anxious about eating or drinking in public settings or in front of others

Panic Disorder

Panic disorder is an anxiety disorder characterized by sudden and intense panic or fear episodes known as panic attacks. A panic attack is a brief but overwhelming surge of intense fear accompanied by significant physical symptoms, seemingly occurring out of the blue. Panic attacks often occur after periods of heightened stress. People with panic disorder may experience the following symptoms:

- Recurrent and/or unexpected panic attacks, accompanied by persistent concern about experiencing future panic attacks
- A state of acute and intense anxiety and fear, accompanied by pronounced physical symptoms that typically last for minutes, sometimes extending to hours
- Profound apprehension, a sense of imminent doom, and sudden fear of losing control or dying
- Fear of being unable to maintain self-control
- Anxiety about the possibility of another panic attack
- Avoidance of locations where previous panic attacks occurred, in an attempt to prevent their recurrence
- Reluctance to go out alone
- Irrational thoughts

100 Fun Activity Ideas

Drawing from my clinical experience, I have compiled a comprehensive list of ideas that I believe will inspire you to discover activities you can enjoy. I also encourage you to contribute your own ideas. As you read through the following suggestions, feel free to mark the ones that resonate with you or capture your interest. You can even create your own mini list from these selections. By creating a personalized and convenient mini-list, whether in your physical journal or digital notes, you will have an easily accessible reference of fun activities. This will make it easier for you to schedule fun activities during your spare time.

Please consult with your doctor if you have any physical concerns about any of these activities and exercise caution in undertaking any activities that may pose a risk to you.

Physical Activities:

1. Get outdoors
2. Skipping
3. Blow bubbles outside
4. Bounce a ball outside, alone or with someone else
5. Go to the gym
6. Engage in a home workout
7. Take a walk in nature

8. Do some gardening

9. Find or create a tranquil garden space to relax and unwind in

10. Go swimming indoors or outdoors

11. Try water aerobics

12. Join a sports team

13. Play an outdoor game

14. Play tennis or badminton

15. Play golf

16. Play Frisbee

17. Go for a run

18. Go for a bicycle ride

19. Fly a kite

20. Go for a dog walk

21. Try a group fitness or dance class

22. Try a martial art

23. Try a water sport like kayaking, sailing, rowing or paddle-boarding

24. Try climbing or bouldering

25. Try fishing

26. Try horse riding

27. Try strength training

Relaxing Activities:

28. Practise deep breathing

29. Enjoy a nice hot or soft drink

30. Read a book

31. Take a nap
32. Treat yourself to a massage
33. Go on a spa day
34. Try aromatherapy
35. Light scented candles
36. Write in a gratitude journal to reflect on positive moments
37. Practice mindfulness
38. Try relaxing yoga or Tai chi
39. Have a picnic in a peaceful place
40. Listen to calming nature sounds or instrumental music
41. Engage in gentle stretching
42. Unwind with a guided meditation or relaxation audio
43. Have a cosy movie night with blankets and snacks

Creative Activities:

44. Painting
45. Pottery
46. Drawing
47. Calligraphy
48. Create personalized greeting cards or handmade gifts
49. Try graphic design or creating digital artwork
50. Try sewing, knitting or crochet
51. Join a local art class

52. Try flower arranging

53. Try woodworking or carpentry, creating unique pieces of your own

54. Read or write poetry

55. Try creative writing

56. Create a personalized scrapbook of cherished memories

57. Start a blog or online journal to share your thoughts and experiences

58. Learn to play a new musical instrument

59. Join a community theatre group

60. Photography

61. DIY

62. Have a clear-out or do some home organization

63. Try out a new recipe or do some baking

Social and Emotional Activities:

64. Schedule a call to catch up with an old friend or relative

65. Plan future outings, events or activities you'd like to do

66. Write a letter to a loved one

67. Volunteer your time to something that is meaningful to you

68. Join a book club

69. Spend an evening with friends

70. Plan your weekend

71. Meet someone for coffee/tea

72. Plan a family get-together

73. Attend a local community event

74. Try a pub quiz, karaoke or games night with family/friends/colleagues

75. Reflect on your achievements

76. Think about your goals for the future

77. Consider the qualities others appreciate in you, and vice versa

78. Reflect on times when you successfully coped with challenges

79. Spend time away from devices and sit quietly for as long as you can

80. Pamper yourself with an at-home facial, skincare routine, manicure or pedicure

81. Practice gratitude by making a list of things you're grateful for

Nature and Scenic Activities:

82. Visit an art gallery

83. Visit a museum

84. Visit the beach

85. Explore a historical library or site

86. Visit an area with beautiful natural scenery

87. Visit a bird-watching spot

88. Visit a national park

89. Visit a botanical garden

90. Visit a waterside setting, seaside, lake or river

91. Take a scenic drive

92. Take a scenic train ride

93. Spend an evening watching stars

94. Try a treasure hunt in nature

Leisure and Entertainment Activities:

95. Listen to an audiobook or podcast

96. Play card games or board games

97. Join a gaming community, do some solo gaming, or game with others

98. Construct a model aeroplane, vehicle or anything you like

99. Attend a play or concert

100. Watch a sports match or comedy show, live or at home

References

Chapter 1

1. P31 *Additionally, people who desire control over their environment . . .*
Stoeber, J., & Otto, K. (2006). Positive conceptions of perfectionism: Approaches, evidence, challenges. *Personality and Social Psychology Review*, 10(4), 295-319. Associated impairment in a large online sample. *Journal of Anxiety Disorders*, 72, 102219.

Wheaton, M. G., Deacon, B. J., McGrath, P. B., Berman, N. C., & Abramowitz, J. S. (2012). Dimensions of anxiety sensitivity in the anxiety disorders: Evaluation of the ASI-3. *Journal of Anxiety Disorders*, 26(3), 401-408.

2. P34 *Some of these have been documented in research studies . . .*
Kessler, R. C., Berglund, P., Demler, O., Jin, R., Merikangas, K. R., & Walters, E. E. (2005). Lifetime prevalence and age-of-onset distributions of DSM-IV disorders in the National Comorbidity Survey Replication. *Archives of General Psychiatry*, 62(6), 593-602.

Dwyer, K., McCallum, J., & O'Sullivan, G. (2011). Posttraumatic stress disorder among ambulance personnel: exploring the relationship with depression, anxiety and job satisfaction. *Journal of Emergency Primary Health Care*, 9(1), 1-10

Xue, C., Ge, Y., Tang, B., Liu, Y., Kang, P., Wang, M., . . . & Zhang, L. (2015). A meta-analysis of risk factors for combat-related PTSD among military personnel and veterans. *PloS one*, 10(3), e0120270.

Hsieh, Y. P., & Purnell, M. (2021). Occupational stress and anxiety among firefighters: The mediating role of resilience. *Journal of Loss and Trauma*, 26(1), 1-11.

Terrill, Z. R., Loflin, M. J., & Worthington, E. L. (2021). Police work and anxiety: A comprehensive review of the literature. *Traumatology*, 27(2), 115-125.

Tawfik, D. S., Scheid, A., Profit, J., Shanafelt, T., & Trockel, M. (2019). Evidence relating health care provider burnout and quality of care: a systematic review and meta-analysis. *Annals of Internal Medicine*, 171(8), 555-567.

Chapter 3

3. P90 *The research supporting the exercises given here is truly astounding.*

Anderson, E. & Shivakumar, G. (2013). Effects of exercise and physical activity on anxiety. *Front Psychiatry*. 4:27.

Aylett, E., Small, N. & Bower, P. (2018). Exercise in the treatment of clinical anxiety in general practice – a systematic review and meta-analysis. *BMC Health Services Research*. Jul 16;18(1):559.

Bartley, B., Hay, M. & Bloch, M. (2013). Meta-analysis: aerobic exercise for the treatment of anxiety disorders. *Progress in Neuro-Psychopharmacology & Biological Psychiatry*. 45:34-39

Conn, V. S. (2010). Anxiety outcomes after physical activity interventions: meta-analysis findings. *Nursing Research*. 59(3):224-231.

Long, B. C., Stavel R. (2008). Effects of exercise training on anxiety: a meta-analysis. *Journal of Applied Sport Psychology*. 7(2):167-189.

Manzoni, G. M., Pagnini, F., Castelnuovo, G. et al. (2008). Relaxation training for anxiety: a ten-year systematic review with meta-analysis. *BMC Psychiatry*. 8, 41.

Perciavalle, V., Blandini, M., Fecarotta, P., Buscemi, A., Di Corrado, D., Bertolo, L., Fichera, F. & Coco, M. (2017). The role of deep breathing on stress. *Neurological Sciences*. Mar;38(3):451-458.

Russo, M. A., Santarelli, D. M., O'Rourke, D. (2017). The physiological effects of slow breathing in the healthy human. *Breathe* (Sheffield). Dec;13(4):298-309.

Seid, A. A., Mohammed, A. A. & Hasen, A. A. (2023) Progressive muscle relaxation exercises in patients with COVID-19:

Systematic review and meta-analysis. *Medicine.* (Baltimore). 102(14):e33464.

Singh, B., Olds, T., Curtis, R., et al. (2023). Effectiveness of physical activity interventions for improving depression, anxiety and distress: an overview of systematic reviews *British Journal of Sports Medicine.*

Toussaint, L., Nguyen, Q. A., Roettger, C., Dixon, K., Offenbächer, M., Kohls, N., Hirsch, J. & Sirois, F. (2021). Effectiveness of Progressive Muscle Relaxation, Deep Breathing, and Guided Imagery in Promoting Psychological and Physiological States of Relaxation. *Evidence-Based Complementary and Alternative Medicine.* 5924040.

Wipfli, B. M., Rethorst, C. D. & Landers, D.M. (2008). The anxiolytic effects of exercise: a meta-analysis of randomized trials and dose – response analysis. *Journal of Sport & Exercise Psychology.* 30:392-410.

4. P91 *Studies also show that optimal breathing . . .*

Dusek, J. A., Otu, H. H., Wohlhueter, A. L., Bhasin, M., Zerbini, L. F., Joseph, M. G., . . . & Libermann, T. A. (2008). Genomic counter-stress changes induced by the relaxation response. *PLoS One*, 3(7), e2576.

Gupta, A., & Epstein, N. B. (2018). Effects of relaxation training on trait anxiety: A meta-analysis. *Journal of Clinical Psychology*, 74(3), 327-342.

Khoury, B., Sharma, M., Rush, S. E., & Fournier, C. (2015). Mindfulness-based stress reduction for healthy individuals: A meta-analysis. *Journal of Psychosomatic Research*, 78(6), 519-528.

Khoury, B., Lecomte, T., Fortin, G., Masse, M., Therien, P., Bouchard, V., Chapleau, M. A., Paquin, K., & Hofmann, S. G. (2013). Mindfulness-based therapy: A comprehensive meta-analysis. *Clinical Psychology Review*, 33(6), 763-771.

Perciavalle, V., Blandini, M., Fecarotta, P., Buscemi, A., Di Corrado, D., Bertolo, L., . . . & Coco, M. (2017). The role of deep breathing on stress. *Neurological Sciences*, 38(3), 451-458.

Lee, Y., Lee, S. H., & Kim, J. H. (2018). Efficacy of diaphragmatic breathing training on physiological and psychological variables in patients with generalized anxiety disorder. *Journal of Psychiatric Research*, 105, 68-72.

Russo, M. A., Santarelli, D. M., & O'Rourke, D. (2017). The physiological effects of slow breathing in the healthy human. *Breathe*, 13(4), 298-309.

Toussaint, L., Nguyen, Q. A., Roettger, C., Dixon, K., Offenbächer, M., Kohls, N., . . . & Sirois, F. (2020). Effectiveness of Progressive Muscle Relaxation, Deep Breathing, and Guided Imagery in Promoting Psychological and Physiological States of Relaxation. *Explore*, 16(6), 377-384.

5. P162 *Anxiety places a significant cognitive burden on its sufferers* . . .

Nadeem, F., Malik, N. I., Atta, M., Ullah, I., Martinotti, G., & Pettorruso, M. (2021). Relationship between health-anxiety and cyberchondria: Role of metacognitive beliefs. *Journal of Affective Disorders*, 284, 32-38.

Risen, J. L., & Gilovich, T. (2007). Magical thinking in predictions of negative events: Evidence for tempting fate but not for a protection effect. *Journal of Personality and Social Psychology*, 92(4), 745–758.

Slovic, P., & Lichtenstein, S. (1968). Anxiety, Cognitive Availability, and the Talisman Effect of Insurance. *Journal of Risk and Insurance*, 35(2), 215-236.

Chapter 5

6. P175 *There is substantial research evidence* . . .

Berggren, N., & Derakshan, N. (2013). Attentional control deficits in trait anxiety: Why you see them and why you don't. *Biological Psychology*, 92(3), 440-446.

Carlbring, P., Apelstrand, M., Sehlin, H., Amir, N., Rousseau, A., Hofmann, S. G., & Andersson, G. (2019). Internet-delivered attention bias modification training in individuals with social anxiety disorder – a double blind randomized controlled trial. *Cognitive Behaviour Therapy*, 48(6), 441-455.

Fox, E. (1993). Attentional bias in anxiety: A defective inhibition hypothesis. *Cognition & Emotion*, 7(2), 107-140.

Hakamata, Y., Lissek, S., Bar-Haim, Y., Britton, J. C., Fox, N. A., Leibenluft, E., & Pine, D. S. (2010). Attention bias modification treatment: a meta-analysis toward the establishment of novel treatment for anxiety. *Biological Psychiatry*, 68(11), 982-990.

Johnstone, K. A., & Page, A. C. (2004). Attention to phobic stimuli during exposure: the effect of distraction on anxiety reduction, self-efficacy and perceived control. *Behaviour Research and Therapy*, 42(3), 249-275.

Kuckertz, J. M., Amir, N., & Boffa, J. W. (2020). The nature, detection, and reduction of attentional bias in anxiety: A review and future directions. *Behavior Therapy*, 51(5), 633-649.

Wells, T. T., & Beevers, C. G. (2019). Attention bias modification for anxiety: Current status and future directions. *Current Opinion in Psychology*, 28, 27-32.

Wells, A., & Papageorgiou, C. (1998). Social phobia: Effects of external attention on anxiety, negative beliefs, and perspective taking. *Behavior Therapy*, 29(3), 357-370.

Hakamata, Y., Lissek, S., Bar-Haim, Y., Britton, J. C., Fox, N. A., Leibenluft, E., Ernst, M.& Pine, D. S. (2010). Attention bias modification treatment: a meta-analysis toward the establishment of novel treatment for anxiety. *Biological Psychiatry*, 1;68(11):982-90.

7. P190 *Studies suggest that exposure to natural . . .*

Beyer, K. M., Kaltenbach, A., Szabo, A., Bogar, S., Nieto, F. J., & Malecki, K. M. (2014). Exposure to neighborhood green space and mental health: evidence from the survey of the health of Wisconsin. *International Journal of Environmental Research and Public Health*, 11(3), 3453-3472.

Bratman, G. N., Hamilton, J. P., Hahn, K. S., Daily, G. C., & Gross, J. J. (2015). Nature experience reduces rumination and subgenual prefrontal cortex activation. *Proceedings of the National Academy of Sciences*, 112(28), 8567-8572.

Bratman, G. N., Hamilton, J. P., & Daily, G. C. (2012). The impacts of nature experience on human cognitive function and mental health. *Annals of the New York Academy of Sciences*, 1249(1), 118-136.

Gascon, M., Triguero-Mas, M., Martínez, D., Dadvand, P., Forns, J., Plasència, A., & Nieuwenhuijsen, M. J. (2015). Mental health benefits of long-term exposure to residential green and blue spaces: A systematic review. *International Journal of Environmental Research and Public Health*, 12(4), 4354-4379.

Tyrväinen, L., Ojala, A., Korpela, K., Lanki, T., Tsunetsugu, Y., & Kagawa, T. (2014). The influence of urban green environments on stress relief measures: A field experiment. *Journal of Environmental Psychology*, 38, 1-9.

Chapter 6

8. P198 *The clinical research supporting this is enormous . . .*

Aldao, A., Nolen-Hoeksema, S., & Schweizer, S. (2010). Emotion-regulation strategies across psychopathology: A meta-analytic review. *Clinical Psychology Review*, 30(2), 217-237.

Gross, J. J. (2002). Emotion regulation: Affective, cognitive, and social consequences. *Psychophysiology*, 39(3), 281-291.

Linehan, M. M. (2014). *DBT Skills Training Manual*. Guilford Press.

Mennin, D. S., & Fresco, D. M. (2013). Emotion regulation therapy. In J. J. Gross (Ed.), *Handbook of Emotion Regulation* (2nd ed., pp. 469-490). Guilford Press.

Marshall, E. C., Zvolensky, M. J., Vujanovic, A. A., Gregor, K., & Gibson, L. E. (2012). Anxiety sensitivity and distress tolerance: joint predictors of anxious arousal and withdrawal-related symptoms. *Journal of Anxiety Disorders*, 26(4), 687-695.

9. P218 *Self-soothing is a particularly helpful . . .*

Dreisoerner, A., Junker, N. M., Schlotz, W., Heimrich, J., Bloemeke, S., Ditzen, B. & van Dick, R. (2021). Self-soothing touch and being hugged reduce cortisol responses to stress: A randomized controlled trial on stress, physical touch, and social identity. *Comprehensive Psychoneuroendocrinology*, 8;8:100091.

Kabat-Zinn, J. (2013). *Full Catastrophe Living, Revised Edition: How to cope with stress, pain and illness using mindfulness meditation*. Bantam Books.

Kline, A. C., Cooper, A. A., Rytwinski, N. K., & Feeny, N. C. (2018). Combining emotion regulation strategies to optimize treatment outcome in adults with anxiety disorders. *Clinical Psychology Review*, 63, 23-45.

Kim, S. H., & Hamann, S. (2007). Neural correlates of positive and negative emotion regulation. *Journal of Cognitive Neuroscience*, 19(5), 776-798.

Knoll, N., Schwarzer, R., Pfüller, B., & Kienle, R. (2008). Self-soothing and health-related outcomes: A meta-analysis. *Applied Psychology: Health and Well-Being*, 1(2), 215-235.

Uvnäs-Moberg, K., Handlin, L. & Petersson, M. (2015). Self-soothing behaviors with particular reference to oxytocin release induced by non-noxious sensory stimulation. *Frontiers in Psychology*, 12;5:1529.

Chapter 7

10. P227 *As early as 1998 . . .*

Dugas, M. J., Gagnon, F., Ladouceur, R. & Freeston, M.H. (1998). Generalized anxiety disorder: a preliminary test of a conceptual model. *Behaviour Research and Therapy*, 36(2):215-26.

11. P227 *Subsequent research, including a study in 2001 . . .*

Dugas, M.J., Gosselin, P., & Ladouceur, R. Intolerance of Uncertainty and Worry: Investigating Specificity in a Nonclinical Sample. *Cognitive Therapy and Research*, 25, 551–558 (2001)

Chapter 9

12. P308 *The impact of exposure to traumatic events . . .*

Hovens, J. G. F. M., et al. (2012). Impact of childhood life events and trauma on the course of depressive and anxiety disorders. *Acta Psychiatrica Scandinavica* 126, 198–207.

Hovens, J. G. F. M., Wiersma, J. E., Giltay, E. J., Van Oppen, P., Spinhoven, P., Penninx, B. W. J. H., & Zitman, F. G. (2010). Childhood life events and childhood trauma in adult patients with depressive, anxiety and comorbid disorders vs. controls. *Acta Psychiatrica Scandinavica*, 122(1), 66–74.

Lochner, C., Seedat, S., Allgulander, C., Kidd, M., Stein, D. & Gerdner, A. (2010). Childhood trauma in adults with social anxiety disorder and panic disorder: a cross-national study. *African Journal of Psychiatry*, 13(5):376-81.

13. P308 *Research indicates that adverse childhood environments . . .*
Glaser, J. P., van Os, J., Portegijs, P. J., & Myin-Germeys, I. (2006). Childhood trauma and emotional reactivity to daily life stress in adult frequent attenders of general practitioners. *Journal of Psychosomatic Research*. 61(2):229-36.
Goldin, P. R., Manber, T., Hakimi, S., Canli, T., & Gross, J. J. (2009). Neural bases of social anxiety disorder: Emotional reactivity and cognitive regulation during social and physical threat. *Archives of General Psychiatry*. 66(2):170-80.

14. P309 *While further research is needed to fully . . .*
Nelson, C. A., Scott, R. D., Bhutta, Z. A., Harris , N. B., Danese, A., & Samara, M. (2020). Adversity in childhood is linked to mental and physical health throughout life. *BMJ*. 28; 371:m3048.
Smith, K. E., & Pollak, S. D. (2020). Early life stress and development: potential mechanisms for adverse outcomes. *Journal of Clinical Child & Adolescent Psychology*, 49(2), 284-296.

Support Organizations

On this page, you'll find a list of organizations that can provide you with help and support if you've experienced trauma or difficult childhood experiences. This help is available to you whether you're currently experiencing these problems or have faced them in the past. These organizations are dedicated to helping people navigate through the challenges that come with these experiences. They can offer a wide range of resources and support to help you on your journey towards healing. Remember, it's never too late to seek help, and there's no shame in reaching out for support.

ASSIST Trauma Care
Specialist help and information for those who've experienced trauma or are supporting someone who has. **assisttraumacare.org.uk**

Birth Trauma Association
Support for those affected by birth trauma. **birthtraumaassociation.org.uk**

Combat Stress
Support and help for armed forces veterans with mental health problems. **combatstress.org.uk**

Disaster Action
Support and information for those affected by major disasters, both in the UK and abroad. **disasteraction.org.uk**

Freedom from Torture
Support for survivors of torture. **freedomfromtorture.org**

MIND
Help, information, and advice for those affected by mental health problems. **mind.org.uk**

The National Association for People Abused in Childhood (NAPAC)
Supporting adult survivors of any form of childhood abuse. **napac.org.uk**

PTSD Resolution
Help and support for veterans and their families affected by trauma. **ptsdresolution.org**

PTSD UK
Information about trauma, including effective treatment, self-help materials, and information on supporting someone with PTSD. **ptsduk. org**

Support for Survivors
Supporting adult survivors of child abuse. **supportforsurvivors.org**

One in Four
Offering advocacy services, counselling and further resources for adults who have experienced trauma, domestic or sexual abuse in childhood. **oneinfour.org.uk**

Acknowledgements

I am incredibly grateful to everyone who has been instrumental in the creation of this book. To each and every one of you, thank you.

To my patients, I am deeply thankful for the trust you have placed in me and for the lessons I have learned from each of you. Being part of your healing process has been a true honour.

My heartfelt appreciation goes to my family for their unwavering support.

I am profoundly grateful to my mother who's shown me the meaning of resilience, as well as the extraordinary capacity of the human spirit to overcome adversity and thrive.

Index

anxiety – *cont.*
  relationship with trauma
    307–23, 344
  snowball effect 86–8
  stopping over-focusing on
    172–94
  and suppression of emotions
    199–200, 224–5
  triggers 28–9, 57, 62, 81,
    100, 122, 202–3, 343
  types of anxiety problems
    372–7
  uncertainty and 229–30
  understanding 19–58
  and the way you think 38–46
  what anxiety is 21
  what it does to your body and
    mind 25–7
  what keeps anxiety going
    36–57
  why you experience it 30–6
aromatherapy 80
attention: biased attention 176
  focusing your attention 43–6,
    181
  how anxiety affects 175–83
  hyper-vigilance 179, 180, 183
  noticing breathing sensations
    190–1
  productive distraction 221–3
  selective and narrowed 179
  self-focused attention 176–9,
    183
  situational refocusing 186
  switching from worst to best
    185–6
  using sensory systems to
    improve 187–91

widening the scope of your
  183–92
Ava 206–8
avoidance behaviours 8, 23–4,
  31, 50, 53–4, 71, 79,
  111–12, 278–97, 301–2,
  344, 348–9, 352
  avoidance of emotions 200–1
  avoidance-based mini-toolkit
    346
  identifying 269–70
  what it is 266–70

B
beach-ball visualization 111–12
behaviours: common anxiety 371
  control behaviours 254–62
  identifying changes in
    351–3
  see also avoidance behaviours;
    safety behaviours
Bella 345, 353–5
belly breathing 92–3
biased attention 176
blood pressure 47, 308
the body: body-based anxiety
  triggers 28, 345
  using to improve the scope of
    attention 188
  what anxiety does to your
    body 25–7
the brain: anxiety and 21–5
  positive feedback and 358
  trauma and 303–4, 324
breathing, anxiety and 172–4
breathing exercises 89–90, 91–4,
  101
  counting backwards 264

trauma – *cont.*
  trauma-related cognitions
    322–3
  traumatic life experiences 30,
    32–4, 35
  what it is 305–6, 338
trauma-focused cognitive
    behavioural therapy
    (TF-CBT) 337
travel anxiety 123
triggers 343
  anxiety 28–9, 57, 62, 81, 100,
    122, 202–3
  anxious thoughts 122–5,
    202–3
  identifying 350
  that cause setbacks 347
Twain, Mark 148

U
uncertainty 274
  acceptance and flexibility in
    the face of 240–4
  addressing general uncertainty
    250–3
  addressing uncertainty specific
    to your anxiety 254–62
  managing uncertain
    predictions 245–7
  navigating 226–64
  problems caused by 231–7
  and resilience 247–50
  uncertainty-management
    toolkit 262
  understanding 228–31,
    237–47

V
validation 261
vision, using to improve attention
    189–90
visualizations, future self 359–61,
    363
voices 194

W
warrior poses 332
Wasim 234
waterfall pose 334
'what ifs' 154–9, 170
work 34, 356
worries 13
worst-case scenarios thinking
    146–54, 170

Z
Zane 317–18, 320
Zara 268–9

About the Author

Dr Kirren Schnack is a clinical psychologist with more than twenty years of experience. She holds a practitioner doctorate (PsychD) in clinical psychology from the University of Oxford.